Love & Joy

Love & Joy

Law, Language and Religion in Ancient Israel

Yochanan Muffs

The Jewish Theological Seminary of America
New York and Jerusalem

Distributed by Harvard University Press
Cambridge, Massachusetts and London

Printed in the United States of America

Library of Congress Cataloging-in-Publication Data

Muffs, Yochanan.
Love and joy, law, language, and religion in ancient Israel/
Yochanan Muffs.
p. cm.
Includes bibliographical references and index.
ISBN 0–674–53931–1 .
1. Law (Theology)—Biblical teaching. 2. Bible. O.T.—Language, style. 3. Assyro-Babyonian literature—Relation to the Old Testament. 4. Bible. O.T.—Criticism, interpretation, Jewish. 5. Rabbinical literature—History and criticism. I. Title.
BS1199.L3M84 1992
296'.09'01—dc20 92–11977
CIP

For Yocheved

Proverbs 31:29

This volume has been published with the support of the Meisel Publication Fund, a fund established by the Meisel children to honor their parents, Philip and Blanche Meisel.

CONTENTS

PART II: LAW AND THE ANCIENT NEAR EAST

PART III: LAW AND METAPHOR

ABBREVIATIONS

AHw	W. von Soden, *Akkadisches Handwörterbuch* (1965–1981)
ANET	J. B. Pritchard, ed., *Ancient Near Eastern Texts* (3d ed., 1969)
AP	A. E. Cowley, *Aramaic Papyri of the Fifth Century* B.C. (1923)
AT	D. J. Wiseman, *The Alalakh Tablets* (1953)
b.	Babylonian Talmud (Talmud Bavli)
BDB	F. Brown, S. R. Driver, and C. A. Briggs, *A Hebrew and English Lexicon of the Old Testament* (1907)
BP	Emil Kraeling, *The Brooklyn Museum Aramaic Papyri* (1953)
CAD	*The* [*Chicago*] *Assyrian Dictionary* (1955–)
D	Deuteronomic/istic Source
DN	divine name
E	Elohist Source
HUCA	*Hebrew Union College Annual*
J	Yahwist Source
JAOS	*Journal of the American Oriental Society*
JBL	*Journal of Biblical Literature*
KAI	H. Donner and W. Röllig, *Kanaanäische und aramäische Inschriften* (1968–1971)
LXX	Septuagint
m.	Mishnah
MDP	V. Scheil, *Actes juridiques susiens* (Mémoires de la Délégation en Perse 22–24)
NJPS	Bible. New Jewish Publication Society Translation (1985)
OB	Old Babylonian
P	Priestly Source
PN	personal name
PRU	J. Nougayrol et al., *Le Palais royale d'Ugarit*
SALPE	Y. Muffs, *Studies in the Aramaic Legal Papyri from Elephantine* (1969)
RS	Ras Shamra (text number)
RSV	Bible. Revised Standard Version (1952–1957)
y.	Palestinian Talmud (Talmud Yerushalmi)

FOREWORD

Reading this collection of articles by Yochanan Muffs is like strolling with a friend through a familiar landscape and, as one listens to him, seeing the familiar landmarks with fresh eyes in unexpected new light. The prophets are here not the messengers of doom one is apt to think them, but daring intercessors trying to mitigate God's righteous wrath. Symbolic expressions of the closeness of God and Israel are explored with point of departure in Jeremiah 13. A look at Mesopotamian religion raises an enlightening question: the possible interpretations of "personal" in the term "personal god." Moving from the section on "God and Man" to that on "Law and the Ancient Near East," it is a surprise to see the pious and compassionate Abraham as noble warlord and diplomat, a role he unquestionably must have had to survive, given the social and political conditions of his time. More technical are the studies of the expression "the money came to me" and of the root DRK. A last section on "Law and Metaphor" explores the implications of terms for love and joy in legal contexts.

To the outsider the first of these studies, the one dealing with the prophets as intercessors, is perhaps the most arresting. It deals with some striking examples of seemingly all too human metaphors for God, with the troublesome matter of punishment deferred to later generations, and it is throughout alive with Muffs' unique ability to accept early anthropomorphic conceptions of God and to articulate their religious value in modern terms.

Muffs begins with Abraham, legitimizing him as a prophet, that is, primarily as someone whose prayers God hears and whom God feels obligated to inform in advance of contemplated destructive punishment, well knowing that this is to invite objection and argument. In Abraham's plea for Sodom—a relatively late piece—the argument is that there might be some righteous people in the city; thus, to destroy it would be to slay the righteous with the wicked, which would not be right and seemly for the judge of all the earth.

In addressing God, Abraham uses the obsequious manner of a courtier addressing his Pharaoh. Not so with the next prophet treated,

Moses. He, although fully aware of God's power, yet argues with Him on a near equal footing and is not above using, as Muffs vividly characterizes it, "strong and audacious rhetorical devices coupled with moral blackmail," to save the people from deserved punishment. The image of God here projected, one that makes Him vulnerable to such strategies is, as one will expect, highly anthropomorphic. God appears as hot tempered, heedless, when angry, of previous commitments, and inordinately concerned about His reputation: that the Egyptians and others might think of Him as only a minor god perhaps. Clearly, these are old traditions from times when such thorough humanizing of the divine image was not felt as reprehensible, and it is a great gain that Muffs in his presentation sees and communicates some of the peculiar values this primitive approach is capable of holding: God's deep and caring involvement with man as "a God Who turns toward man and is interested in man's destiny and in man's reaction to His commandments," a "personal God presenting a full-blown personality."

That the attitude is old, perhaps even uniquely restricted to the Moses tradition is indicated by the fact that none of the later prophets ever argue in this fashion. They pray or fall upon their face when entreating God, and this is in fact the normal approach to deities in the contemporary civilizations such as that of Mesopotamia. Prayer and attempts to arouse the deity's compassion by description of sufferings are the exclusive means to influence him or her. Only one case of argument similar to that of Moses is known, an Old Babylonian letter from a man to his personal god. We shall return to it later and to its possible import for the Moses traditions.

Among the psychological strategies used by Moses is one not hitherto recognized but seen by Muffs in a radical new interpretation of Exod 38:12. After Moses has succeeded in abating God's wrath over the Golden Calf to some extent, God says He will send an angel along to him. Since God up to then had led the people in person, this is clearly meant to put distance between the people and God, who is still very angry with them (Exod 32:3). According to Muffs' new and surely correct interpretation Moses chooses to consider this a slight to him: he is being demoted to dealing with a subordinate, an angel, rather than as hitherto directly with God. He reminds God of promises He has made and eventually obtains God's promise that He will go with him and the people Himself, arguing that otherwise it will not be clear to the other nations that he, Moses, has found favor with God and that the people may be distinguishable among all the people on the earth as His people.

While Moses' intervention has saved the people from immediate extinction, it could not blot out the sin of worshipping the Golden Calf. That must be punished even though punishment is for the moment deferred. "In the day that I punish, I shall punish their sin upon them" (Exod 32:34). The theme of deferred punishment here broached leads Muffs into a highly interesting probe into the "history of ancient Israelite moral sensibility regarding matters of sin and punishment." He recognizes three stages.

In the first of these sin has an objective quality: it is like a cancer that must be cut out and destroyed. In this stage neither repentance nor good deeds or merit of a father will atone for sin. In the second stage sin must still be punished, but mercy toward a repentant and otherwise deserving sinner may allow the punishment to be deferred to a future generation so that the sinner goes free. Finally, in the third stage, sincere repentance and turning away from evil ways will obtain forgiveness.

As Muffs points out, it is the second of these stages that is of great discomfort to the modern reader: to punish innocent unborn children for sins committed by parents who have escaped all punishment seems to a modern sensibility the height of cruelty. Yet, as Muffs shows by clear examples, such deferred punishment was considered mercy by the ancients and must have been characteristic of a certain stage of the moral development of ancient Israel.

The second stage did, of course, not last. By the time of the Babylonian exile the prophets have a different message, more in line with what the modern reader would see as fair. Even so the question remains, how the ancients could once have thought as they did, approving what to us seems unjust in the extreme. Muffs does not go into this in detail but one may perhaps cite the well-known tendency of ancient thought to operate in terms of collectives rather than pluralities made up of individuals. A family or a people is not a congregation of individuals each with their own life and fortunes but rather a living organism, and what happens to any part helps or harms the whole. One survival of such thinking is feuding between rival clans. If a member of one clan is murdered, it does not matter which member of the other clan actually did the killing—anyone in the clan can be killed as revenge. In the Bible, when David sinned by instituting a census, God gave him three possible punishments, only one of which—fleeing from enemies—affected him personally. The others were three years of famine or three days of pestilence. David chose the last, and seventy thousand of the people died. Only then, when it was all over, did it occur to David to ask, "These sheep, what have they done?" That fleeting thought of David, distinguishing between him and his subjects, was likely to create difficulties when applied to wholesale slaughter such as famine, pestilence and other destruction. These difficulties come to the fore in the story of Abraham's plea for Sodom, which is undoubtedly a late insertion. Here Abraham argues that it would be unjust to destroy the righteous with the wicked even though they may number only ten. This view of Sodom as a collection of individuals of different character and conduct is new. On the old view Sodom was uniform, every inhabitant imbued with its essence, and so guilty. By the time of Jeremiah and Ezekiel, the movement to see the old collectives rather as consisting of different individuals was fully realized. "In those days they shall no longer say 'The fathers have eaten sour grapes and the children's teeth are set on edge' but every one shall die for his own iniquity" (Jer 3:29–30) and "The word of the Lord came to me again: 'What mean ye, that ye use this proverb in the land of Israel, saying: 'The fathers have eaten sour grapes and the children's teeth are set on edge? As I live, saith the Lord God, ye shall not have occasion any more to use this proverb in Israel.' . . . The soul that sinneth, it shall die" (Ezek 18:1–4). As will be seen, the statements are directly aimed at the concept of deferred punishment; no longer is the individual to be merged with the mass—he is distinct, does not incur guilt by association.

After considering the problems of deferred punishment Muffs moves on to treat of Samuel, Jeremiah, and Ezekiel, exploring the courage and fortitude of soul it takes to oppose God even though He so wishes, and the inner suffering of the prophet when told not to argue. That God does want the prophet to "stand in the breach against him when anger flares hot in Him and He might be carried away further than He would actually want," is treated by Muffs in the section on "The Turning of Love." This is followed by a section on functional and historical parallels which refers briefly to Mesopotamian concepts of intercession before moving on to consideration of shamanistic elements in the origins of the later prophets with special attention to the Arabic *kahin* and his magic powers. A section on modes of controlling divine anger resumes the questions raised by deferred punishment, seeing the deferment rather as vicarious atonement. I would see that concept as distinct and belonging rather in the context of magic, where a substitute, animal or human, is offered with the intention of tricking the threatening powers.

Muff's study of the prophets is followed by an article dealing with metaphors and symbols for closeness to God, various pieces of clothing and also tattoos. The study begins with the loincloth Jeremiah is told to buy, wear, and then bury near a river in a cleft of a rock, where it becomes thoroughly ruined. The cloth is an image of Israel, which God wore with pride but which is now spoiled.

After thus dealing with symbols for closeness to God, Muffs gives in a review an overview of ancient Mesopotamian religion. Among the features that specially interest him is the concept of the personal god, and he raises the incisive question of whether "personal" is to be understood as "attached to a specific person" or rather as "having personality." I believe that both readings are correct and relevant, but this may perhaps be the point to take a brief look at the older, but in many ways closely related, Mesopotamian civilization to point up differences and similarities.

To begin with, it will be advantageous to distinguish clearly between public and private Mesopotamian religion. Public religion saw the world as a divinely run cosmic state in which the major gods held the administrative offices. The highest authority was an assembly of the gods in which the major decisions regarding nature (floods, famine, etc.) and history (appointment of kings, destruction of cities and kingdoms) were made and announced by An and Enlil. These decisions were unalterable. As Enlil says to his son Nanna in a lament for Ur: "There is no rescinding of a decision, a verdict of the Assembly; changing a verdict announced by An and Enlil is unknown." In later times these verdicts were thought to be written on an unchangeable "tablet of fates." So unchangeable was this tablet that when Marduk under Esarhaddon changed his mind and wanted to reduce the number of years Babylon was to lie waste, the god still had to act according to what was written down; by turning the tablet upside down he was able to read the figure 70 written on it as 11. As to the reasons underlying the gods' decisions, they were sometimes understandable, sometimes not. Sargon and his city Akkadē were destroyed because he began tearing down Enlil's temple to rebuild it without the god's permission. At other times the gods seemed to act on a whim or in a frenzy of vandalism that drove them to destroy their own people and temples, as a lament for Ur depicts. As for means to influence the gods, there was only prayer and music, never argument. Prayer appealed to divine compassion by vivid descriptions of suffering, music soothed distress or anger in the gods, and so their bull harps were seen as calming counsellors. Intercession was almost always by gods—even the harps were considered deities—and did not involve argument. Appeal was typically after the calamity, not before it and preventive. Human prophets, known from Old Babylonian times on, were mere messengers conveying needs of temples and cult and support or warning for the ruler, with no moral dimension to their messages. Consistent with their role as officials in the cosmic state, the gods of the public religion were slightly remote, essentially representatives of their offices with little or no private personal characteristics.

Somewhat different was the case of the Mesopotamian private worship. Central here was the concept of the personal god, that is, a god who had taken a personal interest in a man and his family, suggesting what he should do and giving success to his labors. The relationship to the family continued after the man's death, when the god would transfer his concern to the new head of the family so that he would be referred to as "god of the fathers" or "god of our fathers." The widespread idea that the personal god was a minor god only is mistaken. Great gods such as Sîn, god of the moon, Shamash, god of the sun and of justice, Adad, god of the thunderstorms, and Nergal, ruler of the Nether World, appear in this role.

As the personal god in guiding the head of the house took on the role of effective family head, he was naturally thought of in terms of a father, and with that a special relation of intimacy grew up. The personal god, however high and mighty, was a member of the family and so could be approached as such. It could happen that his ward misbehaved and incurred the god's anger, so that the god turned away and allowed all kind of misfortune to happen. Then it was essential to discover what the wrong was and to confess it publicly. On the other hand, the god might have been merely negligent and so open to blame. In the one such case we know of, the ward is charging his personal god with neglect and argues that faithful worshippers such as him are not easy to find.

We may here be close to an answer to Muffs' question about the sense of "personal" in personal god—does it mean whether "concerned with a person" or "having a clearly articulated personality"? It implies both. The concern for a person brings out personal characteristics in the caring deity, helpfulness and protection, anger at errors committed, forgiveness, and even occasional negligence of duties.

It need hardly be stressed that there is much here that reminds us of the Bible's image of God. God is from the beginning a great god, creator of the Universe, yet He takes a personal interest in Abraham and later in Isaac and Jacob, guiding and protecting them so that He can refer to Himself as "The Lord God of your fathers, the God of Abraham, the God of Isaac, and the God of Jacob" (Exod 3:15). This status of God as the family god of Israel may go some way toward explaining Moses' daring to argue with God like the man arguing with his personal god, like a family member arguing with the head of the family. If the image of God projected in the Bible is seen as originating in, or as influenced by, that of the personal god, God's care for Israel, his anger at its sins, and his willing forgiveness falls readily into place.

As this image was transferred from the relation with an individual to that with an entire people, Israel, a powerful metaphor for the human relation to God, came into being, one insisting on moral and cultic responsibility sanctioned by the "unique theological category" of divine pathos that Heschel understood so well in all its transcendent love and zealous passion.

With "Abraham the Noble Warrior" Muffs turns from the history of religion to the history of law, beginning with a study of Genesis 14, a chapter so thoroughly chewed over by commentators that it would seem impossible to say anything about it that has not been said before—and yet Muffs manages to do just that. He shows for the first time that Abraham punctiliously observes the laws of war and the etiquette of booty restoration of the times insofar as they can be reconstructed from the international treaties of Boghazköy and Ugarit. Thus Abraham, when he has recovered the booty taken from Sodom, has the conqueror's right to keep it. Yet, magnanimously, he gives it back to the King of Sodom in its entirety. Muffs shows that this grand gesture has an exact parallel in records of Shuppiluliuma's noble generosity toward a vassal whose goods he had recovered from the enemy.

Muffs next takes up the neglected subject of rules governing the provisioning of troops and division of booty as they can be seen in surviving treaties. These rules include the obligation of a ruler receiving military help to furnish provisions for the assisting troops. This fits with Abraham's claim to "what the young men have eaten" (Gen 14:24). In the matter of division of booty I would like to see the King of Sodom's request for the recovered persons as an appeal to Abraham's generosity rather than a justified claim. The Ishmerikan treaty cited allows the ruler of Ishmerika to keep as booty the civilian population of a conquered city that has rebelled against his Hittite overlord, so Abraham would have been within his rights to keep the recovered civilians.

The martial aspect of Abraham that comes to expression in Genesis 14 was not an isolated phenomenon. Rather, military capability must have been a *sine qua non* for survival in the milieu in which the patriarchs moved, and Muffs shows how traditions about Isaac and Jacob imply this clearly, more by inference from the way contemporaries react than by direct statement.

Leaving the patriarchs, Muffs next turns to the matter of concrete figurative formulations of abstract legal concepts and the extraordinary persistence and spread of such formulations throughout the ancient Near East, even with occasional difficulties of translation.

One such case is that of Akkadian *maḫāru* and *apālu*, "to receive," payment, which in Aramaic was replaced by *ʿl ʿl*, "to enter in to (someone)." This caused an ambiguity when the phrase was taken over into Hebrew and rendered with *baʾ*, which can mean both "to come" and "to enter." Muffs shows, however, that the proper nuance of meaning and the use of the formula as a term for receipt was fully alive, as he analyzes key examples. Next, Muffs follows up an observation by H. L. Ginsberg that Hebrew *ʿoz* must mean "anger," connecting it with Akkadian *ezzu*, "wrath," and pointing out the parallel of later Hebrew *mēʿēz pana(y)w* with Akkadian *ezziš nekelmû*, "to look at (someone) with anger/wrath." This is followed by a study of the root DRK, showing that it means "to be empowered."

The final two chapters deal with a problem that has fascinated Muffs for years, the use in legal context of terms for strong emotions such as "love" and "joy" for the far less emotionally charged mood of voluntariness. His detailed study begins with a consideration of the manner in which royal and divine donations are presented in the Babylonian boundary stones or *kudurrus* of the first millennium B.C.E. In these documents voluntary giving is expressed in terms of joy. We hear that Nabu-apla-iddinna, for example, "with his bright gaze, shining countenance and sparkling (literally, good) eyes looked upon him (a priest) joyfully [and granted him the priestly revenues]." From these Babylonian materials Muffs turns to biblical and post-biblical documents of varied kinds, showing in example after example how love and joy can express "(a) the free and gracious will that underpins a divine grant to kings or priests; (b) the spontaneity with which man accepts divine grace or the free resignation with which he accepts divine chastisement; (c) the willing and joyful alacrity with which man reciprocates the divine gifts and blessings with his sacrifices, tithes and offerings."

For an Assyriologist it is tempting to pursue the history of the oddly overdone phrasing in the *kudurrus* backward in time. Apparently it can be exemplified as early as Warad-Sîn and his brother Rîm-Sîn, contemporaries of Hammurabi. The goddess Inanna of Zabalam allows Warad-Sîn to build her temple "with her clear brow" (WS 6); the god Nanna looked at his city Ur "with clear brow and heart's joy" (WS 29, 31) when he destined a great fate for it. If we go still further back, to Gudea of Lagash, the phrase introducing a divine benefit is more simple, *igi-zi mu-ši-bar*, "he looked at him (the recipient) truly." Here the benevolence is expressed by *mu-ši-bar*, "looked at him" (dislike or anger is expressed by looking away) and the genuineness of this mood of benevolence is expressed in *zid*, "truly." Here, thus, the phrase is reduced to its essentials, its legal content precisely as pointed out by Muffs: true voluntariness. One might perhaps ask why it was felt necessary to embroider the phrase so heavily. The only explanation that occurs to me is the need to find some external expression of the inner state of mind, one that could be testified to by witnesses. But certainty can of course not be obtained.

In conclusion let me only say that this book by Muffs is indeed, in the full sense, a gift given "with a clear brow and heart's joy," a gift to evoke serenity and joy in its readers.

Thorkild Jacobsen
April 1992

PREFACE AND ACKNOWLEDGMENTS

In the nearly quarter century since the publication of *Studies in the Aramaic Legal Papyri from Elephantine* I have written on a variety of topics related to law and language, religion and emotion, as they existed in the ancient Near East. I have gathered together these studies here with an introduction explaining the development of my interests, as well as a bibliography. Some of the previously published essays saw the light of day in some rather obscure places, and I am happy to be able to make them available again; I have not been able to revise them significantly. About a third of the contents of the volume has not been previously published in English. Chapters 2 and 6, along with the Introduction, have not been published before, and Chapter 1 has previously appeared only in Hebrew. In preparing this collection and the bibliography I have sometimes added notices of recent reprints and translations of scholarly work, but I have not updated the base from which I worked.

* * *

For vocalized Hebrew and Aramaic I have used a form of the transliteration system recommended for the publications of the Association for Jewish Studies. The vowels are represented by the nearest equivalents in the roman alphabet, and the consonants are represented as follows: א is shown by ʾ or, where quiescent, not represented; בּ is shown by *b* and ב by *v*; both גּ and ג are transliterated by *g*, both דּ and ד by *d*; for ה *h* is used; for ו *v* is used where a vowel is not intended; for ז *z* is used, for ח *ḥ*, and for ט *ṭ*; כּ is transliterated by *k* and כ by *kh*; for ל *l* is used, for מ *m*, for נ *n*, for ס *s*, and for ע ʿ; פּ is transliterated by *p* and by פ by *f*; for צ *ṣ* is used, for ק *q*, for ר *r*, for שׂ *s*, and for שׁ *sh*; *t* represents both תּ and ת. The strong dagesh is indicated by doubling (except in the case of *sh* and after the article, a preposition with the article, or relevant forms of the conjunction). For unvocalized Hebrew and Aramaic, where such seemed advisable, and for the other Semitic languages I have followed the usual scholarly conventions. Transliteration is a burden for those at home in

Hebrew, but for single words and short quotations its use has been unavoidable.

* * *

I would like to thank several people for the extraordinary kindness they have shown in helping to put this book together.

My colleague Edward L. Greenstein has offered unstinting and meticulous editorial advice throughout the production of this volume. His wisdom and experience are a precious gift which I cherish highly. I literally could not have produced this volume without his help.

My colleague David Marcus has also demonstrated enormous generosity in sharing his fund of profound knowledge of Semitic languages and literature.

My friend and former student Tikva Frymer-Kensky offered her wise ear and emotional solidarity.

My friend and student Diane M. Sharon has helped me edit this book with great wisdom and skill. She has helped me more than I can express.

I also acknowledge אחרון אחרון חביב my wife Yocheved Herschlag Muffs, to whom this volume is dedicated, for her limitless stores of patience, insight, and love.

At this point, I realize what a deep debt of gratitude I owe to my teachers, especially to E. A. Speiser, Saul Lieberman, H. L. Ginsberg, Thorkild Jacobsen, and Louis Finkelstein; and to my parents, Barnet and Mary Muffs, my first teachers, for the model of their piety and goodness.

I would also like to thank my colleagues at the Jewish Theological Seminary, as well as my many friends in Jerusalem, who generously answered queries on various issues. Above all, I would like to thank my old friend, Chancellor Ismar Schorsch, for his generosity in including this volume among the Seminary's publications.

* * *

I gratefully acknowledge the publishers whose gracious permission enables me to reprint articles in this book which first appeared in their publications.

Am Oved Publishers, Ltd., which, in cooperation with the Jewish Theological Seminary, published a Hebrew-language version of Chapter

1 as "Bein Din Laraḥamim: Tefilatan Shel Nevi'im" in the volume *Torah Nidreshet* (1984). I am responsible for its translation into English.

The Ancient Near Eastern Society, which published Chapter 8 as "Love and Joy as Metaphors . . . Part II: The Joy of Giving," in *Journal of the Ancient Near Eastern Society* 11 (1979); and Chapter 5 as "Two Comparative Lexical Studies," in volume 5 of the same periodical (1973).

E. J. Brill, which published Chapter 7 as "Love and Joy as Metaphors . . . . Part I," in J. Neusner, ed., *Christianity, Judaism and other Greco-Roman Cults: Studies for Morton Smith at Sixty*; and Chapter 3 as "A History of Mesopotamian Religion," in *Numen*.

The Oriental Institute, Oxford University, which published Chapter 4 as "Abraham the Noble Warrior: Patriarchal Politics and Laws of War in Ancient Israel," in the *Journal of Jewish Studies*, Essays in Honour of Yigael Yadin 33 (1982).

Yochanan Muffs
Jewish Theological Seminary of America
April 1992

INTRODUCTION

THE PSYCHOLOGY OF ANCIENT ISRAEL: ASPECTS OF LAW AND RELIGION

This is a book about law and religion. It opens with a study of prophetic intercession as a response to the tensions inherent in monotheism, the struggles between love and justice that seem to take place within Israel's God. The final chapters concern the rich legal vocabulary in which Israelites expressed ideas of freedom and spontaneity. The intervening essays also deal with legal language and concepts in religious contexts.

Law is a synthesis of form and content, yet it is formal only on the surface. I have attempted to spell out some of the primal feelings underlying the law. Law in the biblical pattern of culture is a reflection of God's "urge" to create and God's "need" for kinsmen. God desires to translate the Torah—the plan for a moral world—through the instrumentality of the people God loves, Israel.

I came to the study of law by a rather paradoxical road. I passionately disliked the proscriptive element in what was usually called law—the coercive, the anti-life, the limiting. Then, suddenly, I realized that ancient legal documents were telling a story, and that they told this story by a series of interrelated metaphorical clauses, clauses that had about them a poetic quality. If one would understand the document, one would have to decipher the code. For example, in ancient sale documents we come across three interrelated terms: "My heart is satisfied," "I remove myself from you," and "You are now in control of the property." I was shocked to realize that in the supposedly rigid and prosaic context of a sale document, one regularly found such metaphorical terms. I assumed that the ancients knew what they were doing, and that "satisfaction of the heart" must refer to something well-defined and specific, binding yet not deadening, a mid-ground between primal feeling and abstraction. The key to understanding the metaphor was strict philological method.

In the philological method, position and sequence are of extreme importance. In these documents, "satisfaction" never occurs after "removal"; it is as if the processes are bound together in a temporal chain. One triggers the other. In ancient law, there was an underlying reticence to part with property. Only after the owner was properly seduced with payments and gifts was he ready to relinquish—in metaphorical terms, to "remove himself from"—the property, and to invest the new owner metaphorically with his rights and privileges. We know from ancient law that the seller literally "jumped out of his property" to leave room for the new owner. The new owner then took control by a series of symbolic gestures. He either built and settled the property, walked around the property, donned the seller's cloak, or broke a twig off a tree on the property. At a later time, presumably more sophisticated jurists would feel the need to express these processes more abstractly, but the sensuous aspect of law did not die easily and is still with us in expressions like *habeas corpus* and other concrete remnants of antiquity.

A word of caution. Language hides as well as reveals. The term "satisfaction" hides under the philological cloak of the words *ṭwb lbby*, "My heart is satisfied." Anyone with an elementary knowledge of Hebrew knows that the root *ṭwb* conveys the idea of "goodness." But this can be misleading, for the word *ṭwb* often has little to do with moral attributes. In legal contexts it can express either the notion of satisfaction or the notion of joy. Just as "satisfaction" in certain contexts expresses the idea of receipt and quittance, so in other contexts *ṭwb* expresses "joy," which in legal parlance is to be decoded as free and uncoerced volition. The reader is easily confused by the similarity of these expressions: When does *ṭwb* mean "satisfied," hence "quit," and when does it mean "happy," hence "willing"? The only way to determine this is by position and context. Thus, for example, if we find *ṭwb* at the beginning of a legal document, in the phrase, "A in the joy of his heart sold to B . . . ," we are dealing with an underlying predisposition to sell, not with the receipt of the sale price and quittance therewith. Position determines meaning.

The philological method is also concerned with parallel structures. Parallelism is an excellent way of establishing synonymity and equivalence. This is most clearly seen in the study of parallelism in biblical poetry, but suggestive examples can be found in parallel recensions within biblical narratives, as well as in parallel recensions of the midrash.[1] Thus the cluster, "He did the deed without hesitation/ doubt/ sadness but with the joy of his heart, with alacrity," is often broken up, with one recension spelling out some specific aspects, and other versions specifying other aspects.

An even more subtle use of parallelism may be adduced from the history of legal documents in the Near East. In the Old Assyrian sale documents (from before 1700 B.C.E.) the term for a receipt and quittance is the metaphoric *šabû*, "satisfied." In an identically structured deed from the Old Babylonian period (post-1750 B.C.E.) the term is *libbašu ṭab*, decoded as "his heart is satisfied." The next stage is evident in a Middle Babylonian sale document with the receipt clause *apil zakû*, "received (and) quit." Thus emerges the valuable equation, *šabû=libbašu ṭab=zakû*. Each period uses its own particular linguistic concretization of the root metaphor.

A subheading of parallelism is the antonym. Thus we have the expression, *beṭovato, birṣono*, "in his satisfaction, in his free will," which is parallel to the negative expression, *shelo beṭovato, beʿal korḥo*, "not in his satisfaction, in his sadness (sickness?)." If *ṭov* is decoded as "happy," that is, "willing," the expressions then read, "He did the action joyfully/willingly," "He performed the action sadly/with mental reservations." The negative spells out the positive.

Another example: The Talmud tells us that prophecy does not favor a person who is lazy or sad, but only one who is joyfully ready to translate the divine command into reality.[2] As we shall see, this inner joy expresses itself in two ways: (a) by the smile on the face, which is negatively formulated as "not sadly," and (b) with alacrity of performance, negatively formulated as "not slowly or hesitatingly." Hence the negative formulation "not slowly and not sadly" clearly spells out the two aspects hidden, so to speak, in the positive *ṭovah*, "satisfaction."

In 2 Chr 24:5–10 we have a description of a fundraising campaign unsuccessfully launched by the clergy—*lo miharu ha-leviyyim*, "The Levites did not hurry"—which is contrasted with the successful performance of the people and the officers: *va-yismeḥu kol ha-sarim ve-khol ha-ʿam*, "And all the princes and all the people rushed to perform the deed with alacrity."

As we shall see, the goodness that is joy, hence volition, hides a whole world of expressions dealing with the proper attitude with which to pray, with which to offer sacrifices, with which to give charity, with which God gives the Torah—in short, with the basic gestures and attitudes of ancient Jewish religion. Seemingly dry legal philology informs our theological insight. This is painstaking work. One must not force the material. The clearest indication of correctness is self-evidence.

It was during my work on the cuneiform background of Aramaic common law, which led to *Studies in the Aramaic Legal Papyri from Elephantine* (SALPE), that I discovered the metaphoric and sensuous nature of ancient legal terminology. This is the foundation on which much of my later work is based, specifically the studies on love and joy that could not have been written without the previous legal studies.

When I published my two studies of "Love and Joy" (Chapters 7–8 in this volume), I limited myself mainly to terms of joy as metaphorical expressions of willingness. On reflection, I noticed that in spite of the name of the article, "Love and Joy as Metaphors of Willingness," I did not spend sufficient time on terms of love as expressions of volition. I have therefore added to the second of these chapters a section on "Love in the Liturgy," which deals with this aspect. The two "Love and Joy" studies together could be called the prolegomenon to the history of *kavvanah,* the doctrine of legal and religious intent.

At the same time, in my work on the institution of prophetic intercession, I discovered the principle of the humanity of God. From the late Saul Lieberman I learned of the tragic nature of the Divine Person. The inner-biblical manifestations of divine personhood constitute another important aspect of my work. I have focused on the three major character traits of Yahweh, Power, Love and Justice, and the various clusters in which they are concretized. Power suggests God's creation, God's control of history, and God's imposition of morality on humankind. Love suggests familial imagery as well as divine anger and the modes used to control it, including the intercessory prayer of prophets and the holy fanaticism of saints. The tension between the traits of love and justice leads to the "doctrine of delayed punishment." According to this doctrine, God frees the sinner from his punishment by transferring it to his offspring or to some suffering servant.

The God who appears in the biblical text is not simply a metaphysical idea of non-dependence on nature, as Yehezkel Kaufmann suggests in *The Religion of Israel.* Nor is God the all-powerful principle of salvation. The emphasis must be shifted to the phenomenology of God as person.

Anthropomorphism, the depiction of God in human terms, is one of the most important features of biblical religion and of the three monotheistic faiths derived from it. And although its significance for the understanding of biblical religion is well known, no systematic study has been devoted to its interpretation. God is hardly an idea or a philosophical abstraction. He has a personality as many-faceted as any of the gods of antiquity. His personality expresses itself in His historical and dramatic relationship with His people. Furthermore, God also has a body that cannot be manipulated magically, though it can, at times, be seen.

Once this phenomenology is presented in all its varieties and manifestations, historical and theological questions can be raised. The Near Eastern background of the Bible is crucial for this understanding: the Bible was part of a milieu suffused with personalism, the expression of a growing human self-awareness. If people saw the gods as human, then they probably saw themselves as human beings as well, and not as animals. The new divine projection was another step in humanity's ongoing humanization. Thus the history of monotheism is valuable not only theologically and philosophically but also anthropologically and psychologically.

My major concern has been the psychology of the ancient Israelite. I long ago realized that the best way to study this is to study the divine image, the reflex of human self-understanding. In a sense, I have devoted myself to an historical-phenomenological investigation of anthropomorphic monotheism: its possible Near Eastern background, its innerbiblical manifestations and developments, some of its ramifications in the later monotheistic faiths, and the implications of these studies for a "new theology."

Historical and phenomenological models are Thorkild Jacobsen's various studies of Mesopotamian religion (especially his *Toward the Image of Tammuz*) and Walter Otto's various works on Greek religion. Jacobsen's later studies are of the greatest importance because of his growing concern with the problems of personalism and anthropomorphism in pre-Israelite religions (see Chapter 3). In my work I attempt to synthesize the major studies of the two polar aspects of monotheism: (a) the radical non-identification of the Deity with the world, as represented by the studies of Kaufmann and to a lesser degree by W. F. Albright, G. E. Wright, and before them by Hermann Cohen and the Jewish philosophical tradition of the Middle Ages; and (b) the anthropomorphic-personalistic pole represented by Jacobsen's studies of Mesopotamian religion, the midrashic tradition of Judaism, and modern students of religion from Feuerbach to Buber, Heschel, Cherbonnier, and the neglected modern Jewish thinker, Moshe Maisels.[3]

The creative tension between radical monotheism, which insists that the Deity is not to be identified with the *physis* of the world, and radical personalism, which insists that the Deity is anthropomorphically involved in the world, is especially important. I suggest that God's transcendental nature and His personal involvement in the world are complementary rather than contradictory: only a being in control of nature (including His own nature) can act with the freedom needed to involve Himself in the world of humankind.

The emergence of the biblical God from a Near Eastern milieu can be described by the following model: according to Jacobsen, Near Eastern religion evolved from a divine intransitivity, where the gods were passive manifestations of natural forces, devoid of will and personality, into a divine transitivity, where the gods are seen anthropomorphically with fully developed personalities and wills. Even in the late stage their identification with natural forces and their subjugation to forces beyond themselves had not yet been transcended.

Furthermore, following a suggestion of J. J. Finkelstein, it should be stressed that the will and the love of the high gods were directed mainly to kings—not to everyone.[4] It was the king who was elected by divine love and delegated to concretize the divine plan. Biblical religion, possibly because of its newly realized "transcendence," was able to find more powerful expressions of divine transitivity. First of all, the scope of the divine concern was enlarged: In Mesopotamia, the king was the object of the divine concern and the trustee of the divine command. In biblical religion, it was the whole people that was the object of divine concern and the trustee of God's command. Secondly, the nature of divine concern was stabilized. In Mesopotamia, dynastic succession was never quite secure because kings were chosen individually. In Israel, however, at least according to the official theology, Israel was chosen for all generations. One could say that the "idea" of Israel was chosen at Sinai, rather than any specific genetic representatives of Israel.

Moreover, as many modern scholars have recognized, the covenant between the people and God, the concrete manifestation of God's transitivity and involvement, was based on Near Eastern legal patterns. The treaty pattern is well-known. Less familiar is a pattern taken from the realm of family law—the covenantal formula, "I am your God and you are my people." The negative formulation found at the end of the first chapter of Hosea appears to be based on the common Near Eastern marriage/adoption formula[5]: "I am your husband/father and you are my wife/son." Thus, the political metaphor of Israel's subservience to the power of the divine king is complemented by the familial metaphor of God's husbandhood or fatherhood.

In any case, the interpenetration of law and religion in Near Eastern culture is a basic postulate of modern biblical studies, and so my previous study of ancient Near Eastern sale formulae was a necessary prelude to the study of biblical religion. My original unhappiness with the coercive aspect of the law is partially overcome by putting law in tandem with the poetic and the mystical. Ancient Israel, instead of rejecting the world and worldliness, made God its creator. Worldliness is not an enemy to be vanquished, but a challenge to be faced; the world is to be sanctified and structured according to the rhythms of the law.

NOTES

1. See Shemaryahu Talmon's study of contrasts between the Former Prophets and the Books of Chronicles: "Synonymous Readings in the Textual Traditions of the Old Testament," *Studies in the Bible* (ed. Ch. Rabin; Scripta Hierosolymitana 8; Jerusalem: Magnes, 1961) 335–83.

2. *B. Shabbat* 30b; *b. Pesaḥim* 117a.

3. For the works of these scholars, see the bibliography. Moshe Maisels's *Thought and Truth: A Critique of Philosophy* (New York: Bookman Associates, 1956) was translated and condensed by Abraham Regelson from the Hebrew original, *Maḥshavah ve-emet* (2 vols.; Tel-Aviv: Mitzpeh, 1938–39), written by Maisels under the name M. ʿAmishai.

4. See J. J. Finkelstein, "Bible and Babel," *Commentary* 26 (1958) 431–44.

5. See, for example, the works of Abusch, Greengus, and Yaron cited in "As a Cloak Clings," Chapter 2 in this volume.

CHAPTER 1

WHO WILL STAND IN THE BREACH?: A STUDY OF PROPHETIC INTERCESSION

Introduction

In Israelite prophecy, it is God who turns to man, and the prophet is seen by many as a passive personality, lacking an independent will of his own. The prophet appears secondary to the phenomenon of prophecy because he is the agent of turning, and not the one who turns, and also because at times he is sent against his will by the power of the divine hand that grabs him.

This view is not completely correct, although it finds support in many prophetic statements. Jeremiah, for example, says, "I did not sit in the midst of scoffers and rejoice. Because of your hand, I sit depressed, because you fill me with anger" (Jer 15:17). The same thought appears in Ezekiel: "And the spirit lifted me up and took me, and I went about bitter in the distress of my soul. And the hand of the Lord was strong upon me" (Ezek 3:14). In prophetic speech, the hand of the Lord symbolizes the apperception of a divine force that overwhelms the prophet, takes him up by the forelock, and commands him to speak and to stand up against an inimical people. This power alienates the prophet from society and fills him with gloom and deep depression. The hand of the Lord also symbolizes the submission of the prophet before the overwhelming majesty of the divine personality.

The prophet is thus the instrument of divine severity, the attribute of divine justice. But messengership is only part of the whole picture. The prophet has another function: He is also an independent advocate to the heavenly court who attempts to rescind the evil decree by means of the only instruments at his disposal, prayer and intercession. He is first the messenger of the divine court to the defendant, but his mission boomerangs back to the sender. Now, he is no longer the messenger of the court; he becomes the agent of the defendant, attempting to mitigate the severity of the decree.

This second aspect demands limitless psychic strength, independence of conscience, and intelligence, for, after all, the prophet is opposing the very message that he delivers. In this second role, the prophet is similar to the Baal Shem Tov, who is on intimate terms with his Creator and intuitively knows how to bend Him to his will. Because the prophet has an intimate relationship with the Holy One, Blessed Be He, he is able to approach the cloud of the Divine Presence audaciously.

The clearest example of this divine–human intimacy is Abraham in the story of Sodom and Gomorrah: "Am I going to hide from Abraham what I am about to do?" (Gen 18:17). Amos also speaks of it: "For the Lord God does not do anything without first revealing His plan to *ʿavadav* [His trusted agents], the prophets" (Amos 3:7).

The Hebrew term *ʿeved*, literally "servant," does not reflect any servile status. It is rather an expression of love and friendship. The Book of Isaiah equates the term "servant" with the word "elect": "Behold, my servant whom I have chosen, my elect in whom my soul delights" (Isa 42:1; cf. Isa 41:8). Thus, Moses our teacher, the prototype of prophecy, is also called *ʿeved*, "The Elect": "If it were not for the fact that Moses, His elect, stood in the breach before Him . . . " (Ps 106:23).

Even though the Lord sends prophets against their will to deliver messages to which they object, from Amos 3:7 we learn that there is a divine need to brief the prophet before sending him on his mission. From the Abraham story (Gen 18:17) we learn that Amos' statement is not theoretical, but an actual reality.

In Genesis 18, the Lord is about to destroy Sodom and Gomorrah. However, at the very last moment God recalls that He does not bring evil on the nations of the world without first briefing His prophet. Therefore, God says, "Am I going to hide from Abraham what I am about to do?" As soon as the Lord informs Abraham of His plan for Sodom, Abraham begins to pray and plead. If God is determined to destroy these sinful cities, why does He at the last moment have second thoughts and tell His prophet? Surely He realizes that Abraham might begin to pray, and that a battle of words and unpleasant bargaining is liable to develop!

There is even one case where the Lord actually suppresses His purpose from His prophet because He does not want an argument. When Elisha finds out what happened, he is most resentful of this suppression: "And God hid this from me and did not tell me!" (2 Kgs 4:27). In spite of this difficulty, Elisha intercedes, performs the necessary symbolic actions, and thus brings the stricken child back to life. Even though the prophet knows that God loves him, there is incredible bravery in prophetic prayer—one might say boundless audacity. For how can an ordinary mortal object to the decree of the King, even though he is the King's favorite?

Prophetic prayer is the most characteristic indication of the prophet's total intellectual independence and freedom of conscience. The divine strong hand does not lobotomize the prophet's moral and emotional personality. Prophecy does not tolerate prophets who lack heart, who are emotionally anesthetized. Quite the contrary, one could even argue that, historically speaking, the role of intercessor is older than the messenger aspect of prophecy. After all, Abraham is not a prophetic messenger, yet he is considered a prophet nonetheless. His prophetic nature manifests itself only in his prayer. In Gen 20:7, we hear God's command to Abimelech concerning Sarah, Abraham's wife: "And now return the woman, for her husband is a prophet, and he will pray on your behalf, and you will be cured." There is no better example of prayer and petition than that of Abraham in the case of Sodom, which distinguishes itself in its unbridled audacity against heaven: "Shall the Judge of the world not do justice?" (Gen 18:25).

There is something elemental expressed here. God's hands are tied until Abraham, a human being, makes a request, that is, until a prophet intercedes. Theoretically, this limit to God's total autonomy, at least at this level of transmission of the story, is self-imposed. But it is difficult to refute those who argue that at an earlier time there actually was such a limitation, that at this early time the prophet was a magician, an ancient shaman or, historically speaking, a reflex of the ancient Arabian *kahin*, whose *djiin* was subject to him, and not the opposite. We will return to this problem later.

Moses

For Moses, the father of prophecy, his entire life in the desert was one of sustained prayer to save Israel from the anger of God. At Tabera "the people were complaining in the ears of the Lord, and the Lord heard, and the Lord got angry, . . . and the people cried out (*va-yiṣᶜaq*) to Moses, and Moses prayed to the Lord" (Num 11:1–2). When Miriam, who spoke slanderous words, was stricken with leprosy, "Moses cried out (*va-yiṣᶜaq*) to the Lord, saying, 'O God, heal her!'" (Num 12:13). Crying out (*ṣeᶜaqah*) is a synonym of prayer and petition. Moses also requested mercy on behalf of his brother, and Aaron was saved: "And the Lord became angry with Aaron and wanted to destroy him, and I prayed on behalf of Aaron at that time" (Deut 9:20).

Let us examine two stories of prayer in the life of Moses, the story of the Golden Calf and the story of the spies, which come together into one organic context. In the incident of the Golden Calf Moses says:

> Why, O Lord, should you be angry at your people whom you have taken out of the land of Egypt with great strength and with a strong hand? Why should the Egyptians say, "Out of hate He took them in order to kill them in the mountains and exterminate them from off the face of the earth"? (Exod 32:11–12).

Pay attention to the strategy of the defense attorney who avails himself of all the rhetorical devices of argumentation, legitimate as well as spurious, to save the defendant. How clearly the ancient authorities saw the irony in the tension between "And the Lord spoke to Moses saying, 'Go down, because *your* people has behaved deceitfully'" (Exod 32:7) and "Why, O Lord, are you angry at *your* people which you took out of Egypt?" (Exod 32:11). Suddenly the Children of Israel are no longer the people of God—they are the people of Moses! But the defense attorney reminds the Lord that Israel is not Moses' people, but God's. It is as though Moses is saying, "Don't try to blame me for their sinful behavior. If they have sinned, they are Your people, not mine. If You want to get rid of them, do so, but don't try to erase Your connection to them." The prophets know that their God is a God of truth, and therefore they do not flatter Him.

Here, the defense attorney uses a strong and audacious rhetorical device coupled with moral blackmail; we can paraphrase his approach.

> Don't You know what You are doing to the reputation You have had among the nations of the world as a Great God, ever since they saw with their own eyes the miracles You performed, not in some hidden place but in broad daylight?! You are desecrating Your own name! The gentiles will say, "God deceives His people. He told them that He loved them, but deep in His heart He really hated them. What did He actually do? He took them out of Egypt only in order to kill them in the desert" (Exod 32:12). They will say, "He was not able to complete the act of redemption and hid his aborted redemption deep in the sands of the desert" (Num 14:15–16; see also Deut 9:26–29).

Aristotle's god, whose clearest characteristic is his indifference, would not have been moved by such an egoistic and human argument. But a God Who turns toward man and is interested in man's destiny and in man's reaction to His commandments leaves Himself open to such intimidation. We have two choices: Either an indifferent God who does not reveal Himself through a prophetic revelation because He Himself is devoid of personality and feeling, or a personal God presenting a full blown personality who is worried about what the nations of the world will think. It is the same God, according to Ezekiel, who cannot stand the argument of the nations, namely, "If these are God's people, why have they left their land?" (Ezek 36:20). This God cannot tolerate even the shadow of a doubt that His power may not be sufficient to save the day. Such a doubt is, after all, a desecration, "a dirtying" of His name. In this scenario, God is obliged to sanctify, i.e., to clear His name and reputation while redeeming His people, even though they do not deserve this redemption according to strict justice. Divine need is the decisive factor. The biblical God is anthropomorphic. He who strips God of His personal quality distorts the true meaning of Scripture.

Moses argues further: "Remember Abraham, Isaac, and Jacob, your servants, to whom You personally promised to redeem their children" (Exod 32:13). Here we have a compelling legal and emotional argument. Could it be that God is not as trustworthy as an ordinary human being? When an ordinary mortal writes a deed of gift or a deed of sale or a general contract, he has no right to go back on his word. But the Holy One, Blessed Be He, writes out a deed, enters into a covenant, and before the ink is dry, He reneges on His word. Moses is saying to God,

> You cannot behave in such an arbitrary fashion. After all, You are a King bound by the fetters of Your own justice. You are obligated to realize what You have promised, like it or not! You say, "I will disown Israel. I will make of you a great nation." But Your promise to our fathers was unconditional. Your obligation to the patriarchs is still binding. This specific act of Israel does not cancel Your obligation to the patriarchs. For if You destroy their children, and breach Your contract, how will You ever be able to look the patriarchs in the eye!

Even so, we have not exhausted the strategies of Mosaic intercession. Look carefully at the end of Exodus 32: "And now, if You forgive their sins, good. But if you do not, erase my name from Your book which You have written" (v 32). It looks as if prophetic audacity has won. But this is not the case, for God answers: "And now, go lead this people to [the place] which I tell you. Behold, my angel shall go out before you. And in the day that I punish, I shall punish them for this sin of theirs" (Exod 32:34).

In the following section, we will first investigate the matter of "My angel will lead you out," and then the matter of "In the day that I punish, I shall punish." For both, we will employ a form of quotation and paraphrase.

"My Angel Will Lead You Out"

God says, "My angel [and not myself] will lead you out." And God affirms that the sin has not been expunged, but punishment has been delayed. The transgression still requires retribution. If not now, then later, but payment will be exacted!

There are two antithetical approaches in the Bible regarding the appointment of the angel who leads the Hebrews. The storyteller of Exod 23:20–25 has a positive attitude: The appointment is a blessing. "Behold, I am sending before you an angel to guard you on the road and to bring you to the place that I have prepared for you. Be careful to observe his commands, because he has My authority." But, in the context of Exodus 32, the appointment of the angel is conceived as a terrible punishment. The Lord will not lead the people out personally, but hands over the business of the exodus to somebody else, namely the angel.

Pay close attention to the continuation of our story (Exodus 33:12–23). We have before us a section that has not been understood at all and has been mutilated by scholars and distorted by theologians.

The appointment of the angel as a leader of the people is not simply a punishment for Israel, for, from a formal point of view, there is in this appointment a terrible reproach to the honor of Moses. The fact that the Lord appointed an angel in place of Moses indicates that His anger has not subsided altogether: "If I were to let Myself loose against you for one moment, I would destroy you completely." It is as if Moses is saying, "People will say that the appointment of the angel is a sign of lack of faith, not only in the people, but against me!"

Whether Moses was really hurt or not we do not know. But even if he was not, he uses this formal sign of lack of confidence in his qualities as a leader as a clever device to force the Holy One, Blessed Be He, to cancel His decree. "And Moses said to the Lord: 'Look here, You said to me, once [at the time that You appointed me to be Your prophet], "Lead out [you, Moses, but nobody else] this people." . . . And You said to me, "I know you by name, and you have also found favor in My eyes."'" (Exod 33:12). All these are expressions that indicate the election of the prophet, the confirmation of his authority, and absolute faith in his abilities to translate the Divine command into reality. "You did not tell me at that time that You were going to send somebody along with me" (Exod 33:12). Moses' argument means, "You told me that no angel would mediate between You and me. Rather I assumed that our relationship would be direct. That's why You had better return Israel to its former state, a people whom the Lord brings out personally, not by the agency of an angel or an intermediary, but only by means of a prophet." This is the meaning of Moses' feigned personal insult.

After all, Moses himself did not sin; he is totally innocent. Moses uses God's apparent personal insult against him as a stratagem to restore Israel to its former status. God really is in a bind. If He reconfirms Moses, He has to get rid of the angel. But getting rid of the angel means a clean bill of health for Israel, which God seems unwilling to confirm. God cannot have it both ways.

Moses continues: "If You really want to show publicly that I am Your prophet, [as a sign of good faith in me], show me Your ways that I should know You. And remember, this people here is Your people" (Exod 33:13). Moses indicates that removal of the angel testifies clearly that the people is forgiven completely. "And God said, 'I will lead them personally, and I will give *you* peace'" (Exod 33:14). Moses understands the implication and answers, "If *You* do not lead us out, then do not bring us out at all. [If the act of forgiveness does not include the people as well, I do not accept Your reconfirmation.] And how will it be made manifest that both I and the people have found favor in Your eyes? It is by Your going with us, so that we may be distinguished among all the peoples on the face of the earth" (Exod 33:15–16).

And the Lord said to Moses, "Even this which you have requested, I will do, because you have found favor in My eyes, and I know you personally" (Exod 33:17). God gives in to Moses' stratagem. Moses is not entirely satisfied, because he feels a certain resistance on the part of the Divine. He forcefully demands a concrete sign: "Show me Your presence" (Exod 33:18). He appears to demand a divine theophany, and God seems to give in. The intercessor has won his case. But God is not entirely happy with this situation. It is not altogether proper for the King of Kings that a mere mortal should outwit Him at the game of logic. And so to demonstrate His autonomy after His defeat, God says, "I will have favor on whom I will have favor, and I will love whom I will love" (Exod 33:19). In other words, "Don't think that you have forced Me to do anything. I am powerful, and act according to My absolute will." The Lord appears to be saving His honor after giving in to the cogent and convincing argumentation of Moses.

A similar phenomenon appears later, in First Samuel, after the Lord regrets having elected Saul as king. The defeated Samuel says that it is not God's custom to cancel His decrees. "The Eternal One of Israel will not lie and will not relent and will not change His mind, for He is not a man that He should do so" (1 Samuel 15:29).

"In the Day that I Punish, I Shall Punish"

Now let us turn to explain the last section of the verse in Exod 32:34: "In the day that I punish, I shall punish." A person who understands the end of this verse will have no difficulty understanding the divine revelation of Exod 34:6–7: "The Lord, the Lord, God merciful and kind, slow to anger, and great in steadfast compassion, rewards with loyalty to the thousandth generation, bears sin and iniquity and transgression, but does not entirely expunge the record by visiting the sin of the fathers on the children and their children's children to the third and fourth generation."

This section is organically connected with the section concerning the angel that we have just interpreted. Furthermore, part of this clause is quoted in Moses' prayer in the section about the spies: "The Lord is long-suffering and of great mercy, forgiving iniquity and transgression, and by no means clearing the guilty, visiting the iniquity of the fathers upon the children to the third and fourth generation" (Num 14:18). There is something strange about this quotation. Logically speaking, it is reasonable to assume that words like "bears sin and iniquity . . . but does not expunge the record" would intensify the divine wrath. In the story of the spies, however, we expect not punishment but words of reconciliation. Furthermore, why does Moses omit part of the clause, "who rewards loyalty to the thousandth generation"? As we will see further on, these sections—"On the day that I punish, I shall punish" (Exod 32:34) and the self-revelation of God in Numbers 14—are mutually illuminating. The key to understanding them is in the words, "On the day that I punish, I shall punish."

It is possible to describe the history of ancient Israelite moral sensibility regarding matters of sin and punishment in three stages. (Keep in mind that this schema has no pretension of being anything but a model. There are those who think that this three-stage model adequately reflects reality. Others think that it is simply a satisfying intellectual construction.) To begin, we will deal briefly with stages one and three.

In the first stage, sin has an objective quality. It is like a physical ailment, like a cancer that can only be cured by fire or the scalpel. In this stage, repentance, good deeds, and even the merit of a father do not work. The sin inexorably brings about a punishment, which must be borne. There is no way to cancel this punishment or delay it.

In the third stage, the sin has a subjective nature. It is like a mental disease whose cure is achieved by the repentance of the sinner. Repentance is an inner, psychic process, a type of psychiatric therapy. A clear description of this process is found in Isa 6:10, if we convert Isaiah's negative formulation into a positive one: "And if he sees with his eyes and hears with his ears, his heart will understand, and as a result he will repent and thus cure himself."

It seems that if His sinner/patient takes the first step in the process of repentance, the Lord in His infinite mercy gives the penitent the strength to complete the process of repentance and to stabilize himself in his newly-found self. "Repent, O backsliding children, I will cure your backsliding" (Jer 3:22), or "And you shall take to heart all that has happened to you, as a result of which you will repent to the Lord . . . who will then return your exile . . . then the Lord will circumcise your heart and the heart of your children to permanently love the Lord" (Deut 30:1–6). In this phase, if the patient is cured of his symptoms by the combination of his efforts and those of the Divine physician, the sin no longer exists. The scalpel and fire are no longer instruments of cure, but are simply symptoms of the sickness that brings the sinner to the gates of repentance.

The second stage of this development reflects the tension between stages one and three. The attribute of strict justice makes its demands, and the attribute of mercy makes its demands. Justice says, "There is an objective obligation here—punishment must be exacted." Mercy says, "The sinner has repented, forgive him." The resolution of this paradox is the following: The sinner himself is not punished. The exacting of the punishment is delayed, and it is exacted from his children, in most cases up to the fourth generation. See, for example, the story of Ahab's repentance:

> And it happened when Ahab heard all these things [the chastisement by Elijah], he tore his clothes, dressed himself in sackcloth, and fasted. And he lay down in the sackcloth, and he behaved in a mournful manner. And the word of the Lord came to Elijah the Tishbite, saying: "Have you seen how Ahab has given in to my will [=repented]? Because he has given in to my

> will, I will not bring the evil in his days, but in the days of his son I will bring the evil on his house" (1 Kgs 21:27–29).

The repentance saves the sinner. But the sin must still be paid for and expunged.

A similar example is Josiah's sentence as it is delivered by Hulda the prophetess:

> I hereby bring evil on this place and on its inhabitants, according to the words of the scroll which the king of Judah read. . . . And so you shall say to the king of Judah who has sent you to consult the Lord, "Thus says the Lord, God of Israel, concerning the things that you have heard: 'Because your heart was moved and you gave in to the Lord when you heard that which I spoke about this place and its inhabitants, . . . I have also heard. . . . Therefore, I will gather you up with your ancestors and you will be gathered unto your grave in peace. And your eyes will not see all the evil that I will bring on this place'" (2 Kgs 22:16–20).

Another example is the decree that God made concerning Solomon, and the delay of punishment to the following generation as a result of the merit of the fathers and the holiness of Jerusalem:

> And the Lord said to Solomon: "Because . . . you have not observed My covenant and My laws that I commanded you, I shall rip the kingdom from you and give it to your servant. But I will not do this in your day, for the sake of David, your father. From the hands of your son I will tear it. I will not tear the whole thing from him. One tribe I will give to your son for the sake of David, My servant, and for the sake of Jerusalem, which I have chosen" (1 Kgs 11:11–13).

Similarly, there is the case of Jehu who was righteous in his youth, but who defected in his old age:

> And Jehu destroyed the Baal from Israel. But Jehu did not separate himself from the sins of Jeroboam the son of Nebat, who misled Israel. . . . The Lord said to Jehu: "Because you have done that which is right in My sight, and you have done what I wanted in respect of the house of Ahab, your sons to the fourth generation will sit on the throne of Israel" (2 Kgs 10:28–30).

One could argue that the luckiest thing that could happen to a man is to see four generations of his children. Joseph lived to see grandchildren of Ephraim; Job saw four generations of his progeny. And an Aramean priest from Nerab in north Syria had the following written on his casket:

> Because of my righteousness before him [the god Shahar], he gave me a good name and prolonged my days. On the day I died, my mouth was not closed to words, and with my eyes, what do I see? Children of the fourth generation, who wept for me, being distraught.[1]

It is well-known that legal formulas are like fragments of brick, pulled out of one context only to be incorporated into another. Just as the meaning of the brick depends on the total context, so also the meaning of the formula is determined by the context. In the case of Jehu, the Holy One, Blessed Be He, balanced the righteousness of his youth against the sins of his old age. Note well: It is not written that Jehu experienced in his lifetime four generations of progeny, but rather that four generations will sit on the throne "on your behalf." Here the language is elliptical, and one has to supply "*only* four generations." Furthermore, Jehu's punishment is delayed, but his children after the fourth generation will pay the price.

One might ask how a human being could make peace with such Divine forgiveness. This whole procedure is the height of cruelty—it has nothing to do with mercy, at least according to our modern sensibility. This merely goes to show how different the moral sensibilities of the ancients are from our own. Those wicked people whose punishment has been delayed because of their personal repentance or the merit of their fathers think that it is a good thing, even if their children bear the sins of their parents.

The clearest example of such a reaction involves Hezekiah, who is punished because he showed the ambassadors from Babylon everything that was in his armory. "Behold, the days are coming when everything that is in your house and that your ancestors gathered up to this day will be carried off to Babylon. . . . And he will take your sons whom you shall sire, and they shall be eunuchs in the palace of the king of Babylon" (2 Kgs 20:17–18). The king has sinned, but as an act of divine kindness to the man who did good and was righteous in the sight of the Lord all his days, he is pardoned, and the punishment falls on his children, who are to be eunuchs in the palace of the conquering king. One might expect cries of despair, or at least the tiniest manifestation of dissent. Just the opposite, however, is true. The king's reaction is entirely favorable: "Good is the word of the Lord which you have spoken" (v 19). You might argue that we have here an act of resignation, but pay close attention to the end of the verse: "Hezekiah said, 'If only there will be peace in my day'" (v 19).

These stories have been cited to illuminate the doctrine behind "On the day that I punish, I shall punish." The doctrine of delaying the punishment of objective sin onto the descendants of the actual sinner is a feature of a certain stage of the moral development of ancient Israel.

Sara Japhet has shown that the doctrine of delayed punishment is one of the main elements in the philosophy of history of the editor of the Book of Kings.[2] This orientation was canceled out by the Chronicler, whose guiding principle is entirely different! Each man dies for his own sin. A person who sins is punished immediately. There is no delay of punishment, and the following generation is untouched.

As we said above, the first reaction of the modern reader to the moral doctrine of stage two is one of great discomfort. We can understand the primitive doctrine of stage one: sin has an almost physical reality to it; repentance does not help. Clearly, we have no difficulty understanding stage three: Repentance expunges sin entirely. And indeed, stage two is the most difficult of the options available. The situation is analogous to the following: The atom bomb will destroy us and our family now, in our lifetime; or we will die at a ripe old age, and our children will die in an atomic holocaust. Which of the two alternatives will the sensitive person choose? I think one would prefer the second option, and so, it seems, did the ancients.

This doctrine of delayed punishment, which manifests itself in the expression, "in the day that I punish," is the key to understanding the divine revelation in Exodus 34: "The Lord, the Lord, God merciful and kind, slow to anger." It is often almost impossible to understand the simple historical explanation of a biblical verse once it has been recycled into a new liturgical context and become worn out as an empty figure of speech. This is not to deny the creativity of the liturgical recycling. The synagogue poet cuts here, adds a stitch there, and this is the greatness of the later liturgy. But this liturgical creativity can hide from us the simple historical explanation. In my opinion, this is the simple meaning of the verses: There is available to the righteous an inexhaustible fund of divine grace which they enjoy, as do their progeny after them for a thousand generations. But God also wants to treat the wicked in a kind fashion. God bears their sin but does not expunge it entirely.

How can these two antithetical attitudes function harmoniously? How can the Lord forgive the sinner but not erase the sin? The rabbis understood this difficulty, and in their liturgical recycling they distorted the verse slightly in the direction of divine kindness. God bears the sin and certainly expunges. God does this by holding back the punishment from the fathers and requiring it from their sons and their sons' sons to the fourth generation. This is the meaning of "In the day that I punish, I shall punish."

When Moses prays in Num 14:13–19, we assume that Moses is thoroughly acquainted with God's innermost thoughts. When he deletes the first part of the verse found in Exodus and cites only the last, "he does not clear the guilty by any means, visiting the iniquity of the fathers on the children" (Num 14:18), it is clear that this activity is one of benign intercession, not of categorical condemnation. "He bears sin" (*noseʾ ʿavon*) is an expression of grace. The punishment has been delayed, the people has been forgiven, but the forgiveness is not complete. Clearly, in this context, Moses is certainly not citing anything that will exacerbate divine wrath.

When the spies slander the land (Num 13:27–29), the people rebels and is ready to stone Moses and Aaron (Num 14:1–4). The divine anger overflows: "How long is this people going to vex me? . . . I will strike them with plague and destroy them and make you a great nation in their place" (Num 14:11–22). The answer is known from a similar context in Exodus 32: Moses says roughly, "They will say that God was unable to bring this people to the land" (Num 14:13–16). Moses continues in his prayer: "And now, my Lord, have patience," literally, "And now let the strength of my Lord be great" (Num 14:17).

The language is that of self-restraint and patience, an expression of the attribute of mercy that is latent in God's power. God's power expresses itself in the control of anger and wrath. There is no greater bravery than this. Moses continues and quotes from the words of God. And because the wisdom of Moses is great in the work of prayer, and he intimately knows the mood of his Creator, he omits the first part of the revelation, "he rewards with loyalty to the thousandth generation," which does not fit the situation at this time. Rather he quotes the end of the section, "he bears sin and iniquity and does not expunge the record, but punishes the sin of the fathers on the children to the third and fourth generation" (Num 14:18). Logically speaking, the formula "he punishes the sin of the fathers," situated as it is after "And now, my Lord, have patience" (v 17) and before "as you have carried (*nasaʾta*) this people . . . up to now" (v 19), cannot be anything but an expression of mercy and at least partial forgiveness. It certainly is not an expression of strict justice and total destruction, as it is usually understood.

If we do not explain the formula in this positive manner, we are forced to admit that, when we put in the mouth of the prophet words that are liable to exacerbate an anger beyond all forgiveness, either Moses is a storyteller or he is not quite sane.

More than this, *nasa'* in Num 14:19 is not the *nose'* of Exod 34:7. "And just as you have carried (*nasa'ta*) this people from Egypt up to now" (Num 14:19) means, "And just as you have borne their sin, in other words, did not destroy them, so you shall continue to bear their sin." And when God says, "I have forgiven according to your request" (Num 14:20), the author does not imply a total forgiveness, but rather the divine resolve to bear the sin of a sinful generation until the time He actually punishes them, in other words, until they die a natural death.

There is a good possibility that Ps 99:8 is nothing but a poetic metamorphosis of one of the thirteen attributes of Exodus 34 and of the moral conception reflected in it. This psalm is well-known from the Friday evening service. Moses and Aaron are numbered among God's priests, and Samuel is included among those who call upon the Lord and are answered (Ps 99:6). God speaks to them from a pillar of cloud, and they observe His commandments and the law He gave to them (Ps 99:7). This prayer is intimately acquainted with the details of the ancient battles, especially the victory brought about by the prayer of Moses and Aaron—"O Lord, our God, you answered them." This first line of v 8 is easily understood: they prayed, and their prayers were answered with favor.

The next two lines of Ps 99:8 are more difficult: "You are for them a God who is *nose'*/and also *noqem ʿal ʿalilotam*." These lines are subject to a wide variety of interpretations. Arnold Ehrlich would render, "You were a sustaining God for them, avenging their injuries."[3] According to this, *ʿalilot* refers to actions of the nations who took out their wrath against Israel. Thus the whole verse reflects blessing and kindness. Close to this interpretation is that of the New English Bible (1970): "Thou wast a God who forgave all their misdeeds/and held them innocent."[4] Better and more standard than this type of interpretation is that of the NJPS version: "You were a forgiving God for them,/but You exacted retribution for their misdeeds." Such an approach is also found in the American Standard Translation (1901): "You were a forgiving God to them;/But one taking vengeance on their sins"; and in the Jerusalem Bible (1966): "A God of forgiveness for them, in spite of punishing their sins." The grammar of the verb makes it clear that the view of Ehrlich and the New English Bible is wrong: *noqem ʿal ʿalilotam* refers to the forgiving of the sins of Israel, and not of the atrocities that enemies of Israel have inflicted upon Israel. The concept "to take vengeance" requires the preposition *be* and not *ʿal*. One says, "I am paying back so-and-so for (*be*) his evil," or "I take vengeance for the Children of Israel on (*be*) their enemies." It is impossible to express the idea "to take vengeance" with an idiom like *ve-noqem ʿal ʿalilotam*.

Thus we have before us in Psalm 99 a liturgical recycling of one of the thirteen attributes, a recycling that reflects the duality and tension between divine justice and divine love: "You were a forgiving God to them." In other words, "You are a merciful God; You bore the sin, You delayed the punishment, but You did not expunge their sin; You punish them for their sin." It is possible to formulate the entire matter in an equation: the phrase *noseʾ ʿavon va-feshaʿ ve-ḥaṭṭaʾah* (Exod 34:7) = *ʾel noseʾ hayita lahem* (Ps 99:8); and the phrase *ve-naqqeh loʾ yenaqqeh* (Exod 34:7) = *ve-noqem ʿal ʿalilotam* (Ps 99:8).

The liturgical recycling found in Psalm 99 involves a linguistic reformulation of Exodus 34. However, there is another reinterpretation, which reflects stage three—a conception that is close to that of the rabbis—in Psalm 103. This midrash gives a dramatic and penetrating expression of the unqualified forgiveness of sins. The author of this composition knew the Thirteen Attributes as well as Second Isaiah and the Ten Commandments. However, he radically restructures the original context, not by the creative distortion of the phrase *ve-naqqeh loʾ yenaqqeh* to *ve-noqem*, but rather by polemical rewriting.

Psalm 103 begins: "Bless the Lord, O my soul, and may my whole being bless His holy name . . . Who forgives all your sins and cures all your sicknesses" (vv 1, 3). Pay attention to the identification of sin with sickness. "Who redeems your life from the pit; Who crowns you with love and kindness; Who satisfies your being with goodness; Who rejuvenates your youth like the eagle" (vv 4–5). This last phrase offers a clear echo of Second Isaiah: "Those who hope in the Lord will gather up new strength; they will sprout new wings like eagles" (Isa 40:31). The psalm then introduces the divine attributes by mentioning Moses: "He revealed His ways to Moses, and to the Children of Israel His modus operandi (*ʿalilot*), namely, that the Lord is merciful and kind, long-suffering and of great compassion." There is no doubt that here is a clear quotation from Exodus 34. How different is the literal metamorphosis of Psalm 99 from the creative midrash of the author of Psalm 103! After the reference to the Lord being merciful and kind, we might expect a further statement that the Lord does not expunge the record (*ve-naqqeh loʾ yenaqqeh*), as in similar contexts in Num 14:18 and Nah 1:3. Not so: the author of our psalm polemicizes against the moral conception reflected in the ancient text. Instead of "He will not expunge the sin," as is demanded by the context, the author proposes the opposite thesis: Do not read "He shall not expunge the sin," but rather read, "He will not rage on forever." In place of "He punishes the sins of the fathers on the children," we read "He will not be angry forever." (This last is another echo of Second Isaiah: "I will not rage forever, I will not be disturbed for all time," Isa 57:16.)

The author of Psalm 103 then continues:

> He has not rewarded us according to our sins, nor has He punished us according to our iniquities. As far as the heavens are from the earth, so has His lovingkindness been manifest to those who worship Him. As far as the East is from the West, so He has removed from us all our sins. . . . For He knows our nature, He is mindful that we are but dust. Man is like the grass, his days are like the flowers of the field. The wind passes through him and he is not, and his place shall not recognize him. But the kindness of the Lord is forever toward those who worship Him and His lovingkindness is for their sons' sons and for those who observe His covenant, and those who remember His commandments and do them (Ps 103:10–12, 14–18).

Here the author incorporates a subtle quotation from the Ten Commandments that is similar in its language, but not entirely in its content, to the verse in psalms: "The kindness of the Lord is forever . . . toward those who worship Him." This passage is a restructuring of "I do kindness to the thousandth generation for those who love Me" (Exod 20:6). In general, in the Bible, those who fear the Lord are identical with those who love the Lord.[5] Similarly, "those who observe His covenant and those who remember His commandments" is a quotation based on "those who observe My commandments" from the Ten Commandments (Exod 20:6).[6]

If you should ask why the Lord bestows so generously His lovingkindness without commensurate repentance by the people, the answer is that it is an expression of divine arbitrariness. It is the nature of the King to do whatever He wants, and nobody can oppose His will. When He wants, He imposes a strict corvée. And when He wants, He proclaims a gracious jubilee and an amnesty for all sins. As it says in our composition, "The Lord is in heaven, where He firmly set His throne, and His kingship exercises dominion over all" (Ps 103:19). H. L. Ginsberg writes in a discussion of Ps 96:11–13 and of Ps 98:5–9: "So . . . for the summons to the nations, the heavens, the earth, the rivers, the forests and the trees of the field to whoop, Psalms 96 and 98 give a good reason: an infinitely kind and good King has come to tend them."[7] In Psalm 103 the covenant world of Israel acknowledges the Lord's infinite goodness toward its members.

Samuel

The second of the great prophetic intercessors was Samuel. How many times he prayed and was answered! The first time was in Mizpah (1 Samuel 7). The Philistines conquered Israel, the ark of the Lord was taken into captivity, and the destiny of the nation was hanging in the balance: "And Samuel said, 'Gather all Israel to Mizpah, and I will pray on your behalf to the Lord.' . . . And Samuel cried (*va-yiṣᶜaq*) unto the Lord and the Lord answered him" (1 Sam 7:5, 9). The Israelites won the battle, not on account of their military prowess, but because of the prayer of the prophet. Note how this event was preserved in the collective consciousness of the people: before Judah Maccabee fought his decisive battle against the Greek garrison occupying Jerusalem, he gathered the people to Mizpah for prayer, "because Mizpah was a place of prayer in antiquity in Israel" (1 Macc 3:46).

Samuel prayed on another occasion. Critical scholarship has not given adequate attention to this prayer. Everyone remembers the grim scene of Saul's battle against Amalek (1 Sam 15:7–33). The king did not observe the command of the prophet to destroy the Amalekites totally, and this was the occasion for the break between Saul and Samuel (1 Sam 15:35). Many scholars have said that the tension between the prophet and the king was not the matter of the ban or *ḥerem*, but was due to psychological and political factors; the aging prophet is jealous of the political power now concentrated in the hands of the king. If we follow Yehezkel Kaufmann, what we have here is the eternal tension between church and state, or between the institutions of prophecy and of kingship: "Samuel made peace with the kingship, he even gave it his blessing. But we see through the battle with Saul that the institution of prophecy never quite agreed to give up its dominant status, and to subjugate itself to the kingship."[8]

Many readers of this story are shocked by the fanatic cruelty of Samuel and more would seem to side with the king than with the prophet. But such a conception of the story is more than a little distorted. Pay close attention to the simple meaning of Scripture: "And the word of the Lord came to Samuel, saying 'I regret having made Saul king because he has defected from My cause and has not observed My word'" (1 Sam 15:10–11). God is sending Samuel on the awful mission to cancel Saul's kingship. And what is the personal reaction of the prophet? "And Samuel was very disturbed (*va-yiḥar*), and he cried out (*va-yiṣᶜaq*) to the Lord all night."

"And Samuel was very disturbed." Is it possible for flesh and blood to be angry with God? *Va-yiḥar* expresses sadness and depression as well as anger: "Are you good and angry (*ḥarah*) over the gourd?" (Jonah 4:4). Or, "And Cain was disturbed greatly (*va-yiḥar*) and fell on his face" (Gen 4:5). Pay attention to the end of that verse: to fall on one's face is not an expression of anger but of sadness, as Ibn Janaḥ correctly recognizes. The clearest example of this usage is found in Joseph's response to his brothers: "Now, do not be depressed and do not be disturbed (*ve-ʾal yiḥar*) with yourselves that you sold me to Egypt" (Gen 45:5).

What is the meaning of "And he cried out to the Lord all night"? "To cry out" (both *ṣʿq* and *zʿq*) is an expression of prayer, as, for example, in "Why are you crying out (*tiṣʿaq*) to me? Command the Children of Israel and let them travel" (Exod 14:15). Samuel assimilated the divine decree, and his personal reaction was one of sadness and depression. He gave voice to his personal feelings in prayer and intercession. And we are not dealing here with a short prayer—"and he cried out . . . *all night"*—a long and stormy war of words.

It is true that in the beginning Samuel opposed the request of the people to give them a king. But he gave in to their request and anointed Saul as the first king in Israel. How many inner psychic dislocations can a man suffer? The prophet, possibly under divine command, suppressed his personal opposition to the kingship, and finally made peace with it. Now, God demands of him to cancel the kingship of Saul. Isaac Abravanel (1437–1508) understood the psychological reason for the prophet's sadness in this matter: "He was very angry because Samuel loved Saul with his whole being . . . and the king was the work of his hands. For after all, it was Samuel who anointed him to be king over all of Israel and who loved him with the love of the creator for his creation. Therefore, he became angry and sad when he saw that the divine anger was directed against Saul."[9]

Samuel, as a free and independent personality, voiced opposition as strongly as possible to the divine decree and attempted to rescind it in a fiery prayer that lasted all night. Unfortunately, Samuel did not win, for on the next day he went out to announce the evil decree. But deep in his heart he did not make peace with the decree: "And Samuel did not again see Saul until the day of his death, for Samuel mourned over Saul, even though the Lord had regretted that He had ever made Saul king over Israel" (1 Sam 15:35).

In other words, even though the Lord changed His mind about having made Saul king, Samuel mourned over the king's fate. He was so depressed that it was only a divine reproach that awoke him from his depression: "And the Lord said to Samuel, 'How long are you going to mourn over Saul, seeing that I have rejected him. . . . Fill your horn with oil, and let us get ourselves [a new King]'" (1 Sam 17:1).

The prophet reacts to this divine command by saying, "How can I go? If Saul hears about it, he will kill me!" I tend to agree with Abravanel that this reaction is "an insincere bluff, for Samuel did not want to anoint a man in the lifetime of the king, and it was a horrible thing in his eyes, the commission that he destroy the work of his hands. . . . Therefore, to get out of this awful commission, he says, 'How can I go, for he will kill me?'"[10]

Even when Samuel is standing in the house of Jesse, ready to anoint a new king, there stands before his mind the tall and handsome figure of the king. The prophet announced that which he did not want to announce. The tension between his personal will and the will of the Lord brings about horrible psychic depression. For how can one and the same man be the announcer of the evil that the king's time is up and also the petitioner for the recision of that decree?

Jeremiah

There are two prophets, Moses and Samuel, known for their efficacious prayer. One must take the power of their prayer seriously; echoes of it are still heard in Psalms: "Moses and Aaron are among His priests, and Samuel among those who call upon His name; they call upon the Lord, and He answers them" (Ps 99:6). "Calling" (*qrʾ*) in this context clearly refers to prayer. Jeremiah seems in contrast to be totally filled with anger and condemnation, as if he were an enemy of Israel, though this is hardly an adequate description of the reality. Pay attention to the famous prophecy concerning Shiloh:

> Shall you steal and murder and commit adultery, swearing falsely, offering incense to Baal, running after foreign gods whom you do not know, and come and stand before me in this temple of mine, and say "We're saved . . . "? Is this temple of mine a den of thieves? . . . Go into my sanctuary which is in Shiloh where I caused my name to dwell in former times, and see what I did to it . . . and I will do to this temple of mine that which I did to Shiloh (Jer 7:9–14).

It would seem that there could hardly be a greater expression of hate than this speech. What was Jeremiah's personal reaction to this speech? Scripture does not spell it out, but there is a clear hint in God's warning:

"And as for you, don't you dare pray on behalf of this people, and do not express supplication and intercession on their behalf . . . because I am not listening to you" (Jer 7:16). God well knows the likely reaction of the prophet. He knows the prophet is ready to plead for mercy immediately after he finishes announcing the decree against the people—but God is in no mood to listen. In the case of Samuel it is said, "And he cried out all night." In Jeremiah God says, "Don't pray!" How will the prophet find the catharsis for the love that is stored up in his soul if he does not have the opportunity to pray?

How do we know that Jeremiah ever prayed on behalf of the people? In chapter 14, the same prophet who poured out his wrath on the people now stands at the head of the people as its intercessor. In this chapter we have a national dirge lamenting a drought. Let us break down the chapter into its logical components and learn some important things about prophetic intercession.

The composition opens up with a description of the drought (Jer 14:1–6). It continues with the national confession: "If our sins (*ʿavonenu*) testify against us, Lord, act for Your name's sake" (v 7). Note the plural form of "our sins." Here the prophet joins himself to, and identifies with, the sinfulness of the people. He does not say, "your sins" or "their sins." The dirge continues with a section distinguished by its seeming impropriety: "Oh, Hope of Israel, Savior in time of sorrow, why are You like a sojourner in the land, like a fly-by-night stranger? How can You be like a shell-shocked soldier, like a warrior who cannot bring salvation?" (Jer 14:8–9). After such words of blasphemy, which can only be spoken by a religious spirit of the greatest sensitivity, Jeremiah ends this section with the statement, "You are in our midst, O Lord, we are Your precious possession; do not abandon us" (Jer 14:9).

And again God forces the prophet to repress his pleading: "To me says the Lord: Do not pray on behalf of this people, for even if they fast, I will not listen to their supplication" (Jer 14:11–12). This time, the prophet does not give in to the divine command but continues his battle of words. If God is not ready to listen to a confession that combines outrageousness with gentle supplication, maybe God will listen to an argument of reason. Now the plea takes on a more philosophical nature: "And I said, '*ʾAhah*, Lord God, behold the prophets say to them (the people), "You shall not experience sword, and you shall not have famine, for I will plant a perfect peace in this place"'"(Jer 14:13).

It is a little difficult to follow the line of the argument. Luckily, what is unclear in Scripture in one place is spelled out in another. One key to the solution is the expression *ʾahah*. Biblical dictionaries do not clearly distinguish the three particles *hoy*, *ʾoy*, and *ʾahah*, but each word has its clearly defined semantic field. *Hoy* is not an expression of pain as much as an exclamation: Pay attention! Listen to what I have to say! For example, "*Hoy*, sinful people, nation heavy with iniquity!" (Isa 1:4). *ʾOy* is an expression of pain and fear: "*ʾOy* (woe is me), for I am finished" (Isa 6:4). *ʾAhah* expresses prophetic opposition to a divine decree: "I fell on my face and cried out, '*ʾAhah*, Lord God, are you going to destroy the whole remnant of Israel by pouring out your wrath on Jerusalem?'" (Ezek 9:8).

Another example from Jeremiah will help us understand the verse in chapter 14 under discussion. "Behold, on that day, says the Lord, the king and his officers will lose their mind and the priests will be shocked. . . . And I said, '*ʾAhah*, Lord God. Is it You who have misled this people . . . by saying "Peace is yours"?'" (Jer 4:9–10)—by letting them think that the false prophets' promises of peace are true? Most scholars have some difficulty with this passage, for how can the prophet defend the false prophets and the people, and blame the Lord? The emendation, "And the false prophets will say 'How could you have deceived us?'", is incorrect for two reasons: (1) *ʾahah* is almost always the style of the prophet when he is opposing divine action; (2) the false prophets would not say "You have seduced this people and Jerusalem," they would have said, "seduced us." It is possible to understand chapter 14 in the context of chapter 4. In order to clear the people from the sin and the punishment, the prophet transfers the accusation from the people to the Lord, claiming, "You are responsible for their sins, for You have seduced this people into following a perverse path. After all, it was You who allowed the false prophets to speak. How can You possibly blame them if You Yourself seduced them into sinning?"

God is not moved by this sophisticated argumentation. After all, the people are mature individuals who have free will: "*I* did not send them [the other prophets], *I* did not command them, and *I* did not speak to them; they are prophesying a false vision for you, the product of *their* self-deception" (Jer 14:14). People are free, and God does not seduce anybody to sin. Nevertheless, the prophet does not give in. If the philosophical argument does not work, he can always fall back on divine mercy. "Have You really rejected Judah? Has Your whole being truly rejected Zion? Why have You struck us, and there is no cure? We have hopes for peace, and none is forthcoming" (Jer 14:19). But evidently God has had enough of these arguments, for He closes the argument: "Even if

Moses and Samuel were to intercede before me, I would not be moved" (Jer 16:1).

Every prophet finds catharsis in prayer. Sometimes he is answered, as Amos was (Amos 7:3), and sometimes he is not answered, as Samuel was not. In any case he has an outlet for his personal pain. If he is not answered, then he can at least mourn. But look at the horrible fate of Jeremiah: Not only is his prayer not answered, but he is denied the consolation of prayer. His mouth is closed by divine injunction. This double aspect of prophecy places the prophet under an onerous psychological pressure. If there is no resolution to this polarity, the prophet collapses or goes crazy. This is what we learn from the fate of Jeremiah. The prophet cannot take this tension, and for a moment he breaks out and curses God—a clear sign of his breakdown: "Why is my pain interminable, and my wound incurable? . . . Why have You been to me like a dry gulch, an unreliable source of water?" (Jer 15:18).

At this moment the prophet stops being a prophet. He has a failure of nerve. The end of the section testifies to the correctness of this interpretation: "If you repent, I will restore you to your position. You shall serve Me . . . and be My mouthpiece again" (Jer 15:19).

"If you repent" (*ʾim tashuv*)—the implication is that the prophet has sinned. "I will restore you . . . , and you shall serve Me"—this indicates that for some time the prophet had forfeited his prophetic status. "You shall be My mouthpiece again." The passage ends with, "I will make you, vis-à-vis this people, a fortified wall of brass" (Jer 15:20).

We have before us a dedication almost identical to Jeremiah's first dedication in chapter 1. But the prophet would need a second dedication only if he had stopped being a prophet. The prophet curses and blasphemes the Lord, and in spite of this, God restores him to his original position. This would seem to entitle us to infer that God does not oppose prophetic independence that expresses itself in stormy prayer. The answer to this problem is found in Jer 18:20: "Shall goodness be paid off with evil? For behold, they have dug a pit for me. Be mindful of how I stood before You to speak good on their behalf, to deflect Your anger from them." In order to justify his demand to punish his oppressors, and to explain that this demand is not simply an expression of smallness of soul and personal vendetta, the prophet reminds God of all his selfless entreaties. How much can any one person take? One might say that the task of prayer is "to deflect Your anger from them." The prophet mentions prayer as something that God reacts to positively. And yet there is no real prayer without independence and opposition.

This idea is only implied here. It is spelled out with exceptional clarity by Jeremiah's great student, the prophet Ezekiel.

Ezekiel

Most definitions of a true prophet are rather superficial, holding roughly that his prophecies come true. This definition is based on the passive function of the prophet. The question is, whether or not there is in the Bible a more subjective, psychological definition, based on the autonomous personality of the prophet.

A clear subjective definition is found in Ezekiel. God is looking for a true prophet but does not find one. Exactly what is a true prophet like? "And I searched [among the candidates for prophecy] for a man, a fence-mender, somebody who would stand in the breach against Me on behalf of the land, that I not destroy the land. But I did not find one, and I poured out My wrath upon them" (Ezek 22:30–31).

We have here a profoundly subjective definition. The first function of the prophet is to announce the punishment and to call on the people to repent. In this role, the prophet acts as the messenger of the Lord. But if the people does not heed the prophet's words and does not mend the "fence" of its moral being, the Lord will come as an enemy through the "breach." The function of the prophet is now to go up in the breach, to build a protective wall, and to prepare for the battle against the Lord. The prophet is like a mighty warrior, but his only strength is his eloquence, the strength of the prayer, which may deflect the Lord from destroying His people.

The notion in Ezekiel 22 is spelled out in Ezekiel 13, which is similar to it both in form and content. "Like foxes in the ruins were your prophets, Israel; you did not rise in the fortifications to create a protective wall on behalf of the house of Israel, and to be ready for the battle on the day of the Lord" (13:4–5). Here, most of the commentators obfuscate and do not see the image in all its clarity. The breach, as in chapter 22, is the breach of sin. The enemy is not the army of the gentiles that is placing a siege around Jerusalem. The Lord Himself is the enemy, the warrior who is setting His face against Jerusalem to destroy it.

This reading of these two passages sheds light on the real nature of prophecy. God does not want to destroy the people even in the hour of His greatest anger. In the depths of His heart He desperately hopes that the prophet will fight against Him and force Him to cancel His decree. The prophet who is lacking in autonomy and bravery of spirit causes the destruction of the world. But who can take upon himself this double burden of prophecy? It is enough for one person to be the messenger of the divine court. Is it at all possible for the same man to be the messenger and at the same time to plead with the Lord to rescind the message? It is not only possible, but essential. Not only does prophecy not annihilate the personal independence of the prophet, it demands such autonomy as a prerequisite for the prophetic role. Only boundless spiritual bravery allows the prophet to suffer the great loneliness of one who stands in the breach and at the same time to call on the people that does not listen.

All prophets prophesy, but only Ezekiel is able to bring to conscious expression the process of prophetic confrontation with the divine emotion. He achieves this, not by means of an abstract definition such as we moderns delight in, but rather by a graphic depiction. It may seem strange that Ezekiel, who defines the role of the intercessor so clearly, seemingly does not himself pray, but is rather the classical example of one who is the mouthpiece of divine anger alone. The picture is, however, more complicated than this. Listen to the heart-wrenching cry of the prophet after the death of Pelatiah: "And as I prophesied, and Pelatiah son of Benaiah fell dead, and I fell upon my face, and I cried out with a loud voice, and I said, '*ʾAhah*, Lord God, are You about to destroy the remnant of Israel?'" (Ezek 11:13). The reaction of the prophet is shock. In chapter 1 of Ezekiel, the act of falling on the face expresses the shock of seeing the presence of the Lord (Ezek 1:28). The prophet is overwhelmed, and the Lord has to get him on his feet and bring him to sufficient consciousness to be able to speak with him (Ezek 2:1–2). In chapter 11, the second falling is a falling of opposition and defiance. We earlier clarified the exact nuance of *ʾahah* as an expression of prophetic opposition. This falling is a type of prayer. For example, in the story of Korah's rebellion God says to Moses and Aaron, "Get yourselves out of this community, and I will destroy them instantly." Their response is to fall on their faces and say, "God, God who has placed the breath of life in all flesh, is it fair for one man to sin and you be angry at the whole community?" (Num 16:21–22). Similarly, after the failure of Joshua's campaign against Bethel, we read that Joshua "rent his clothes and fell on his face to the ground before the ark of the Lord. . . . Then Joshua said, '*ʾAhah,* Lord God, why have You brought this people across the Jordan only to give them into the hands of the Amorites to destroy us?'" (Josh 7:6–7). There are times when the prophet, in spite of the severity of the situation, has nothing to say any more. In that hour of desperation, he utilizes the final weapon in his armory: the silent prayer of falling on his face.

Amos is also among the intercessory prophets. The prophet opens with a prayer: "Who will stand up for Jacob, for he is so small?" (Amos 7:2). The words are still in his mouth when God cancels His decree: "The Lord has changed His mind in this case; there will be no [calamity]" (Amos 7:3). In the next scene, the Lord shows Amos another somber vision: "Thus the Lord God showed me; and behold, the Lord God called to contend by fire; and it devoured the great deep and would have eaten up the land" (Amos 7:4). This time, Amos uses stronger language, and the Lord cancels His decree yet another time: "God has relented about this, too. It shall not be, says the Lord God" (Amos 7:6). Twice Amos prays and succeeds in his prayer. But the third time the Holy One, Blessed Be He, says, "I will not continue to forgive them any more" (Amos 7:8).

The Turning of Love

The essential nature of prophecy is the turning of God from His eternal silence to establish a creative relationship, a permanent conversation with Israel. And if, because of the indifference of Israel, the divine pathos turns into disappointment, and the disappointment turns into anger that overflows all boundaries, then the divine initiative is placed in great jeopardy. The Deity who left His hidden palace of silence now takes out His anger on the very people He so loved.

If there is no balance in the divine emotion, if justice gets the upper hand over mercy, then the world is placed in great danger. Therefore, God allows the prophet to represent in his prayer His own attribute of mercy, the very element that enables a calming of God's feelings.

In a more radical formulation: God originally sent prophets to Israel to demonstrate to them His great love. Even at the moment of His anger, He manifests His love by listening to the prayers of the prophets, prayers that control and calm His anger.

Because of this, the midrash depicts God crying when Moses hands over his soul to die: "God said, Who will stand against Me on the day of wrath? (cf. Ps 94:16). This means, Who shall protect Israel in the hour of My anger? And who will stand up in the great eschatological war for My children? And who will speak up for them when they sin against Me?"[11]

Look at the phrase "the eschatological war for My children." It is clearly derived from Ezekiel 13. This war is with God Himself. How does the prophet participate in this war? By his prayer the prophet controls the divine anger. Here is a clear example of the deep understanding the rabbis had for the simple meaning of Scripture. Here the rabbis interpret the prophecy of Moses in the light of the thought of Jeremiah and Ezekiel. They are anticipated in this by the poet of Psalms: "And [the Lord] said He was about to destroy them, if not for the fact that Moses, God's elect, stood in the breach against Him to deflect His anger from destroying" (Ps 106:23). A similarity between the language and the thought of Ezekiel and the passage in Psalms is unmistakable. Clearly, Moses' whole life was a battle of words, his attempt to prevent the anger of the Lord from destroying the people. The author of Psalms singles out this first attempt to save the people after the debacle of the Golden Calf. If it had not been for the prayer of Moses in that instance, all of later Jewish history would have been nipped in the bud. The midrash spells out the implications of Psalm 106:

> God said to Moses after the incident of the Golden Calf, "Let me at them, and my anger will rest on them and I will get rid of them." Is Moses holding back God's hand, so that God must say "Let go of me"? What is this like? A king became angry at his son, placed him in a small room, and was about to hit him. At the same time the king cried out from the room for someone to stop him. The prince's teacher was standing outside, and said to himself, "The king and his son are in the room. Why does the king say 'stop me'? It must be that the king wants me to go into the room and effect a reconciliation between him and his son. That's why the king is crying, 'Stop me.'" In a similar way, God said to Moses, "Let Me at them." Moses said, "Because God wants me to defend Israel, He says, 'Let Me at them.'" And Moses immediately interceded for them.[12]

We said above that a close partnership exists between God and the prophet for the sake of stabilizing the divine emotion. If divine stringency gets the upper hand, it is the prophet's responsibility to activate God's love. The rabbis concretized this partnership by means of an analogy: "It is written that the Lord spoke to Moses face to face. [Read, 'mood juxtaposed against mood.'] God said to Moses, 'Did I not make a condition with you, that when you are angry with them, I will soothe *your* anger, and when I am angry with them, you will soothe *My* anger'" (*Shemot Rabbah*, 35:2).

According to Ezekiel, the function of the prophet is like that of a scout at the outbreak of war: "In a land on which I bring war the people of the land shall elect one man from its midst and shall appoint him as a lookout for them. And he shall see the war coming on the land and blow the horn to warn the people" (Ezek 33:2–3).

The function of the prophet is to see the approaching enemy and to warn the people. A true prophet is not merely one who watches on the wall, but also one who tests the wall. If the wall, namely, the ethical behavior of the people, is broken, the prophet issues a warning and makes a vigorous protest concerning the danger. By contrast, the false prophet does not test the wall. He treats the wall with total neglect. Because he sees no breach in the wall, he is unable to fulfill the third function of the prophet: "And I searched among them for . . . a fence-mender, somebody who would stand in the breach against Me on behalf of the land that I not destroy it" (Ezek 22:30). That is to say, the false prophet does not stand in the breach to push away the divine enemy by means of the power of prayer in his mouth.

According to Ezekiel, a prophet who is not a national intercessor is a false prophet. The rabbis walked in the footsteps of the Bible. They expanded this notion and criticized seemingly true prophets who predicted only evil, who may have seen the breach but did not stand in it to ask mercy for Israel, to deflect the attribute of justice from destroying the people. A prophet who does not recognize the deep love inherent in divine justice has a faulty conception of prophecy. Thus, it is possible to explain the talmudic attitude toward Elijah, the annoyance with the prophet's intransigence, with his refusal to defend Israel. We find in the midrash:

> God says, "What are you doing here, Elijah?" (1 Kgs 19:9). Elijah should have said, "Lord of the Universe, behold: Your children, the sons of Abraham, Isaac, and Jacob, have done what You wanted." Elijah did not say this. Instead he said, "I have been zealous for the Lord" (1 Kgs 19:10). God began to speak to Elijah words of consolation. He said, "When I went down to give the Torah to Israel the only ones who accompanied me were the angels who desired Israel's welfare," as it says, "Go out and stand in the mountain before the Lord, . . . and after the noise was fire, . . . and after the fire, the sound of great silence" (1 Kgs 19:11–12). Three hours later, Elijah was still in the same mood. Once again he said, "I have been zealous for the Lord" (1 Kgs 19:14). God then said to Elijah, "You shall anoint Elisha . . . to be prophet after you (1 Kgs 19:16). And that which you wanted to do [to destroy Israel], you cannot do" (*Yalqut Shimʾoni*, 2. 217).

We also find in a midrash:

> Moses said, "Listen here, you rebels" (Num 20:10). God said to Moses, "Therefore you shall not bring this community into the land" (Num 20:12).

> Isaiah says, "I am living in the midst of a people of impure speech" (Isa 6:5). Immediately after this statement, he finds in his hand a glowing coal. How do the rabbis interpret this glowing coal (*riṣpah*)? R. Simeon bar Nahameni comments, "*Riṣpah* is to be interpreted as *reṣoṣ peh*, 'break the mouth,' that criticizes my sons."
>
> Elijah says, "Because the children of Israel have left Your covenant" (1 Kgs 19:14). What is said to him? "And you shall anoint Elisha ben Shafat . . . as a prophet in your place" (1 Kgs 19:16) (*Yalqut Shim'oni*, 2. 218).

Another midrash: "There were 365 pagan temples in Damascus, where each god had his day to be worshiped. There was one special day when all of them were worshiped together. On that day, God said to Elijah, 'Before you start criticizing my children, go to Damascus and criticize *them*'" (*Yalqut Shim'oni*, 2. 218).

We are shocked by the sharpness of the criticism directed at a true prophet like Elijah because he did not recognize the love underlying divine justice and did not exercise the power of prayer on behalf of Israel, even if we say that hiding in this motif is an enlargement of the words of Ezekiel.

Perhaps the rabbis had a biblical precedent. The Bible does present the case of a true prophet whose prophecy is not perfect because he does not know mercy. This prophet is Jonah. Jonah is a prophet like Elijah, and almost his contemporary. He is the one who asks the Lord to take his soul because death is preferable to life if divine justice is not concretized before his eyes. In many important aspects, the rabbinic Elijah is a recycling of the biblical Jonah. And what is the lesson of Jonah? A criticism of Elijah may be implied here. Therefore, the rabbis dared to criticize acts of fanaticism like these, not only in Elijah, but in every prophet who knew only to rebuke, but not to intercede.

And if we should say that there are degrees in prophecy, that the greatest of the prophets is intimately acquainted with prayer, and the least of the prophets seems to be ignorant of prayer, this insight was already anticipated by the rabbis. They said that there are three types of prophets: one who worries about the honor of the father but does not worry about the honor of the son; one who worries about the honor of the son but does not worry about the honor of the father; and one who worries about both the honor of the son and the honor of the father. Elijah worries about the honor of the father and does not worry about the honor of the son: "I have been zealous for the Lord of hosts" (1 Kgs 19:10). Jonah worries about the honor of the son but does not worry about the honor of the father: "And Jonah got up to run to Tarshish from before the Lord" (Jonah 1:3). Jeremiah worries about both the honor of the father and the honor of the son: "We sinned and rebelled, but You did not forgive" (Lam 3:42).[13]

But what happens if an intercessor does not arise to worry about the honor of the son, to stand in the breach with his prayer, to deflect the anger of the Lord from destroying? According to the rabbis, the Holy One, Blessed Be He, rises from His chair of strict justice and goes to sit upon His chair of mercy. It is as if the Lord Himself removes the toga of the prosecutor and puts on the toga of the defense attorney. The Holy One, Blessed Be He, appropriates to Himself, so to speak, the role of the intercessor, and pleads for Israel in His very own court. This, it seems, is the meaning of the passage in Second Isaiah, "And [the Lord] saw and was displeased that there was no redress. He saw that there was no man, he gazed long, but no one intervened. Then His own arm won Him triumph, His victorious right hand supported Him. He donned victory like a coat of mail" (Isa 59:15–17, NJPS). This passage was thus interpreted by Abravanel: "To stand in the breach against Himself." Earlier commentators remarked that God's power and absolute authority will save Himself. Abravanel cites the idea without agreeing with it.[14]

A paradoxical situation is created. The attribute of mercy, internalized in the role of the prophet, seemingly fights with another aspect of God's personality, namely His anger. Perhaps the same idea is expressed in Second Isaiah in the following passage: "For I had planned a day of vengeance, and My year of redemption had arrived. Then I looked, but there was none to help. . . . So My own arm wrought triumph, and My own rage was My aid" (63:4–5, NJPS). This last passage is a parallel to Isa 59:15–17. Possibly "the helper" in chapter 63 is none other than the missing man of chapter 59. And possibly, on the basis of the formal structural similarity between these two verses, we will be able to understand why the rabbis were able to interpret the verse, "For the Lord will judge His people and relent concerning His servants" (Deut 32:36) in this way:

> [Of what does this verse speak?] When God sees that there are no people who plead for their case like Moses, as it says, "And He was about to destroy them, if it were not for Moses His elect" (Ps 106:23), then He sees that there is no man to request mercy of Him like Aaron, as it is written, "And he stood up between the dead and the living, and the plague was stopped" (Num 17:13). Another interpretation: When He sees that there is no one to request mercy on their behalf like Phinehas, as it says, "Phinehas got up and prayed" (Ps 106:30).[15]

Functional and Historical Parallels

Most of the sources that have to do with messenger and intercessory prophecy are derived from the ancient Near East. In the matter of intercessory prophecy we have singled out specifically the *kahin*, the pre-Islamic Arabian shaman, but our discussion will be lacking somewhat if there is no mention of the rich literature about prayer found in the Assyro-Babylonian world.[16] Landsberger demonstrates decisively that the classic term for intercession is *āḥiz/ ṣābit abbūti*, literally "assuming a fatherly attitude on behalf of someone."

At times the king intercedes before the gods of his own city, or a god of a low level intercedes before the high gods. If the Akkadian expression were to be translated into Hebrew it would appear in the form *ʾaḥaz ʾavot*. It actually appears in the *Rule of the Community* (*Serek Ha-Yaḥad*, 1QS), one of the Dead Sea Scrolls: "You shall not have someone who speaks kindly on your behalf among all the intercessors, *ʾoḥazey ʾavot*."[17] The expression *ʾoḥazey ʾavot* in this context refers not to minor gods, as in Mesopotamia, but to angels who can pray for human beings.

From a functional point of view there are similarities between the late Jewish angel, the biblical prophet, the Mesopotamian king or god, and the Babylonian *āḥiz abbūti*. The borrowing of words from one language to another is a phenomenon that requires further discussion. Wherever you find the borrowing of words, you will find the borrowing of concepts as well. Some would say that monotheism lowered the gods of idolatry to the status of angels.[18] The god Bethel was, for example, reduced in biblical faith to the status of an intercessory angel (see Gen 31:13; Jer 48:13).

As to which of the prophetic roles is older, the shamanistic or the messenger, we know from Mari that that is difficult to determine. One thing, however, is clear: The fusion of these two traditions is the decisive process in the history of Israelite prophecy. Ancient Israelite messenger prophecy stopped turning to kings alone in matters of ritual and began to turn to each individual, not for one moment, but for all time, not only in matters of ritual, but also in matters of morality. This new mode of prophecy was the instrument of the relationship between Israel and its God. The kahinic mode of prophecy was selfish by its very nature. It requested advice for individuals. It found lost donkeys for individuals. It revived the dead for individuals. It promised children for individuals. It cured leprosy for individuals. This prophecy served its various customers for a price. When the kahinic prophecy was combined with the messenger mode of prophecy, it did not lose its ancient character. It even caught some of the new spirit and produced a new type of Baal Shem Tov. From this time, prophecy concerned itself not only with individuals for a price—"There is no more bread in our bags, therefore we have no gift to bring to the prophet" (1 Sam 9:7)—but on its own initiative prophecy began to concern itself with the whole people, and certainly not for a fee.

It is possible to formulate the process in modern language, and to say that the private institution became nationalized. The polarity between, on the one hand, consultants for individuals, and, on the other hand, the active and outrageous advocates of the divine court who try to rescind the evil decree, finds beautiful expression in the lives of two of the most magical prophets, Elijah and Elisha. At one point, for example, Elijah is a messenger prophet who chastises Ahab: "After murdering, you want to inherit?!" (1 Kgs 21:19). At other times, Elijah brings the rain and revives the dead. And even Moses, the classic messenger whose main function is the chastisement of the people and the broadcasting of the divine word, even he brings forth water from the rock. His magical power makes war and breaks war like some Arabian *kahin*. Moses, chastiser and messenger, becomes a *kahin*; and Elijah the *kahin* becomes a messenger and chastiser. In the creative tension between the shamanistic elements and the messenger elements is found one of the secrets of the greatness of the Israelite prophets.[19]

This marriage between the shaman and messenger was made in heaven. Messenger prophecy became a powerful expression of the great love of the God of the absolute will. But this absolute love is dangerous if it does not find an ideal partner who always does what God wants, because every slight deviation from the divine command turns the love to boundless hate. If it were not for the institution of the intercessor in its new Israelite garb, who would calm the anger hidden in the heart of the frustrated divine lover?

It is worthwhile thinking about the great danger inherent in the idea of one God whose power is absolute, whose judgment is absolute, and whose love is absolute. If absolute love is frustrated, the reaction of God is absolute anger: "If you remember our sins, O Lord, nobody will survive" (Ps 130:3). Therefore, there is a need for many modes of calming divine anger. Prophetic prayer is a matter of persuasion and dialogue. What did they do when prayer did not work, when the rational arguments of Moses and Aaron were of no avail, when even one rhetorical word is not found in their mouths? "They fell on their faces" (Num 17:10). This gesture is nothing more than a marvellous mode of asking for mercy—prayer without words. And if prostration does not work, incense does: "And Moses said to Aaron, 'Take the censer and put on it fire from the altar. Take incense and go quickly through the camp and atone for them because the anger has gone out from the Lord. The plague has begun.' . . . And [Aaron] stood between the dead and the living, and the plague was controlled" (Num 17:11, 13).

There is another mode of calming the divine anger, and that is the vicarious expression of it. The Bible tells us of the cult of Baal Peor and about the orgies of prostitution connected with that cult: "And Israel became attached to Baal Peor, and the Lord was angry with Israel. And the Lord said to Moses, 'Take all the leaders of the people and string them up before the Lord in the presence of the sun.' And the anger was becalmed from Israel" (Num 25:3–4). It is as if God tells His messenger what He needs in order to becalm His anger. Immediately after this, "And behold, a man from the children of Israel drew near and brought to his brothers a Midianite woman in the sight of Moses, and in the sight of all the congregation" (Num 25:6). The orgy of sexual abuse with the daughters of Midian brought about calamity on the people, a calamity that was atoned for only by a holy lynching. "And Phinehas saw and got up in the midst of the congregation, and he took a spear in his hand . . . and he pierced the two . . . and the plague was stopped" (Num 25:7–8). The same concluding expression is used in the story of Aaron and the incense.

What is God's reaction when a human being takes the law into his own hands? "And the Lord spoke to Moses saying, 'Phinehas the son of Eleazar the son of Aaron the priest turned my wrath away from the children of Israel when he was zealous for my sake among them, that I not consume the children of Israel in my jealousy.' Wherefore, say, 'I give him my covenant of peace'" (Num 25:10–12). A human being becomes involved in the balance of divine emotion, and the divine anger is vented by the actions of that person, and not by the action of God. It is as if Phinehas saves God from an act which, if He had done it, He would have regretted.

This human involvement in the inner emotional life of the deity has a paradoxical advantage, a positive side effect: "I hereby give him my covenant of peace." We have before us an etiological story which attempts to explain why it was Phinehas and not another priest who was granted the perquisites of the priesthood and its rights. The same process of mollifying the deity is found in 2 Samuel 21. Saul broke the agreement which Joshua made with the Gibeonites, and as a punishment there was a famine in the land for three years. "And David said to the Gibeonites, 'What shall I do for you and how should I atone that you might remove the curse from the inheritance of the Lord?' . . . 'Let seven men from his sons [i.e., sons of the man who sought to exterminate us] be given to us and we will impale them before the Lord'" (2 Sam 21:3–6). There is a possibility that the dismemberment of Agag in the presence of the Lord is another primitive means of soothing the anger of the Lord.

A creative, polemical recycling of the story in Numbers 25 is also found in Psalm 106, which is thought to be rather late. This psalm seems to express opposition to the legitimacy of human expression of the divine anger. We have seen above that prophetic prayer and its functional equivalents of prophetic prostration, priestly incense, and priestly zeal (*qnʾ*) are effective ways of holding back the divine anger. Instead of saying, "Phinehas the son of Eleazar the son of Aaron the priest has turned my wrath away . . . by his vicariously expressing my zeal," as Numbers (25:11) has it, the author of the psalm says, "They yoked themselves to Baal Peor, they ate sacrifices for the dead, they vexed me with their deeds, and the plague broke out among them; then Phinehas got up and prayed and halted the plague" (Ps 106:28–30). Do not read, the psalmist tells us, "And Phinehas expressed the divine wrath in an act of manslaughter," but read instead, "And he prayed," with words, and not by the shedding of blood. The psalmist is put off by the act of zealousness dripping with blood, and so replaces it with conversation, dialogue, and rational means of persuasion. Certainly this is not an isolated example.

Modes of Controlling Divine Anger

We have seen the active role the prophets take in balancing divine justice and divine love. The softening of divine anger reveals itself in the following ways:

(1) God does not destroy the generation in the desert immediately. He exacts payment little by little, until the whole generation has died off. This act of kindness was called "bearing" (*nasaʾ*) the sin (Num 14:19).

(2) God does not punish the sinner himself, but transfers the punishment to another human being in the same generation. This kindness is sometimes called "transferral" (*haʿavarah*). For example: "And David's heart smote him. And afterward, he went out and counted the people. And David said to the Lord, 'I have sinned greatly in what I have done.

Now, Lord, please remove (*haʿaver-naʾ*) the sin of your servant, for I have done foolishly'" (2 Sam 24:10).

David was saved because he repented. But punishment for the sin had to be exacted: "So says the Lord, 'I give you three choices. Pick one that I will do for you'"(2 Sam 24:12). God suggests three possibilities: seven years of famine; three months of running away from enemies; or three days of plague in the land. And this is conceived by the author as a kindness! Compare also what is told of David when he did what he did with Bathsheba and Uriah the Hittite. David heeds the prophetic chastisement and repents: "And David said to Nathan: 'I have sinned before the Lord.' And Nathan said to David: 'God has transferred (*heʿevir*) your sin. You shall not die'" (2 Sam 12:13). The sinner repents and is not punished. But the record of the sin must certainly be requited, and from whom? The Lord transferred the punishment to the little one yet to be born: "Because you have acted in contempt for the enemies of the Lord [a euphemism for the Lord Himself] in this matter, the son born to you will surely die. And Nathan went to his house. And the Lord smote the child that the wife of Uriah had borne to David, and he was sorely stricken" (2 Sam 12:14–15).

Notice the frequency of plague in these cases. Possibly the chapter concerning transference of the punishment of the suffering servant belongs here: "Indeed, our sickness He bore, and our pain He carried. . . . My servant shall vindicate many and shall bear their sin" (Isa 53:4, 11). It is impossible to agree with the opinion of Yehezkel Kaufmann, who denies categorically the existence of the idea of vicarious atonement in the Bible.[20]

The doctrine of punishment and its transference to another constitutes the basis of Christian faith. This doctrine is distinctly Jewish. For us, however, it is not the ultimate principle, but a secondary idea which is, nevertheless, a perfectly legitimate one, and there is no purpose in repudiating it. If you want proof for the legitimacy of the idea of the transference of punishment, look at the rabbis' approach to the ten saints killed by the Roman government. According to the midrash, Satan appeared before the Holy One, Blessed Be He, and asked in an outraged fashion why the Judge of the whole world did not require punishment from the brothers of Joseph. After all, it is written in the Torah, "He who steals a man and sells him shall surely die" (cf. Deut 24:7). And, indeed, it was the brothers of Joseph who stole him. Why were they never punished? Or is it really true that they were never punished for this sin? Why does the Holy One, Blessed Be He, overlook the sin of the brothers, and the punishment demanded by their dastardly deed? Once the complaint of Satan is heard, God's arguments are put to an end, and He transfers the punishment that the brothers of Joseph deserved to ten saints of a later generation. We hear about them in many midrashim and also in the medieval liturgy.[21]

In light of the doctrine of vicarious atonement in Isaiah 53 and in rabbinic literature, it is possible to depict the Christian myth concerning the doctrine of vicarious atonement in the form of a midrash:

> The attribute of strict justice stood before the throne of the Holy One, Blessed Be He, saying: "Lord of the universe, mankind is stained by sin. They deserve to be destroyed." Immediately thereafter, the attribute of mercy prayed for mankind, saying: "They are Your children, Your chosen ones! How can You destroy the apple of Your eye?" Said the Holy One, Blessed Be He: "The attribute of justice makes sense, and the attribute of mercy makes sense. The scales are balanced. But God's mercy prevails, and God is unable to destroy them. But if the sin still needs to be requited, let my firstborn son atone for them."

Here before us are the roots of the myth of the martyred death of Jesus that constitutes the basis of Christianity. The idea of the transference of punishment, which is a secondary idea in rabbinic Judaism, becomes central in Christianity. For Jews, the center of their theology is repentance and good deeds and the divine forgiveness that comes in the wake of repentance.

(3) The third way the Lord controls His attribute of strict justice reveals itself in the verse, "He is merciful, He erases sin, He does not destroy, He restrains His anger many times, He will not express all His anger" (Ps 78:38). Here we do not have absolute mercy, but an act of divine restraint. "He does not destroy" completely—but there is some destruction. "He will not express all His anger"—but He does express some of His anger.

The idea expressed in the words, "He will not express all His anger," is opposed in the statement, "I will not give expression to My anger, and I will not return to destroy Ephraim, for, after all, I am God, not a man. . . . Therefore I cannot come in anger" (Hos 11:9). A new consciousness is here born in the mind of God. He reviews His previous behavior, and it is as if He says to Himself: "All those methods of self-restraint are noble in man but are not sufficient for God. It is fitting for God to give up this human pettiness of vengeance no matter how restrained and controlled." God simply decides not to get angry.

Finally, the attribute of love rules unopposed. Divine love triumphs over divine anger. This victory is most poignantly formulated in several midrashim concerning the creation of humanity.

The rabbis were acutely aware of this dialectical tension in the act of loving: the painful need to love and to speak, on the one hand, and anxiety that this love will not be properly received, on the other. This is the inner dialectic of the human personality and it is impossible to avoid it. Mankind can only overcome this tension by an act of bravery. We are not dealing here with a leap of faith, but with a leap of action: Communicate! Love!

> Said Rabbi Berechia: When God was about to create Adam, He saw saints and wicked men emanating from him. God said: "If I create him, the wicked will be born from him. If I do not create him, how will the saints ever be born from him?" How did God resolve this conflict? He consciously repressed the thought of the wicked from His mind, turned up the decibels of the attribute of mercy, and took the chance of creating humanity.[22]

> Rabbi Judah said Rav said: When God was about to create Adam, He created one group of angels and He said to them, "What's your opinion? Shall we create man in our image?" And they said to Him, "Master of the universe, what is he like?" And He told them. And they answered him, "Master of the universe, what is man that You consider him, and the son of man that You are mindful of him?" (Ps 8:5). God was so angry with the angels that He stretched out His little finger and burned the cosmic nay-sayers to a crisp. And so it happened with the second group of angels. The third group was a bit wiser. "The earlier ones, what did they effect by their protest? The whole world is Yours. Whatever You want to do, do." When they got to the generation that dies in the flood, the generation of the tower of Babel, whose deeds were really rotten, they said: "Weren't the first groups of angels right after all?" God answered them sharply: "Even to old age will I suffer, and even for eternity will I bear their sins" (Isa 46:4).[23]

The argument between the angels and the Holy One, Blessed Be He, constitutes a dramatic concretization of the inner tension in the mind of God. The angels give expression to the fear and danger inherent in the divine experimental communication. There is always the possibility that wicked people will be born, who will not participate in the divine-human communication. Their ears are dead. God, on the other hand, represents the demand of love to find for itself an expression in the world, whatever the consequences. Thus, according to the first midrash, it was the qualities of mercy and love that made the creation of humanity possible, whereas in the second midrash, divine forbearance is demonstrated, for

God seems to be ready to suffer the emotional frigidity and the perverse stubbornness of the wicked in order to have the opportunity of communicating with a few saints.

Love is an act of bravery and tolerance at the same time. Humanity created in the image of the divine personality does not reach its completion without the creative leap of loving communication. It is a great mystery that psychologists have not understood the importance the Bible has for them. In the image of the biblical God we have a definition of personality that is remarkably close to the modern definition. It is a little known secret that the modern Western definition of personality has its roots in the biblical revolution. The new idea in the Bible is not the idea of one God, but rather the revelation of a new concept of personality. The divine personality is, to a great degree, the mirror image of man's understanding of himself. And if you should react in horror, and say, "You are promulgating heresy," I can reformulate the problem slightly and say, "God is defined as personality, and humanity is created in God's image." Judaism conquered nature and put in its place the personality that revealed itself in an act of love. Everything that formerly had a natural quality to it took on, in Judaism, a personalistic cast. The cosmic sphere is now personal, moral, communicative, and loving.

What is the target of this divine turning towards humanity? What is the content of the conversation? What does prophecy ask of man? It is possible to concretize the answers in a poetic image:

> Once there was a great playwright, the cosmic Shakespeare. And once He saw His whole essence in a play. And the need to bring this play into fruition was an unbearable urge, an expression of His innermost being. But unfortunately, the platonic idea of the play cannot turn into reality without a stage, lights, actors, and an organization. What did our playwright do? He got up, built the stage, equipped it with lights and a curtain, and with everything necessary for the production of this Play of Plays. And where did He get the actors from? It was not an easy matter to find the gifted actors who possessed the sensitivity to translate the divine intuition into reality. For after all, He was handing over to them His very essence. Would they understand Him? Would they be sympathetic to His inner vision? So He invited one troop of actors and tested them out with some bit parts, but they were not adequate to the task. He then brought in another team of actors, and this one failed as well. Finally, He tried out another, younger troop of actors, even though it was lacking in experience. The playwright loved this group of actors, chose it, and handed over to it the vision of His life. We are dealing here with modern improvisational drama. Everything was not spelled out in black and white. What He did was to give the actors chapter headings and allow them (he did not demand it of them) to improvise that which was

> not spelled out, interpret the ambiguous and translate the hints into sentences and chapters. He promised them that He would always be there in the wings of the stage, and if they departed too radically from the script, He would set them on the right path by means of hints delivered by His agents. The play has begun, the actors have appeared, and the dramatist still haunts the wings of the theater, desperately worried about the fate of His play.

What does this mean? Poetically speaking, God is the playwright whose whole essence is locked up in the play—in the cosmic program called the Torah—which lay inert in the divine desk thousands of years before the creation of the world. And when the time came, He looked in the Torah and created the world.

The Torah says, "I was the instrument of God's creation." It is customary that when a human king builds a palace, he does not build it without consulting with an architect. And an architect does not move without consulting a blueprint to know where he is going to put the rooms, where the windows go. So the Holy One, Blessed Be He, looked in the Torah and created the world.

A Jew is not a slave who nourishes his master as in Mesopotamia, but a creative partner in the translation of the divine intuition into a concrete moral order. The Torah says, "By the beginning, God created the world" (Gen 1:1). There is no beginning other than the Torah. Therefore, the Holy One, Blessed Be He, created the world as a backdrop for the divine activity, provided it with lights, water, and food, only after which He created humankind. God tested humanity with many tests; He gave them one commandment (*mitzvah*) and they failed the test—ten generations from Adam to Noah, and ten generations from Noah to Abraham—and God refined humanity and finally chose Abraham and his descendants, and ultimately he chose Israel and gave them a Torah, the quintessential distillation of God's own psychological attributes. Israel rose up and translated the Torah into reality, and when they wandered from the right path, God sent His prophets to set them straight on the way. Humanity is indeed a partner in this play, for when they observe the Torah, they become partners with God in the act of creation.

NOTES

1. The Nerab Inscription (KAI 226), lines 3–6, trans. F. Rosenthal, *ANET*, 661.
2. S. Japhet, *The Ideology of the Book of Chronicles and Its Place in Biblical Thought* (Jerusalem: Mosad Bialik, 1976; in Hebrew) 136ff.

3. A. B. Ehrlich, *Mikra ki-Pheschuto* (3 vols.; Berlin: Poppelauer, 1899–1901; rpt. New York: KTAV, 1969; in Hebrew) ad loc.

4. The translation reflects several emendations; the change to *niqqam* is acknowledged in L. H. Brockington, *The Hebrew Text of the Old Testament. The Readings Adopted by the Translators of the New English Bible* (Oxford University Press and Cambridge University Press, 1973) ad loc., but the NEB rendering also reflects a transposition not noted by Brockington: *ʾel noseʾ ʿal ʿalilotam hayita ve-niqqam*; compare the treatment of this verse in N. H. Tur-Sinai, *Peshuto shel Miqra* (Jerusalem: Kiryat Sefer, 1967; in Hebrew) ad loc.

5. B. Bamberger, "Fear and Love of God in the Old Testament," *HUCA* 6 (1929) 39–53.

6. For the problem of dating this psalm, see A. Hurvitz, *The Transition Period in Biblical Hebrew* (Jerusalem: Mosad Bialik, 1976; in Hebrew) 107–30. For various formulations involving the attributes "kind" and "merciful," see Hurvitz, pp. 104–5.

7. Ginsberg, "A Strand in the Cord of Hebrew Hymnody," *Eretz Israel* 9 (W. F. Albright Volume, 1969) 45–50 at 47; on the relationship between the Psalms and Second Isaiah, see Ginsberg, pp. 48–50.

8. Y. Kaufmann, *Toledot ha-ʾEmunah ha-Yisraelit: Mime Qedem ʿAd-Sof Bayit Sheni* (Tel Aviv: Dvir, 1937–1956) part I, vol. 2, 162.

9. Isaac Abravanel, *Peirush ʿal-Ha-Neviim Ha-Rishonim* (Jerusalem: Torah Ve-daʿat, 1955–56; in Hebrew) 252.

10. Abravanel, *Peirush*, 252–53.

11. S. Buber, ed., *Midrash Tanḥuma* (Vilna: Rom, 1885; rpt. Jerusalem, 1946) ad *Parashat Ve-ʾetḥanan.*

12. M. A. Mirkin, ed., *Shemot Rabbah* (Tel Aviv: Yavneh, 1959) 42:9; further references are given in the text.

13. S. Schechter, ed., *Avot de-Rabbi Nathan* (Vienna, 1887; rpt. New York: Feldheim, 1945) 47.

14. Abravanel, *Peirush*, 272–73.

15. L. Finkelstein, ed., *Sifre Devarim. Siphre ad Deuteronomium* (Breslau, 1935; rpt. New York: The Jewish Theological Seminary of America, 1969) 378, ad *Parashat Haʾazinu.*

16. The classic discussion is that of B. Landsberger, "Das gute Wort," *Mitteilungen der Altorientalischen Gesellschaft* 4 (1928–29) 294–321. On the uses of *aḫāzu* and *ṣabātu*, see CAD s. vv.

17. 1QS 2.9; see P. Wernberg-Møller, *The Manual of Discipline* (Studies on the Texts of the Desert of Judah 1; Leiden, Brill, 1957) 53–54 and references; E. Y. Kutscher, "The Aramaic Calque in Hebrew," *Tarbiz* 33 (1964) 118–30 at 125–26.

18. See the interesting work of J. J. M. Roberts, "Divine Freedom and Cultic Manipulation in Israel and Mesopotamia," *Unity and Diversity* (ed. H. Goedicke and J. J. M. Roberts; Baltimore: Johns Hopkins University Press, 1975) 181–90.

19. It is not unimportant that Moses, Aaron, and Miriam are members of a single family. In ancient Arabia, the role of *kahin* is a matter of inheritance rather than election. The fact that Moses, the first messenger, exhibits kahinic qualities is an example of what Yehezkel Kaufmann calls a "border phenomenon" between pagan culture and Israelite monotheism. On Moses as *kahin*, see *The Religion of Israel* (trans. M. Greenberg; Chicago: University of Chicago Press, 1960) 227–29, and I. L. Seeligmann,

"On the History and Nature of Prophecy in Israel," *Eretz Israel* 3 (M. D. U. Cassuto Volume, 1954) 125–32 (in Hebrew).

20. See Kaufmann's *The Babylonian Captivity and Deutero-Isaiah* (*History of the Religion of Israel. Volume IV, Chapters 1, 2*) (trans. C. W. Efroymson; New York: Union of American Hebrew Congregations, 1970) 128–49, esp. 142–43, 148–49.

21. For the story of the ten saints, see the text in A. Jellinek, ed., *Midrash Eleh Ezkerah* (Leipzig: Colditz, 1853), or in J. D. Eisenstein, ed., *Ozar Midrashim: A Library of Two Hundred Minor Midrashim* (2 vols.; New York: Eisenstein; in Hebrew, 1915), s. v. *ʿEsreh haruge malkhut*; there is a recent translation by D. Stern, *Rabbinic Fantasies: Imaginative Narratives from Classical Hebrew Literature* (ed. Stern and M. J. Mirsky; Philadelphia: The Jewish Publication Society of America, 1990) 143–65.

22. J. Theodor and Ch. Albeck, *Midrash Bereshit Rabbah* (Berlin: Itzkowski, 1903–29) §8.

23. *B. Sanhedrin* 38a.

CHAPTER 2

AS A CLOAK CLINGS TO ITS OWNER: ASPECTS OF DIVINE–HUMAN RECIPROCITY

The relationships between God and Israel are reflected in a wide number of quasi-legal formulas modeled on ancient Near Eastern sources. In ancient Near Eastern law, the relationship between husband and wife was established by the clause, "I shall be husband, you shall be wife, for now and for all time." Conversely, a divorce was established by the opposite, "I am not the husband, you are not the wife." Analogously, when a man adopted a son, he declared, "I am the father, you are the son, from this time forth and for all time."[1] The relationship was dissolved by its opposite.

Similar to these two family-establishing relationships was the relationship between God and Israel as depicted by the prophet Hosea. At the end of chapter 1 the Lord declares, "You are not My people, and I will not be your [God]" (Hos 1:9). Thus we see in Hosea that the God–Israel relationship was conceived in an almost identical fashion to two kinds of familial relationships in the ancient Near East and Israel: marriage and adoption.

In chapter 2, the allegory of chapter 1 is spelled out in a more realistic fashion. The prophet says, "She is not my wife, and I am not her husband..., lest I strip her naked as on the day she was born" (Hos 2:4–5), a symbolic action which is associated with both divorce and the cessation of father–son relationships at Nuzi and Ugarit.[2] Similarly, when the wife is taken back at the end of chapter 2, the positive formula, "You will call me husband" (Hos 2:18) is re-employed, and God generously bestows upon His new/old bride all the moral attributes that she lacked in the first marriage. These are given her as her dowry: "And I will espouse you with righteousness and justice, and with goodness and mercy, and I will espouse you with faithfulness; then you shall be devoted to the Lord" (Hos 2:21–22, NJPS). Armed with these moral gifts, the second marriage can hardly be a failure.[3]

Furthermore, this reciprocity is re-established by the calling of names: "I shall show mercy to *Lo Ruḥamah*, and I shall say to *Lo ʿAmmi*, 'You are My people,' and he will say, '(You are) my God'" (Hos 2:25). These dual declarations approximate what I call the double-ring ceremony of Deuteronomy 26, of which we shall speak later.

What are the origins of these husband–wife, father–son, God–Israel relationships? Logically speaking, Hosea presents us with the negation of a postulated positive form. His "You are not My people and I am not your God" points to the existence of an older formula, "I am your God and you are My people," which is found for the first time in Exodus 6. The verse reads, "I revealed Myself to your fathers Abraham, Isaac, and Jacob under My name El Shaddai, but My real personal name, YHWH, I did not make known to them" (Exod 6:3). By implication, I am revealing it to you here, now, on this day.[4] A few sentences later, we hear the divine declaration, "I will take you out of the travails of Egypt, I will deliver you from your slavery, I will redeem you with outstretched hand and with great portents, and I will take you to be My people and I will be your God" (Exod 6:6–7). The proximity of the revelation of the new name to the first occurrence of the family-establishing formula cannot be fortuitous. The more intimate familial status that Israel now enjoys with the Lord is dramatically expressed by that new first-name basis that the parties now enjoy. Israel no longer calls God by His name El Shaddai, but by His real personal name, YHWH. This observation was already made by Judah Halevi in *The Kuzari*.[5] Judah Halevi says the use of the name YHWH in this context is like a person calling his friend Reuven or Shimʿon. In other words, God is not called Deus any more, He is called Zeus!

There is yet another step to the prehistory of this clause. In Exodus 6, God establishes a relationship with a people already in existence. Therefore, He can legitimately say, "You are my people." However, in the time of Abraham, there is as yet no people, so in Genesis 17 when the Lord makes a covenant with Abraham, He simply says of Abraham's children, "I will be their God" (Gen 17:8). When the people emerges, the tripartite formula emerges with it. However, even though both sides are represented, all the initiative is God's. After a period of maturation, the formula becomes two-sided: "And you have declared YHWH to be this day your God, . . . and YHWH has declared you this day to be His precious chosen people, as he promised you, on the condition that you observe all His commandments, and he will set you high above all the nations and make you an object of *tehillah*, *shem*, and *tifʾeret* [renown, glory and splendor], and you will be a sacrosanct people to YHWH the Lord as He promised" (Deut 26:17–19).

Mordecai Friedman correctly saw a reflection of a growing egalitarianism in Hosea's two-way declaration, "I shall say to *Lo ʿAmmi*, 'You are My people,' and he will say '(You are) my God'" (Hos 2:25).[6] The same process is at work in Deuteronomy 26.

The formula in Deuteronomy has a significant echo in Jeremiah 13. Israel is elected to be an object of *shem*, *tehillah*, and *tifʾeret*, "glory, renown and splendor," and to be above all people. The advantages are all Israel's. Notwithstanding the slightly nationalistic theology in Jeremiah, the formula is redirected from an anthropocentric bias to a theocentric one.

God commands Jeremiah to buy himself a new linen loincloth (Jer 13:1), which one must assume is much like someone buying a new outfit in order to look good. Then Jeremiah is commanded to stuff the loincloth under a rock in the river Perat (modern Wadi Phara, near Jeremiah's Anathoth) and let it rot. Later on in the chapter, this symbolic action is spelled out by the statement: "As a garment cleaves to the body of a man, so I have caused the whole House of Israel to cleave to My body . . . for My glory, My renown, and My splendor" (Jer 13:11). The chagrined lover takes his anger and frustrated love out on the suit of clothes. Israel was created to reflect God's glory, and the Lord rightly gets angry when Israel does not perform this service to the Divine. This is no longer a statement of human nationalism, but of Divine Pathos. Parenthetically, it should be noted that the Lord wearing Israel like a suit of clothes is a concept that we shall see later anticipates certain mystical or gnostic ideas of "God's garment." Both the technically correct translation of *ʾezor* as "loincloth" and the anachronistic gloss "suit of clothes" have been used, in order to clarify the twofold focus of Jeremiah 13. The "loincloth" image brings out the closeness described here—God *cleaves* to Israel and Israel *cleaves* to God—while the "suit of clothes" or cloak image emphasizes the attendant splendor, the splendor of God reflected by Israel.

Although the image of clinging is found in Jeremiah, it is anticipated by the Deuteronomic school, which, alone of all the Pentateuchal sources, stresses the idea that God chose Israel to cleave to Him, *ledovqa bo*.[7] Thus, Jeremiah, in transcending Deuteronomy, does so using Deuteronomic building blocks. In Deuteronomy, man is commanded to cleave to God. In Jeremiah the metaphor is restructured theomorphically: God causes Israel to cleave to *Him*.

The rabbis in the midrash were well aware of the significance of the metaphor in Jeremiah 13. On the verse, "Holy shall you be" (Lev 19:2), the rabbis in the *Tanḥuma* comment:

> Why "shall ye be holy, for I am holy"? Because I caused you to cleave to My loins. As the girdle clings to the loins of man, so I have caused the whole House of Israel to cling to Me. The Holy One, Blessed Be He, said to the whole House of Israel, "I am not like flesh and blood." A human king does not allow ordinary citizens to be called by his name. Just consider the fact that when a man, wanting to insult his friend, calls him, "You damned Augustus," he immediately incurs the death penalty for this indignity; but Israel has God's name incorporated in theirs, just as the Holy One, Blessed Be He, is called "The Holy One," so God called Israel holy, and Israel incurs no guilt.[8]

In chapter 33 of Jeremiah, we see that the Lord cannot abide the destruction of His suit of clothes: "And I shall return the exile of Judah, . . . and I shall purify them of their sins which they have committed against Me, . . . and [this act of redemption] shall be for Me for *shem sason* [joyful glory], for *tehillah* and *tif᾿eret* [renown and splendor], for all the nations of the world who will hear all the good things I am doing for them, and they shall be stunned and excited for all these good things" (Jer 33:7–9). Midrashically, the *shem, tehillah,* and *tif᾿eret* of Deuteronomy have undergone two recyclings, the first from Deuteronomy to Jeremiah, and the second from Jeremiah 13 to Jeremiah 33. Jeremiah 33 resurfaces in a new form in Isaiah 61: "The Lord has appointed me . . . to declare an amnesty for prisoners and a moratorium to slaves. . . . To give them a turban [*pe᾿er*] for ashes [*᾿efer*], the oil of joy [*shemen sason*] for mourning, the garment of glory instead of the spirit of heaviness" (Isa 61:1–3). The *shemen sason*, "oil of joy," echoes Jeremiah's *shem sason*: a garment of glory instead of a depressed spirit.

In the societies of the ancient Near East there is a wide spectrum of relationships of dependency. Almost everybody is dependent on somebody else. The main types of these dependent relationships are father–son, husband–wife, master–slave, creditor–debtor, king–subject, God–people. All the parties to the relationships have responsibilities and a certain number of rights, depending on where one stands on the spectrum. The lowest slave or debtor is not devoid of rights, even though he has more obligations than rights. Even the most subservient has the right to food, shelter, and protection. It is not for naught that the subservient population of a Roman household is called the *familia*, and the head of this group of clients is called a *pater familias.*

Let us return for a moment to an aspect of family law. The extended family in the ancient world also included slaves. Slaves were entitled to their master's concern, and thus were assimilated to the status of children. In the ancient Near East, it was not strange for a slave to have written on his hand the name of his master.[9] A reflex of this is found in Isaiah: "Another shall mark his arm 'the Lord's,' and adopt the name 'Israel'" (Isa 44:5, NJPS). In a later chapter in Isaiah, God says, "I have engraved you on the palms of My hands" (Isa 49:16, NJPS).[10]

The two tattoos immediately strike a receptive chord with anyone acquainted with later midrashic thought. We hear in the midrash of two sets of cosmic phylacteries, of God's and of Israel's. Just as God's name was inscribed on Israel's phylacteries, so Israel's name was inscribed on God's.[11] The tattoo was a more primitive form of a phylactery. Abraham Epstein has pointed out that the imagery in Proverbs, which normative Judaism applied to the phylacteries, was interpreted by early Jewish Christians, Samaritans and some Karaites as referring to a tattoo.[12] Thus, the structural/functional equivalence between the tattoo and the phylactery seems to be established. The wearing of the hat / phylactery / tattoo is a means of "wearing" the divinity. One "wears" God on one's head; one "wraps" God on one's arm; one "imprints" God on one's flesh. The same means of coming close to the beloved is available to God, who wears Israel on His head and wraps Israel around His arm. To the extent that each of these symbolic gestures brings God and people closer, to that extent they are functionally and structurally equivalent.

Magical phylacteries are attested all through the ancient world.[13] Phylacteries can be seen as a type of magical garment: The person who wears the phylacteries is wearing God's law.

In the same vein, God wears Israel as a suit of clothes. In one passage in Isaiah it is said that God holds Israel in His hand like a cap that can be worn on the head if so desired (Isa 62:3). In another passage, Israel wears God as a crown of glory (Isa 28:5). The cap or crown represents Israel in the first example, and God in the second. The personal garment stands for the person.

This synecdoche is familiar in the ancient Near East. The use of the hat as a symbolic representation of the deity in his non-iconic form is well known from Near Eastern royal inscriptions.[14] In the Aramaic inscriptions from Zinjirli, for example, the hats literally represent the various deities who are partners to the treaty.[15] A similar praxis is known from the Middle Babylonian *kudurru* documents, where the symbols of the gods, especially their hats, stand in place of an iconic representation.

In summary, we have before us a series of symbolic representations of the divine–human interaction: the double tattoo, the double phylactery, the double hat, and Israel as Divine Garment. It matters little, logically, who is the wearer and who is the clothes. Each cleaves to the other. In the later Jewish hymn *ʾAnʿim Zemirot*, we see a grand orchestration of each of these themes: *Peʾero ʿalay u-feʾeri ʿalav*, "His hat/*tefillin*/splendor is on me and my hat/*tefillin*/splendor is on Him."[16] In Biblical Hebrew, the word *peʾer* means both "splendor" and "hat." On one level, the poet is recapitulating the images in Isaiah in which God wears Israel as a hat and Israel wears God as a hat. On another level, "hat" is a metonym for *tefillin*. This medieval hymn interweaves strands of biblical and rabbinic imagery within a mystical framework.

In the world of late antiquity, the symbolic use of clothes (hats, crowns, sandals, belts) plays an unusual role in religious thinking. While a comprehensive treatment is impossible here, we will dedicate a few words to this problem.[17]

It is tempting to see in the tattoos, hats, garments, and, of course, phylacteries the origins, or at least the background, of later somatic mysticism, namely, the mystic vision of the Divine Soma that was represented by *Merkavah* mysticism. Clearly, the author of *ʾAnʿim Zemirot* was basing himself on this biblical material. Whether the term "mysticism" is appropriate for the biblical phenomenon may be questioned by some, but no other term seems to fit the material. While the psychological content of this somatic mysticism is unclear, it is apparent that the various traditions concerning the divine garments in late antiquity are an intimate part of this framework.

In the ancient world it was not unusual for a god or a king to exchange clothes with the elect. Thus, in a mystical vision recorded in the pseudepigraphal Third Enoch, when God elects Enoch to be the lesser YHWH He fashions him a crown and a mantle of glory and appoints him over the whole heavenly domain.

> R. Ishmael said: Meṭaṭron, Prince of the Divine Presence, said to me: Out of the love which he had for me, more than for all the denizens of the heights, the Holy One, blessed be he, fashioned for me a majestic robe, in which all kinds of luminaries were set, and he clothed me in it. He fashioned for me a glorious cloak in which brightness, brilliance, splendor, and luster of every kind were fixed, and he wrapped me in it. He fashioned for me a kingly crown in which 49 refulgent stones were placed, each like the sun's orb, and its brilliance shone into the four quarters of the heaven of ʿArabot, into the seven heavens, and into the four quarters of the world. He set it upon my

> head and he called me, "The lesser YHWH" in the presence of his whole household in the height, as it is written, "My name is in him."[18]

As a mark of special favor, God lets His elect wear His robe, His sandals, and His belt.

> A youth [*naʿar*] comes out to meet you from behind the throne of glory. Do not bow down to him—for his crown is as the crown of his King, and the sandals on his feet are as the sandals of his King, and the robe [*ḥālûq*] upon him is as the robe [*ḥālûq*] of his King . . . his eyes blaze like torches, his eyeballs burn like lamps; his brilliance is as the brilliance of his King, his glory is as the glory of his Maker.[19]

We have before us a type of mystical investiture. In some traditions, God's name is also written on the garment, although this is not required.[20] There are also non-mystical investitures, like the one we find in Pseudo-Philo, where God invests Joshua with the garment of leadership.

> And in that time God established his covenant with Joshua the son of Nun, who was left from the men who had spied out the land; for the lot went forth upon them that they should not see the land because they had spoken badly about it, and on account of this that generation died. Then God said to Joshua the son of Nun, "Why do you mourn and why do you hope in vain that Moses yet lives? And now you wait to no purpose, because Moses is dead. Take his garments of wisdom and clothe yourself, and with his belt of knowledge gird your loins, and you will be changed and become another man. Did I not speak on your behalf to Moses my servant, saying, 'This one will lead my people after you, and into his hand I will deliver the kings of the Amorites'?"
>
> And Joshua took the garments of wisdom and clothed himself and girded his loins with the belt of understanding. And when he clothed himself with it, his mind was afire and his spirit was moved.[21]

In a different type of mystical vision, according to Scholem, God wears a cloak embossed with the name of Israel.[22] This is what we would call non-allegorical physical mysticism. The image conveys no allegorical significance, nor does it attempt to convey a psychological truth. It is simply mystical vision taken quite literally. This is true of most Jewish visionary mysticism.

On the other hand, in the rabbinic midrash we see a different approach. Here we are in the world of psychological exegesis. Everything in this tradition is a symbol of divine–human intimacy dramatically or mythically presented.

A common theme in normative rabbinic midrash is the concern of the Divine Monarch with His royal garments. The content is clear: God loves Israel as much as the king loves his favorite clothes. We cite here one of these midrashim, collectively referred to as the genre of *Mashal La-melek*, taken from Ziegler's classic study:

> Rabbi Abin said, "There was once a king who had a set of royal purple garments, and he would command his servant, saying: 'Shake them out, fold them well, and pay close attention to these garments.' The servant said to the king, 'My Lord, why is it that of all the royal garments that you have, you only seem to be worried about this set?' Said the king, 'It is because this is the set of clothes I wore the first time I was crowned king.' So said Moses before the Holy One, Blessed Be He, 'Master of the Universe, of the seventy original nations of the world, why are you concerned only with Israel?' Said the Lord to Moses, 'Because I first appeared as King when I split the Red Sea for them.'"[23]

Clearly, Israel in this similitude is structurally equivalent to God's clothes. Israel is considered to be God's royal garment, and God cherishes Israel as much as the king cherishes his favorite robes. The statement is completely unmystical. There is no hidden or allegorical meaning conveyed. The clothes are simply an object of tremendous feeling. Contrast with this the use of garments in gnostic mysticism as described by Hans Jonas.

> In our narrative ["The Hymn of the Pearl"] the garment . . . acts like a person. It symbolizes the heavenly or eternal self of the person, his original idea, a kind of double or *alter ego* preserved in the upper world while he labors down below: as a Mandaean text puts it, "his image is kept safe in its place". . . . It grows with his deeds and its form is perfected by his toils. Its fullness marks the fulfillment of his task and therefore his release from exile in the world.[24]

In this mystical tradition, the garments represent the ideal transcendental person of the believer. The believer encounters his garments after he dies. It is obvious that we are dealing with a religious experience different from that expressed in the midrash.

For a number of reasons, the ideal form for expressing Jewish theological ideas is the *Mashal La-melek*.[25] First of all, it is analogical, which means it avoids philosophical speculation. The genre of *Mashal La-melek* is usually supercharged with emotion. The use of the king as the central figure would seem to be contradictory to such an emotional tone. One would not expect that a *mashal* about a king would be used to convey tenderness, for example. But that is the paradox of the continuum of *din–raḥamim*, "justice–mercy." Wherever you find God's power you also find His gentleness.[26]

We do not have an adequate conception of what kingship meant in the ancient world. We usually see the king in terms of an autocrat, but the ancients did not see their kings in this light. This is beautifully illustrated by an ancient West Semitic royal inscription in which the king says, "To one person I was a father, to another I was a mother, to another one I was a brother. The person who had never seen the face of a sheep, I gave him a flock. The person who had never seen the face of a calf, I gave him a herd. . . . The person who had never seen a shirt from his youth, in my days he was covered in linen."[27] Or, to cite another royal text:

> Baʾl made me a father and a mother to the Danunites. I have restored the Danunites. I have expanded the country of the Plain of Adana from the rising of the sun to its setting. In my days, the Danunites had everything good and plenty to eat and well-being. . . . I have been sitting upon the throne of my father. I have made peace with every king. Yea, every king considered me his father because of my righteousness and my wisdom and the kindness of my heart. . . . In my days, there was, within all the borders of the Plain of Adana, from the rising of the sun to its setting, even in places which had formerly been feared, where a man was afraid to walk on the road but where in my days a woman was able to stroll, working with spindles, by virtue of Baʾl and the gods (*El*). And in all my days, the Danunites and the entire Plain of Adana had plenty to eat and well-being and a good situation and peace of mind.[28]

In Mesopotamian royal inscriptions, kings pride themselves not merely on how many cities they conquered, but on what specific benefits they bestowed upon their people: How many aqueducts they built, how they stabilized prices, how just they were, how they prevented the rich from oppressing the poor, how they were fathers to the orphan.[29] The whole of Jewish theology is there—God the King is just, He is kind, He is a great and gracious provider.[30] The king symbolizes the benign uses of power. He was a father, a mother, a nurturer. As the psalmist sings, "When my father and my mother abandon me, then the Lord will take me up" (Ps 27:10).

This is the secret of the Jewish prayer formula, *Barukh attah ʾadonai, ʾelohenu melekh ha-ʿolam . . .*, "Blessed are You, O Lord our God, King of the universe." Kingship both in the blessing and in the *Mashal La-melek* is an expression of kindness rather than severity. It is the combination of strength and kindness that is God's hallmark and seal.

We are looking at two different orientations here as we survey rabbinic midrash and the mystical tradition. Gnostic–Manichaean mysticism is allegorical, with little apparent psychological content. The midrash is psychological mythmaking.

It would be interesting to ask what, for example, is the orientation of Jeremiah 13. Is it simply visionary–literal mysticism? Or does it lead into the midrashic genre cited above? We think that both are true. Jeremiah 13 conveys deep emotion, namely God's love for Israel. Its truth is human, psychological, and poetic, and it does not attempt to indulge itself in metaphysical speculation. At the same time, while the term "mysticism" may not strictly apply to the biblical imagery, there is no question that the imagery is visionary. Fortunately, we are not in the position of having to reject one tradition or accept another. We glory in the exuberant variety of our religious expression. This is its truth and its power.

NOTES

1. See T. Abusch, "Ishtar's Proposal and Gilgamesh's Refusal: An Interpretation of *The Gilgamesh Epic*, Tablet 6, Lines 1–79," *History of Religion* 26 (1986) 143–76, especially 153 (on Tablet 6, Line 9); cf. S. Greengus, "The Old Babylonian Marriage Contract," *JAOS* 89 (1969) 505–32, especially 517, 518, 522; R. Yaron, *The Law of the Aramaic Papyri* (Oxford: Clarendon, 1961) 40; K. Baltzer, *Die Bundesformular* (Neukirchen: Neukirchener Verlag, 1960). On adoption, see S. Paul, "Adoption Formulae: A Study of Cuneiform and Biblical Legal Clauses," *Eretz Israel* 14 (H. L. Ginsberg Volume, 1978) 31–36 (in Hebrew); the same paper in English in *Maarav* 2 (1980) 173–85.

2. F. Thureau-Dangin, "Trois contrats de Ras Shamra," *Syria* 18 (1937) 245–55, at 250. See also M. Friedman, "Israel's Response in Hosea 2:17b: 'You Are My Husband,'" *JBL* 99 (1980) 199–204.

3. Cf. H. L. Ginsberg, "Book of Hosea," *Encyclopedia Judaica* 8:1012–25.

4. There seems to be in the P source a tendency toward greater self-revelation by God. God was originally known by the general name Elohim; to Abraham God reveals Himself as El Shaddai; to Moses and the Israelites God reveals Himself as YHWH. El Shaddai was, in this context, God's personal name; however, it is clearly superseded by YHWH in intimacy. See F. M. Cross, Jr., *Canaanite Myth and Hebrew Epic* (Cambridge: Harvard University Press, 1973) 298.

5. Rabbi Judah Halevi, *The Book of Kuzari*, trans. H. Hirschfeld (New York: Pardes, 1946).

6. M. Friedman, *Jewish Marriage in Palestine: A Cairo Geniza Study* (2 vols.; New York: The Jewish Theological Seminary of America, 1980–81).

7. M. Weinfeld, *Deuteronomy and the Deuteronomic School* (Oxford: Clarendon, 1972; rpt. Winona Lake, Indiana: Eisenbrauns, 1991) 8, 83, 333.

8. See M. M. Kasher, *Torah shelemah* (New York: American Biblical Encyclopedia Society, 1949; in Hebrew) ad Lev 19:2.

9. R. Yaron, *The Law of the Aramaic Papyri*, 36. For further examples of the ancient Near Eastern practice of the writing of the master's name on the slave's hand, see CAD, Q, 186a.

10. A. Ḥakham sees the action as poetically analogous to that of a lover who draws the face of his beloved on his hand; see *Book of Isaiah. Chapters 36–66* (Daʿat Mikra; Jerusalem: Mosad Ha-Rav Kook, 1984; in Hebrew) 533.

11. L. Ginzberg, *The Legends of the Jews* (Philadelphia: The Jewish Publication Society of America, 1909–38) 6.58, 328.

12. Prov 3:3: "Bind them on your neck, write them on the tablet of your heart"; Prov 6:21: "Bind them continually on your heart, tie them about your neck"; Prov 7:3: "Bind them on your fingers, write them on the tablet of your heart." Cf. *Kitvei Avraham Epstein* (Jerusalem: Mosad Ha-Rav Kook, 1950; in Hebrew) 176ff.; W. W. Hallo, introduction to Briggs Buchanan, *Early Near Eastern Seals in the Yale Babylonian Collection* (New Haven: Yale University Press, 1981). Some present-day Coptic and Armenian Christians tattoo the cross on the palms of their hands as an act of piety, thus continuing an ancient tradition. See the recent article of M. Bar-Ilan, "Magical Seals on the Body," *Tarbiz* 57 (1988) 37–50.

13. See the chapter on Samaritan phylacteries and amulets in M. Gaster, *Studies and Texts in Folklore, Magic, Medieval Romance, Hebrew Apocrypha and Samaritan Archaeology* (London, Maggs Brothers, 1925–28; rpt. New York: KTAV, 1971) 1.387–461 and 3.109–30.

14. For a study of the divine horned cap, see E. Unger, "Diadem und Krone," *Reallexikon der Assyriologie* (ed. E. Ebeling, D. O. Edzard et al.) vol. 2 (Berlin: de Gruyter, 1975) 201–11.

15. Y. Avishur, *Phoenician Inscriptions and the Bible. 2. A Selection of Phoenician Inscriptions* (Jerusalem: A. Rubenstein, 1979) 223.

16. Also call *Shir ha-Kabod*, "Song of Glory," this thirteenth-century alphabetic acrostic is a synagogue hymn ascribed to Judah he-Hasid of Regensburg. See "Anim Zemirot," *Encyclopedia Judaica*, 3.21–23.

17. For the use of divine garments, see R. Eisler, *Weltenmantel und Himmelszelt* (Munich: Beck, 1910), cited by G. Scholem, *Jewish Gnosticism, Merkabah Mysticism, and Talmudic Tradition* (2d ed.; New York: The Jewish Theological Seminary of America, 1965) 61.

18. 3 (Hebrew Apocalypse of) Enoch 12, trans. P. Alexander in *The Old Testament Pseudepigrapha. 1. Apocalyptic Literature and Testaments*, ed. J. H. Charlesworth (Garden City, New York: Doubleday, 1983) 223–315 at 265.

19. Cairo Genizah Hekhalot text A/2, quoted by Alexander in *The Old Testament Pseudepigrapha. 1. Apocalyptic Literature and Testaments*, 268n. Cf. also Scholem, *Merkabah Mysticism*, 59. Compare this with Ahasuerus' investiture of Mordecai in Esth 6:7–11, cf. 8:15.

20. Scholem, *Merkabah Mysticism*, 60.

21. Pseudo-Philo, *Biblical Antiquities* 20:1–3, trans. D. J. Harrington in *The Old Testament Pseudepigrapha. 2. Expansions of the "Old Testament" &c.*, ed. Charlesworth (Garden City, New York: Doubleday, 1985) 297–377 at 328–29.

22. Scholem, *Merkabah Mysticism*, 60.

23. I. Ziegler, *Die Königsgleichnisse des Midrasch, beleuchtet durch die römische Kaiserzeit* (Breslau: S. Schottlaender, 1903) 11; cf. also S. Buber, ed., *Midrash Tanḥuma: ein agadischer Commentar zum Pentateuch von Rabbi Tanchuma ben Rabbi Abba* (Vilna: Rom, 1885; rpt. 1946) Exodus, 107.

24. H. Jonas, *The Gnostic Religion* (2d ed.; Boston: Beacon Press, 1963) 122; see also G. Widengren, *Mani and Manichaeism* (London: Weidenfeld and Nicholson, 1965) 63–65. Note also *iṣtelo*, "garment," in rabbinic literature, on which see Ziegler, *Königsgleichnisse*. Israel is often considered the royal mantle of the Divine King; the root of this conception in Jeremiah 13 was seen by the rabbis in the *Midrash Tanḥuma* to Jeremiah 13, quoted by Kasher, *Torah shelemah*, ad loc. Probably related to these garments are the "robes of the saints," the heavenly robes the saints put on after death as a symbol of their transformed state or even a replacement for their bodies, that are so important in the "Martydom and Ascension of Isaiah," trans. M. A. Knibb in *Old Testament Pseudepigrapha. 2. Expansions of the "Old Testament" &c.*, ed. Charlesworth, 143–76; Knibb provides a note at Ascension 1:5, p. 157, where he also discusses the New Testament references to robes—note especially Rev 3:4–5; 6:11; 7:9. For the use of garments in Mandaean literature, see E. S. Drower, *The Canonical Prayerbook of the Mandaeans* (Leiden: Brill, 1959) 7.

25. For an excellent treatment of the relationship between *mashal la-melek* and the anthropomorphic God, see the penetrating work of D. Stern, "The Function of the Parable in Rabbinic Literature," *Jerusalem Studies in Hebrew Literature* 7 (1985) 90–105 (in Hebrew), especially p. 97; see also the anthology edited by Stern and M. J. Mirsky, *Rabbinic Fantasies: Imaginative Narratives from Classical Hebrew Literature* (Philadelphia: The Jewish Publication Society of America, 1990); Stern there mentions the structural similarity between my study of prophetic intercession (Chapter 1) and his own work. Other *mishlei melakim* need to be studied in the light of Near Eastern law and lore.

26. For discussion of the tension between mercy and justice, see Chapter 1 in this volume.

27. The Kilamuwa Inscription, KAI 24, lines 10–13; for a translation, see F. Rosenthal, in *ANET*, 654–55, or Y. Avishur, *Phoenician Inscriptions . . . 2. A Selection*, 209.

28. The Azitiwada Inscription, KAI 26, A.I.3–6, 11–13, II.1–9; I follow the translation of F. Rosenthal in *ANET*, 653–54, except for the phrase *dl plkm*, "working with spindles"; see also Avishur, *Phoenician Inscriptions . . . 2. A Selection*, 223.

29. See, for example, the Prologue to the Code of Hammurapi, especially column 2, lines 39–41: "provided abundantly to his people"; cf. the translation by T. J. Meek in *ANET*, 164.

30. See, for example, Mal 3:6: "Please, just test Me, said the Lord of Hosts. I will surely open the floodgates of the sky for you and pour down boundless blessings. . . ." See also Pss 81:11, 16; 104; 145:15–16, among many others.

CHAPTER 3

A HISTORY OF MESOPOTAMIAN RELIGION*

Thorkild Jacobsen's *The Treasures of Darkness*[1] is a truly remarkable achievement, comparable in many ways only to Walter Otto's studies on Greek religion. Jacobsen's masterly recreation of the spiritual life of ancient Mesopotamian man is well known from his previous works, especially from his contribution to *Before Philosophy*, a work that has done more than almost any other to transform the study of the ancient Near East from an esoteric occupation of a few specialists to an organic and legitimate branch of the Western humanities.[2] Jacobsen's combination of philological pre-eminence with uncanny empathy into the intellectual and religious life of the Sumerians and rare felicity of expression—qualities which distinguish all his previous writings—manifest themselves in this great work in all their power.

Those of a more positivistic bent may claim that he makes the ancient texts too resonant poetically and a bit too profound intellectually. However, in a field where the qualities of aesthetic appreciation and philosophic sensitivity have been too infrequently represented, it seems wiser to err in the direction of seeming over-explication. Whether one differs with Jacobsen on specific details or even general orientation, one must admit that we have before us a model of scholarly and humanistic interpretation, one that treats the ancient texts with the seriousness and penetration they deserve.

The book is not to be taken simply as a gathering of his previous studies in the field; this has been attempted elsewhere.[3] Nor does its uniqueness lie in the richness of new material and wide-ranging documentation it presents or in the fact that we now have in written form most of his great lectures: on the "Personal Gods," Enuma Elish, the Gilgamesh Epic, and others. To my mind, the greatness of the book lies in the creative integration of the wide range of methodological approaches

---

* This chapter first appeared in *Numen* 25 (1978) 80–84.

that Jacobsen has used over the years into a new organic whole, one that transcends any of the methodological structures or grids used before.

Each of his previous studies has been distinguished not merely by a richness of factual information, but also, and especially, by the creative use of some new methodological focus. Rarely does one find such a careful attempt at doing justice to such a wide range of approaches—from the almost materialistic (the gods Laḫmu and Laḫamu are but personifications of the geological process of silting and being silted) to the almost mystical (the use of the "numinous" in his more recent publications); from the ecological (while all Tammuz figures represent the principle of fertility, their specific representations differ from area to area according to the central economic concern of each area: hunting, cattle breeding, date cultivation, etc.) to the psychological or even the psychoanalytical (his brilliant treatments of the psychology of Inanna, the theme of parricide in the Enuma Elish, maturity in the Gilgamesh Epic); from the use of the mythopoetical in *Before Philosophy* to the literary-aesthetic interpretations of the Akkadian epics. And above all, Jacobsen shows a constant preoccupation with the process of humanization (or humanification) by which originally "intransitive" nature gods become more and more "transitive"—human, humane, and articulated personalities distinguished by an outgoing will and purpose.

What is truly exciting about this book is the subtle manner in which these various methodological foci interpenetrate and complement each other, thus creating a multileveled texture of rare beauty and sophistication. In Enuma Elish, for example, Tiamat is not merely the personification of the salt waters of the Persian Gulf mating with the sweet waters of the rivers, but also a representation of the passivity of the older generation of gods who resent the creative restlessness of youth. The story also has a clear psychological aspect: Marduk is involved in an act of parricide—he kills his parents. Not quite, warns Jacobsen—note that Marduk does not kill his immediate parents; note also the sympathy with which Tiamat is depicted, as a woman with motherly feelings. Now, just at the moment when through the skill of Jacobsen we are totally involved in the literary and psychological aspects of this piece of world literature—and under the spell of his "New Criticism" have forgotten that this work of art is not merely an expression of eternal and transcultural human values—we are suddenly confronted by another level of interpretation, where the psychological ambivalence of the poet toward the act of parricide is given a profound and unexpected political interpretation. To our great joy, however, the political interpretation, instead of canceling the psychological-literary approach, enhances and complements it. The whole book abounds in such surprises.

Without a doubt, one of Jacobsen's major contributions in this book is his discussion of the "personal god," a religious phenomenon that seems to have originated in Mesopotamia and spread from there not only to Egypt but to Israel as well. At this juncture, it may be useful to raise a few questions concerning the implications of the term "personal." A personal god may be either (a) a god who is concerned with my person or (b) a god with a clearly articulated person(ality). Jacobsen clearly opts for the first meaning. Furthermore, he points out that the Mesopotamian personal god, as a personification of Lady Luck, had little or no personality of its own.

One is therefore tempted to ask what relationship, if any, exists between this personality-less "personal" god and the process of "humanification" by which intransitive nature gods emerged into anthropomorphic transitive gods with articulated wills and personalities? At first glance, the term "personal" in the concept personal god seems to link this new phenomenon to the humanification process, a thesis central to all of Jacobsen's studies. However, further reflection would seem to cast doubt on this association.

Furthermore, the relationship between the Mesopotamian personal god and the personal god of Israel is also somewhat problematic. Yahweh is not a personal god simply because He is concerned with the person of Israel. He is a personal god because He is a most highly articulated personality—in fact, probably the most articulated personality of all Near Eastern deities. Indeed, if one is looking for connections between Israelite personal religion and the Near East, one could postulate a linear development, not from the Mesopotamian personal god, but rather from Jacobsen's "transitive" high gods to Israel's super-transitive deity. Whatever the case may be, the problem deserves some clarification.

A few observations concerning the human reaction to the personal gods may now be in order. If Jacobsen finds the idea of the personal god to be a positive religious contribution, he is clearly disturbed by the human reaction to this type of god, a reaction that found its literary expression in the personal penitential prayers. He is perplexed by a seemingly improper human intimacy with the divine and by a rather ostentatious display of pseudo-humility, which he takes to be an unconscious expression of an overblown sense of self-importance. What has happened to the traditional (and theologically "proper") sense of awe before the divine and the transcendent? At least in the Old Testament, says the author, this audacious parading of pseudo-humility is, more often than not, balanced by more sincere expressions of human sinfulness and real lack of self-worth.

Jacobsen's negative reaction to the seeming lack of awe in these personal confessions may be a reflection of a modern or Western sensibility in which such a familiarity with the divine can hardly "co-exist" with a proper sense of awe. The fact is that the ancients may have reacted differently. The arguments that Abraham, Moses, Samuel, Jeremiah, and Job have with God may seem strange and more than a bit improper to the modern Western sensibility, but they are certainly typical of biblical religiosity. The rabbis of the Talmud, who certainly experienced divine awe, speak to and about God with an audacious familiarity that Moslems and Christians may find positively irreligious. Kierkegaard had a similar problem in dealing with the too human intimacy with the divine reflected in some Islamic legends.[4] Jacobsen's evaluation of the human reactions in the Mesopotamian compositions may indeed be correct. My remarks, therefore, are only intended to offer an alternate, subjective vantage point rooted, shall we say, in a more "oriental" tradition.

After the sublime chapters on the Gilgamesh Epic and Enuma Elish, the last chapter, on the spiritual life of the first millennium, is disappointing. Jacobsen sees little in the religious literature of this period that is of positive religious significance and much that he dislikes: the growing brutalization of the divine image, possibly a reflex of human despotism; the growth of astral religion; the obsession with death and the underworld and many other "unpleasing" phenomena. Even the interesting later tendency to view the various gods and their functions as aspects of one deity is not treated with any real enthusiasm. (Contrast the importance of such developments for the historian of biblical monotheism.) Furthermore, it seems a bit strange that after having rejected the humility of the second-millennium penitential prayers as a pseudo-humility, Jacobsen seems to reject the apparently real humility of first-millennium kings as "passivity" and "quietism." On the contrary, one could make a good case here that a new type of piety is emerging that has real affinities with similar phenomena in the Old Testament (as Jacobsen himself points out).

Jacobsen ends his study on a more "positive" note quoting, without comment, Nebuchadrezer's prayer to Marduk. The idea that without the deity's help man cannot serve him properly, expressed in the concluding lines, "Cause me to love Thy exalted rule/ Let the fear of Thy godhead be in my heart," seems to be a new and positive breakthrough in the religious thought of the Near East, one that deserves a broad comparative treatment. It is an idea that appears at about the same time in Israel and becomes a dominant (although not sufficiently investigated) theme in later Jewish liturgy and Christian theology. This idea is a fine example of the type of personal religion that began to emerge in this seemingly barren period. The piety of Nabonidus and the deeply personal prayers of his mother also merit discussion in this context.[5] It seems that something fine and new was beginning to break through the archaic stereotypes of the older Mesopotamian traditions. Are these positive innovations, as well as the many barbarizations that Jacobsen has pointed out, somehow to be connected with the growing "Aramaization" of Mesopotamian culture? Could it be that the relatively greater evocativeness of some of this later material for the biblicist and the student of West Semitic culture and religion has to do with the non-Mesopotamian quality of some of this material? Whatever the case may be, this later period and its religious traditions were not all "bad," and even if they were, they deserve a broader treatment.

My few questions and qualifications in no way detract from the greatness of this book. It is a masterwork of one of the great humanists and scholars of our age. Its publication is a source of great joy both to the scholarly world and to the general public.

NOTES

1. T. Jacobsen, *The Treasures of Darkness: A History of Mesopotamian Religion* (New Haven: Yale University Press, 1976).

2. The most famous "Oriental Institute essay" was published in two forms: the better known form is the Pelican paperback—Henri Frankfort, H. A. Frankfort, J. A. Wilson, and T. Jacobsen, *Before Philosophy: The Intellectual Adventure of Ancient Man. An Essay on Speculative Thought in the Ancient Near East* (Baltimore: Penguin, 1949); the older form, by the same authors with W. A. Irwin, is called *The Intellectual Adventure of Ancient Man: An Essay on Speculative Thought in the Ancient Near East* (Chicago: University of Chicago Press, 1946) and includes a chapter on ancient Israel. Portions of the book have been reprinted elsewhere. Jacobsen's chapters, on Mesopotamia, are the same in all versions.

3. T. Jacobsen, *Toward the Image of Tammuz and Other Essays on Mesopotamian History and Culture* (ed. W. L. Moran; Harvard Semitic Series 21; Cambridge: Harvard University Press, 1970). This book includes a bibliography and a lexical index. Jacobsen has since published another major volume, *The Harps That Once . . . : Sumerian Poetry in Translation* (New Haven: Yale University Press, 1987).

4. Søren Kierkegaard, *Concluding Unscientific Postscript* (trans. David F. Swenson with Walter Lowrie; Princeton: Princeton University Press, 1941) 369n; he cites an

Islamic story about intimacy with the divine in counterpoint to his own view that "as between God and a human being . . . there is an absolute difference."

5. See the translations by A. L. Oppenheim in *ANET*, 560–63.

CHAPTER 4

ABRAHAM THE NOBLE WARRIOR: PATRIARCHAL POLITICS AND LAWS OF WAR IN ANCIENT ISRAEL*

Probably no chapter of Scripture has been so thoroughly studied as Genesis 14. It is a notoriously seductive chapter, tantalizing the scholar with a real name here and a seemingly historical name there. Nevertheless, the search for a solution has not abated, as is attested by an unceasing flow of articles and monographs.

In spite of some rough spots in composition, Genesis 14 reads as a relatively organic whole.[1] The war was a necessary backdrop to the heroic deeds of Abraham, who as a warrior, allied by pact with Lot, Aner, Eshkol, and Mamre, with his troops 318 in number, restores not only the plundered goods of Lot but those of his allies as well. Decisive in battle yet noble in peace, Abraham refuses to take a share in the booty—neither property nor slaves, neither string nor sandal-lace—his only concern being the rations of his troops and a legitimate share for his allies.

The major thrust of this study is an examination of the details concerning the division of the booty and Abraham's concern with the shares of his allies and the rations of his troops. It will be demonstrated that each element of Genesis 14 has its exact counterpart in the laws of war and in the etiquette of booty restoration attested sporadically in the international treaties of Boghazköy and Ugarit. The Israelite narrator brings together all these ancient laws of war and peace in his depiction of Abraham as the most noble of warriors. As noted by the great legal theorist Hugo Grotius, this nobility in war constitutes the literary high point of the story.[2]

---

* This article first appeared in *Journal of Jewish Studies* vol. 33, nos. 1–2 = *Essays in Honour of Yigael Yadin* (1982) 81–107. It was first presented at the World Congresses of Jewish Studies in 1965 and 1973. My thanks to Rabbi Benjamin Scolnic, my research assistant, for his aid.

Furthermore, a re-examination of the secular treaties between Isaac and Abimelech, and between Jacob and Laban, clearly demonstrates that military activity, following Near Eastern traditions of law and chivalry, is a common—but often neglected—theme in the lives of all the patriarchs as depicted by many of the tradents in the Book of Genesis.

A Biblical Narû

Before we address our main concern, a few words are in order regarding the literary form of the chapter of which the booty-division pericope is an integral part. Stylistically, Genesis 14 seems to be the biblical reflex of the *narû*, an Old Akkadian literary form; the *narû* is a historical romance whose original purpose was the glorification of monarchs such as Sargon I and Naram-Sin, and evidently of other later kings of equal fame. Unlike the Old Babylonian omen literature, with its almost scientific concern for empirical fact, the Old Akkadian *narû* must be seen as a form of historiographical literature rather than as pure history.[3] Furthermore, the genre was quite alive in the Neo-Babylonian/Neo-Assyrian period, as can be seen in the Spartoli Tablets—documents of great importance for the proper understanding of our chapter. It was Michael C. Astour who reintroduced this body of evidence into the scholarly discussion of Genesis 14.[4] The parallelism between the Spartoli Tablets and Genesis 14 is striking. Both texts deal with wars between confederations of kings; both are introduced by the stereotypic *inūma–inūmišu*, "when–then."[5] Some kings like Bera and Birsha, as well as the city of Bela, probably have artificially constructed names. Others have excellent Near Eastern credentials: Tidal, the King of Goyim, was probably none other than the Hittite king Tudḫalia of the Umman-Manda; Chedorlaomer, King of Arioch and Elam, was probably none other than Kuter-Naḫḫunte of Aruku. It should also be noticed that even these historical names come from a wide range of historical strata. It is to the credit of Roland de Vaux to have recognized the importance of this aspect of Astour's studies of the Spartoli Tablets, correctly seeing them as a late biblical reflex of the Old Akkadian genre and applying them to Genesis 14.[6]

Significantly, the *narû* romance was still alive whenever Genesis 14 was written. While the Babylonian *narû*s celebrate the military exploits of kings, actual and fictitious, Genesis 14 glorifies Abraham, not merely as a hero of faith but as a man of heroic deeds and king-like nobility.

Neither String Nor Sandal-Lace

Our investigation of Genesis 14 begins with the declaration of Abraham: "I have sworn by uplifted hand to the Lord, God Most High . . . that I would not take anything that belongs to you, *miḥuṭ ve-ʿad serokh-naʿal* not even so much as a string or sandal-lace." As E. A. Speiser pointed out, the Hebrew phrase is based on a much older Near Eastern formulaic tradition represented in the Elephantine Aramaic as *miḥam ve-ʿad ḥuṭ*, "be it blade of straw or piece of string," a partial reflex of the older Akkadian *lu ḫāmu lu ḫuṣābu*, "be it a blade of straw or a splinter of wood."[7] These three historically related idioms are but dialectal variants of the same general theme: the complete and total division of property. In spite of the semantic identity of the phrases and their partial functional overlap, the terms are used in contrasting contexts: the Aramaic term is used in the division of marriage property in case of divorce,[8] while the Neo-Assyrian *lu ḫāmu lu ḫuṣābu* has been found in the liquidation of partnership holdings.[9] Until recently, none of the phrases has been found in a context like that of Genesis 14, namely, the division of booty. Was this particular usage simply an innovation of the narrator or was it actually based on an older cuneiform model, in which the Akkadian *lu ḫāmu lu ḫuṣābu* was used in a diplomatic narrative in much the same way that the Hebrew phrase "be it string or sandal-lace" is used in Genesis 14?[10]

In the historical prologue to the treaty between Shuppiluliuma of Hatti and Mattiwaza of Mitanni, the Hittite overlord reminds his vassal that he has never encroached on the other's border, and that while the Assyrians and others had impoverished the land of Mitanni, the Hittites had never taken from his property *ḫāmu* or *ḫuṣābu*![11] Thus we see that the terms *ḫāmu* and *ḫuṣābu* are at home in north Syrian and Hittite international treaties. If they are found in one such context, it is likely that they will also be found in a context similar to that of Genesis 14.

Just such a text is found in the archive of international treaties at Ugarit.[12] In it, Niqmaddu of Ugarit, who had been plundered by his neighbors, summons his suzerain, Shuppiluliuma, to come to his aid (lines 1–14). After all, had they not agreed that "my enemies are your enemies and my allies, your allies"?

> Thus (spoke) the Sun, Shuppiluliuma, the Great King, king of Hatti, the mighty one: "When Ituraddu, king of Mukish, Addunirari, king of Nuḫashshe, and Akieteshub, king of Niʾi, rebelled against the Sun, the Great King, their master, and gathered their forces, seizing villages belonging to Ugarit, pressing on against Ugarit (itself) and taking as booty property be-

longing to Niqmaddu, king of Ugarit, laying waste to Ugarit, then Niqmaddu, king of Ugarit, went and sent to Shuppiluliuma, the Great King, saying: 'Let the Sun, the Great King, my master, save me from the hand of the enemy; I am the servant of the Sun, the Great King, my master. With the enemy of my master I am an enemy and with the ally of my master I am allied.[13] Behold the kings are pressing in against me.'"

As soon as Shuppiluliuma hears of the plight of his ally, he immediately sends troops, consisting of his grandees and princes, who drive the enemy out of Ugarit and restore Niqmaddu's plundered goods (lines 15–19).

išmēma[14] *šarru rabū annā qabāsu ša* ^{I}*Niqmaddi*
išpurma ^{I}*Šuppiluliuma šarru rabū*
mārē šarri u amēli rabūti adu ṣābē
$^{i\d{s}}$*narkarbāti ana māt* ^{al}*Ugārit u ṣābē* $^{am\bar{e}l}$*nakri*
ištu libbi māt ^{al}*Ugārit uḫtabbitū*

As soon as the Great King heard these words of Niqmaddu, Shuppiluliuma, the Great King, dispatched princes and nobles together with forces and chariots to Ugarit, and they drove out the enemy forces (from) Ugarit.

In the next lines, we have nicely co-ordinated clauses (*iqiššunūti . . . iqiššunūti*) reflecting a ceremonial exchange of goods somehow connected with the formal disposition of booty. It seems that the "silver, gold, and copper" presented by Niqmaddu to the Hittite lord came from the very property of Niqmaddu that had just been returned to him by the Hittites (lines 20–28).

[*u gabba* (?)] *ša*[*llāte*][15] *ša ilteqūni*
[*u ana* ^{I}]*Niqmaddi iqiššunūti*
[*u* ^{I}*Niqma*]*ddu š*[*ar māt* ^{al}*Ug*]*ārit mārē šarri u amēli rabūti*
[. . .]? *danniš uktebbissunu kaspē ḫurāṣē erē*
[. . . *iq*]*iššunūti u una* $^{\bar{a}l}$*Alalaḫ*
[. . . *ana m*]*uḫḫi* ^{d}*Šamši šarri rabi bēlišu ikšuda*
[. . . *aka*]*n*(?)[*n*]*a ana* ^{d}*Šamši šarri rabi bēlišu*
[. . . *n*]*a*(?) *ina abāti ša nukurti*
[. . . *lā*] *summuḫ*[16] ^{I}*Niqma*[*ddu*]

[And all their] boo[ty] which they had taken, they presented as a gift [to] Niqmaddu. [And Niqma]ddu, ki[ng of Ug]arit, the princes and nobles . . . he rendered great homage to them, presenting them with silver, gold, and copper. And having come to Alalakh [before the pres]ence, to the Sun, the Great King, his master, thus he declared before the Sun, the Great King, his master: . . . in seditious matters . . . Niqmaddu was [not] involved.

Although the next lines of the document are damaged, what is preserved seems to contain a declaration in which Shuppiluliuma assures Niqmaddu that he does not want *ḫāmu* or *ḫuṣābu* of Niqmaddu's goods, and most probably, his land.

[u ᴵŠuppilulium]a šarru rabū
[. . .]ša māt ᵃˡUgārit
[. . . ḫāma u] ḫuṣābu [mimma]
[ša ᴵNiqmaddu] la [ilaqqi / iqerrib]

[And Shuppiluliumla, the Great King, [saw] the loyalty [of Niqmaddu, and as far] as what belongs to Ugarit, . . . [Shuppiluliuma, the Great King will] not [touch/take anything, be it straw or] splinter.

This reconstruction, substantially that of Nougayrol, is supported by the logic of the context. Hence, we have a case where an overlord has donated cities to a vassal, and in response to a call for aid from the vassal against whom the cities have now rebelled, the king has now retaken some of those cities. However, the cities do not seem to return automatically to the vassal; therefore, a formal reconfirmation of the territories seems to be a legal necessity. The document of this reconfirmation[17] would consist of an historical prologue that would describe just how the vassal's property was lost and would continue with the declaration that the overlord desires neither *ḫāmu* nor *ḫuṣābu* of his vassal. Then there would be a formal reinvestiture of the properties and, finally, a recital of the necessary oaths and curses. The *ḫāmu–ḫuṣābu* clause is thus the necessary psychological introduction and legal motivation for the last and most essential part of the document. The narrative quality of the text should not obscure its essentially legal function.

Abraham seems to follow a kingly etiquette since structurally his relationship to Lot and the king of Sodom is identical with the relationship between Shuppiluliuma and Niqmaddu.[18] Can we infer from this parallelism that Abraham had actually made a treaty with Lot and/or his allies, a treaty in which Abraham was the suzerain and they the vassals? The question cannot be answered with any degree of certainty.[19] In Genesis 14:13, Abraham appears with his *baᶜale berit*, "allies," Aner, Eshkol, and Mamre. Elsewhere (Gen 23:25–32), he enters into a treaty with a local monarch following good local custom. Yet if induction leads to the attractive conclusion that the kings of Sodom, Gomorrah, and Admah—very much like Aner, Eshkol, and Mamre—were covenanted vassals of the patriarch, the text as it stands remains inconclusive.[20] While Lot and the kings may not have been allies formally bound by treaty to their suzerain, Abraham graciously considers the kings his protégés—probably because of their association with his nephew—and treats them with the same degree of concern and magnanimity as Shuppiluliuma treated Niqmaddu. To say more than this would be overstepping the limits of the inductive method.

As mentioned above, Grotius anticipated a great deal of this discussion. In his study of the laws of war, he attempts to establish the right of conquerors in his own day to appropriate the territory of the vanquished. As usual, he argues on the basis of legal precedents taken not only from classical but also from biblical antiquities. Grotius shows that, indeed, Abraham had a right to the conquered property, but that, out of the magnanimity that was typical although not frequent among ancient kings, he freely relinquished that clear right. The examples that Grotius gives demonstrate that Abraham's behavior in Genesis 14 was not unique to the Hebrew saint, but was the common attribute of all noble conquerors.

> Marcus Cato conducted himself in much the same fashion as after the victory in Spain, saying (almost in the very words of Abraham) that no part of the spoils of war would be acquired by him, save only those things which he had eaten or drunk. He added that, in taking this stand, he was not casting reproach upon those other leaders who would accept the profits assigned to them from the said spoils, but merely preferred for his own part to vie in virtue with the most virtuous rather than in wealth with the wealthiest.[21]

Not every conqueror in the ancient world was an Abraham or a Marcus Cato. But even if a king took his share of the booty, his magnanimity and fairness could be expressed in the concern that he demonstrates towards his friends and allies.[22]

Abraham the Ally

To the best of our knowledge, previous investigators of Near Eastern covenant forms—Akkadian, Hittite, or biblical—in their descriptions of the essential components of the treaty-form have not discussed stipulations concerning the provisioning of troops or the laws of booty-division. This omission is not only true of Korošec and others who have considered the treaty-form to be rather fixed, but even of McCarthy, who correctly sees it as more flexible.[23] Logically speaking, such stipulations should have been at least as important as those regulating the return of political prisoners, for even in the most sophisticated political or diplomatic contexts, one of the main functions of war is the taking of booty. As we have seen, the absence of such regulations from the actual treaties is more apparent than real. Their relative rarity is probably fortuitous and due to the hazards of excavation, a fact that may account for the minimal discussion of the subject in scholarly literature. Furthermore, since many of the more recent studies of the Mesopotamian treaty-form are motivated by inner-biblical concerns, great emphasis has been placed on the components like the historical prologue, curses and blessings, land-grants, periodic reading, etc., that are immediately relevant to a proper understanding of the treaty between God and Israel; the division of booty and the provisioning of troops are not so clearly germane.

In at least one Hittite treaty, viz. that between Murshilish II and Tuppi-Teshub of Amurru, there are clear stipulations concerning the obligations of the vassal to provide food and drink for the overlord's troops when engaged in the defense of an ally.[24] Similar stipulations are to be found in the Hittite version of a treaty between Shuppiluliuma and Aziru of Amurru, recently restored and translated by Goetze.[25]

> [And if someone presses Aziras hard . . . or (if) somebody starts a revolt, (if) you (then) wri]te to the king of the Hatti land: "send troops (and) charioteers to my aid! I shall h[it] that enemy for [you]. . . . I, the Sun, dispatched notables of the Hatti land, troops (and) charioteers of mine [*from* the] Hatti land down to Amurru land. [If] they march up to towns of yours, treat them well and furnish them with the necessities of life. Before [the people of Amurru land] let them walk like brethren! Treat [the Hi]ttites well.

In one Akkadian text from Hatti we find the expression *akal ḫarrānišunu*, "the rations for the road" = Hebrew *ṣedah ladderek*, used for the *per diem* rations allotted to an ally's troops.[26]

Thus, when Abraham comes to the aid of his protégé Lot and of Lot's friends (or allies), he asks only for what is rightfully his in insisting that the king of Sodom (and most probably his allies) be responsible for the rations of his soldiers. Although Abraham does not intend to enrich himself from the expedition, his magnanimity does not include voluntary self-impoverishment. Such magnanimity was a requirement neither of secular treaty nor of Israelite piety.

In the collection of Akkadian treaties edited by Weidner, we find treaties including not only stipulations concerning the provisioning of troops but also those that regulate, in various ways, the proper division of booty between overlord and vassal. The treaty between Muwatalli and

Sunashshura of Kizzuwatna is most illustrative. One of the relevant passages reads as follows:

> If some city within the land of the Sun initiates hostility, just as it [that city] is an enemy of the Sun, so shall it be an enemy of Sunashshura. Together they shall wage war against it. The goods/property of the city, the booty (*maršit āli šallātu*) that the army of Sunashshura seizes, it shall take as its own. No one shall put a claim against him. [Nevertheless], that city remains the territory of the Sun. If some city within the land of Sunashshura initiates hostility, just as it [that city] is an enemy of Sunashshura, so it shall be an enemy of the Sun.[27]

These provisions seem to indicate that each party—whether vassal or overlord—has a legal right to the booty that his army seizes. This right holds true even if the vassal has taken booty from a Hittite city. However, lest one side claim that taking booty from a city somehow also invests the plunderer with rights to the city itself, the treaty clearly stipulates that the city still remains the property territory of its original owner.[28]

We have thus found a parallel to part of Abraham's answer, namely to his refusal to take anything, be it string or sandal-lace. Is there a parallel to the king's offer, "Give me the people, but keep the goods yourself"? The recently re-edited Ishmerika Treaty gives the following stipulations concerning the booty-rights of the Ishmerikan vassals who come to the aid of their Hittite overlord:

> When a city in the midst of the land sins, then you, the people of Ishmerika, shall step in, enter, and destroy the city and its male population. The conquered civilian population [non-combatants, women, and children] you shall keep for yourself.[29]

We are reminded of the biblical distinction between *rekush*, "property," and *nefesh*, "slaves," with the king of Sodom playing the role of the overlord in asking for the human population while offering Abraham the property, which in this particular tradition went to the vassal. There were obviously different traditions in existence, but the objective distinction of categories is virtually identical in Hittite and Hebrew traditions.

Now, all of these parallels with second-millennium documents would seem to confirm the position of scholars like Albright and Speiser who argue for the antiquity of much of the material in Genesis.[30] When Mendenhall[31]—and before him, Bickerman[32]—called attention to the parallels between the Hittite treaties and the biblical covenant, many assumed that these similarities constituted iron-clad proof of the antiquity of the covenant form in Israel. While the covenant may be of hoary antiquity on independent grounds, we know that many of the elements of the Hittite treaty were preserved in Neo-Assyrian treaties. Therefore, Weinfeld,[33] Frankena[34] and others are correct in pointing out that the covenant form—at least in Deuteronomy—could just as well have been borrowed at a later date from Neo-Assyrian sources or from Aramaic adaptations of the Neo-Assyrian treaty literature.

Consider a case in point—during the last few years, scholarly attention has been drawn to the eighth-century Aramaic treaty between Bir-Gaʿyah, the king of KTK, and Matiʿel of Arpad. The similarities between this treaty and contemporary Assyrian and earlier Hittite and Akkadian treaties from Ras Shamra have been investigated. Present are all the well-known promises of mutual aid and the stereotyped lists of curses known from the Akkadian sources. What we also find—in a slightly broken context, but one clear enough to yield its meaning—is a requirement concerning the obligations of Matiʿel to furnish the king who comes to his aid with the necessary provisions. Sefire I B stipulates the obligation of the vassal to come to the aid of his overlord. Line 38 reads: "And if you do not give (me) my bread [provisions] . . . and do not offer [them], you will have broken this treaty."[35] Clearly, we have before us an eighth-century Aramaic reflex of a second-millennium treaty stipulation. It is from such late reflexes that the provender regulations of Genesis 14 may have been derived.

Line 39 of the same treaty is a crux that both Fitzmyer and Donner have left partly untranslated. In Fitzmyer's edition, the beginning of the line is clear: *[ltk]hl ltśʾ lḥm*, "You will not be able not to deliver the bread."[36] Fitzmyer separates *lḥm* from the following *ʾnḥ kʾym yqm lk*, reading an impossible *kʾym* in the second part of the line. H. L. Ginsberg suggests that we read the *kaph* with *ʾnḥ* as *lḥm ʾnḥk* (there are no word dividers in the text). The line would thus be translated: "You will be unable not to deliver (= you must deliver) the bread of your feudal service whatever is available to you/as much as you are obliged to."[37] The term *ʾnḥ* is used here as a verbal noun with its second-millennium Syrian-Akkadian meaning, rather than in its later Aramaic one; it can hardly denote "groanings," as it does regularly in Hebrew and Aramaic. Nor does the regular sense of the Akkadian *anāḫu*, "to be exhausted," fit the context much better. However, in the Akkadian of Alalakh, Amarna, and most commonly at Ras Shamra, *anāḫu* is the regular term used for "to perform feudal service for an overlord."[38]

In short, we have seen that each element of the laws of war found in Genesis 14 has its parallel in ancient Near Eastern tradition. This would seem to make Abraham not merely a pious man but a noble warrior and a politically astute maker of treaties.

At this juncture two different but related lines of development suggest themselves: (a) An examination of several other biblical traditions relating to the division of booty that will round out the picture and further illuminate some problems specifically connected with Genesis 14. (b) An investigation of the military and political implications of the laws of war as they manifest themselves in the lives and covenants of the patriarchs.

Inner-Biblical Parallels

There is an ancient law that lays down that booty must be divided equally between those who personally fought and those who are left behind, be they soldiers who guard the camp (1 Sam 30:24) or simply noncombatants, members of the *ʿeda*, "congregation" (Num 31:27).[39]

Let us first examine Numbers 31, the chapter that deals with the war against Midian. Moses was specifically commanded by the Lord, "Take an inventory of the booty that was captured, man and beast, . . . and divide the booty equally between the combatants who participated in the campaign and the rest of the community" (Num 31:26–27). Further on, the narrative reads: "The commander of the troop divisions, the officers of thousands, the officers of hundreds, approached Moses. They said to Moses, 'Your servants have made a check of the warriors in our charge, not one of us is missing. So we have brought as our offering to the Lord such articles of gold as each of us came upon, armlets, bracelets, signet-rings, earrings and pendants, that an expiation may be made for our persons before the Lord'" (Num 31:48–50). Contrast the behavior of the upper echelons to that of the rank and file: "But in the ranks everybody kept his booty for himself" (v 53). Is the noble action of the officers comparable to Abraham's giving a tithe to Melchizedek?[40]

A related operation is mentioned in Joshua's final injunction to the troops of Reuben, Gad, and the half-tribe of Manasseh: "Return to your homes with great wealth—with very much livestock, with silver and gold, with copper and iron, with a great quantity of clothing. Share the spoil of your enemies with your kinsmen" (Josh 22:8).

In light of the preceding, an examination of 1 Samuel 30 is in order. David, buffeted from one situation to another, finds it impossible to continue playing his cat-and-mouse game with the Philistine king Achish. Claiming to have attacked the Negev of the Kenites and the Negev of the Jerahmeelites (both in Judean territory), while actually attacking the Amalekites, enemies of the Judeans and Philistines alike (1 Sam 27:8–11), David was actually defending Judahite settlements. Due to the realistic suspicions of Achish's generals, David is not only prevented from joining the Philistine troops but barely escapes with his life (1 Samuel 29). He returns home to Ziklag, only to find the city burnt and plundered, his two wives and the families of his men taken into captivity by the Amalekites (1 Sam 30:1). David, held responsible for this fiasco, "was in great danger, for the troops threatened to stone him [cf. Num 14:10]; for all the troops were embittered on account of their sons and daughters" (v 6). This is certainly the nadir of his career. But David sought strength in the Lord his God (v 6) and was encouraged by a positive omen that he would overtake the Amalekites.

From now on, the onus in the story is on David to prove himself as a leader and overlord to his men, his protégés (very much like the relationship between Abraham and Lot in Genesis 14). Only by the successful restoration of his men's booty, wives, and families does he extricate himself from this tight situation: "And David rescued (*va-yaṣṣel*) all that the Amalekites had carried away; and David rescued his two wives. Nothing of theirs was missing—young or old, sons or daughters (= parallel *miḥut ve-ʿad serokh naʿal*!), spoil or anything else that had been carried off—David recovered everything; David took all the flocks and herds, which (the troops) drove ahead of the other livestock: and they declared, 'This is David's spoil'" (1 Sam 30:18–20). Thereupon follows the quasi-rebellion of some mean and churlish fellows who want to deprive the non-combatants of their rightful share of the booty—a suggestion that is nipped in the bud by David's converting into binding law the ancient custom that the booty has to be divided without discrimination against non-combatants. The story does not end here, for this particular law is sandwiched between the mention of David's booty and the end of the chapter (vv 21–31), which tells us what he did with his booty. Instead of keeping it for himself, he sends gifts to over sixteen different towns in the Judean territories that had probably been the object of Amalekite depredations. Whether bound by formal treaty or not, he actually makes a token reparation with his private booty for the goods lost. Even tokens to this huge list of towns could hardly have left David with much of the cattle designated by the popular acclamation, "This is David's spoil" (v 20). David is indeed a noble warrior—in enforcing the equitable law of booty division between combatants and non-combatants, and by actually returning his rightful share of the booty to those who had been plundered. Shades of Abraham![41]

In 1 Samuel 25, David seems to have thought that his unsolicited protection of Nabal's flocks and shepherds entitled his men to a gift of food and drink on the joyful occasion of the sheep-shearing festival. On hearing that his men were turned down, David in an outburst of rage is ready to turn Nabal's celebration into a veritable blood bath. Though David's right to provisions was an unwritten one stemming from an informal relationship, he was infuriated that his request should be so churlishly ignored. Instead of being seen as a loyal protector, he was actually accused of being one in a long line of hoodlums who rebelled against the rightful authority of their king. Perhaps Nabal's accusation was too close to the truth for David to bear. If not for the wise intervention of Abigail, David might have aborted his meteoric rise to the kingship. As things happened, David was seen as a staunch ally of the Judean settlements bordering the Philistine territory. He was their unofficial protector and they his unofficial protégés to whom, as we have seen, he later attempted to indemnify losses sustained by Amalekite victims.

Whether or not scholars are correct in seeing the patriarchs as either foreshadowings, or more specifically reflexes of Davidic times,[42] objective similarities between Davidic deed and patriarchal practice suggest themselves. That David was a noble—and at times ignoble—warrior is taken for granted. Abraham, on the other hand, is hardly ever depicted as a man of military might; his characteristics of political astuteness and military activity have usually been considered as an anomaly in a chapter filled with anomalies. But as we have seen, every aspect of Genesis 14 heretofore taken as an anomaly corresponds quite exactly to inner-biblical usage and ancient Near Eastern tradition. Once Abraham is seen in this light, it will become clear that the other patriarchs were also no strangers to political and military activities.

Patriarchal Covenants

Although the stories of the binding of Isaac and the brave intercession over the fate of Sodom and Gomorrah tend to stamp Abraham with the seal of radical spirituality, the various Pentateuchal narrators/tradents were aware of the aspect of the patriarch that we have called his worldly, political-military side. While some of the tradents of the patriarchal narratives may have played down the role of the patriarch as a warrior, the weight of tradition impelled them to preserve passages like Gen 21:22–23 (E), where Abimelech is significantly accompanied by his general Phicol, and Gen 26:26, where Abimelech, Phicol, and Ahuzzat, Abimelech's counselor, come forward.[43] In these passages Abimelech seeks to enter into a pact of non-aggression with the patriarchs.[44] Clearly, the patriarch's presence in the land constituted something of a threat to the Philistine king. (Having God as an ally hardly detracted from Abraham's military strength.) The fact that Abimelech's general was at the Genesis 21 negotiations made him an active party to the treaty: it is he who will have to do the fighting in case of a breach of covenant.[45] All this evidence clearly suggests that the patriarch was not simply a powerless resident-alien of the land. A similar pact of non-aggression between Abimelech and Isaac is the subject of the J narrator in Genesis 26. Although Isaac seems, at least superficially, to have been a rather colorless figure, he was anything but a weakling. Isaac enjoyed almost magical success in agriculture.[46] Although the year was one of famine, "Isaac prospered in the land and reaped a hundredfold the same year": "The man grew richer (*va-yigdal*) and richer (*gadel*) until he was very rich indeed (*gadal*)" (Gen 26:13). Furthermore, it was Isaac's remarkable proliferation in Abimelech's territory that intimidated the Philistine king and caused him to say, "Go away from us, you are too numerous (*ʿaṣamta*) for us" (v 16), and that finally prompted Abimelech to arrange a *détente* with the patriarch. In a similar fashion, as judged correctly by McCarthy, it is Laban in Genesis 31, usually seen as stronger than Jacob, who finds Jacob so alarming that he initiates the treaty proceedings.[47] As we shall see, this is not an isolated example of Jacob's redoubtable military aspect.

As far as content is concerned, the four secular covenants in Genesis (14; 21:22–34; 26:1–33; 31:44–54) deal with the following subjects: (a) booty restoration etiquette; (b) booty division rights; (c) the *per diem* rations due to the troops of an ally; (d) the regulation of boundaries (Genesis 31); and (e) stipulations concerning the superior status of daughters of one party married to another (Genesis 31). As already seen, (a), (b), and (c) are known either from the Akkadian treaties of Ras Shamra or those of Boghazköy; boundary regulations are often found in covenants from Boghazköy or Alalakh. The only element which may seem strange in the treaty context is the regulation of the superior status of the daughters of one of the treaty partners. This "strangeness" is the result of certain stereotyped notions concerning the supposedly monolithic nature of the "covenant pattern." But, as McCarthy rightly pointed out, such a "pattern" was more flexible than is usually assumed; the contents of the treaty and the various genres incorporated into its structure varied according to the interests of the contracting parties.[48] The Hittite treaty, on rare occasions, also regulated the status of wives and concubines. This was certainly the case in the treaty between Shuppiluliuma and Mattiwaza.[49] Thus, Laban's condition that Jacob not mistreat his daughters nor take other wives besides them is well within the traditional purview of the Near Eastern secular treaty.

Along with the substantive parallels between the secular covenant in Genesis and similar Near Eastern treaties, there are also some linguistic and formalistic similarities that are hardly fortuitous. Characteristic of the treaties in Genesis 21, 26, and 31 is the significant fact that in several cases it is the stronger party who takes the oath.[50] The sacrifice of animals as part of the covenant ceremony is attested not only at Mari[51] but also at Alalakh[52] and Sefire.[53] The presence of the king's general at the covenant ceremony is known not only from the Bible but also from Alalakh.[54] The term *šqr*, with the technical meaning "to break covenant," is common both to the Bible and early Aramaic treaty usage.[55] The closest parallel to the *gal/maṣṣebah* witness-stele of Genesis 31 are the *bethel* monuments of Sefire, which, although not specifically called "witnesses," may actually function as such.[56] Furthermore, the name Miṣpah and the concomitant interpretation, "May Yahweh keep watch/look . . . " (Gen 31:49), given by the E tradent to the *maṣṣeba* witness-stele, is virtually identical with the appeal to the gods at the opening of the Sefire treaty: *pqḥw ʿynykm lḥzyh ʿdy br gʿyh* [*ʿm mtʿʾl mlk ʾrpd*], "Open your eyes [O gods!] to gaze upon the treaty of Bir-Gaʿyah [with Matiʿel, the king of Arpad]."[57] Clearly, the biblical *ṣph* is but the equivalent of the Aramaic *ḥzh*.

Military Traditions Relating to the Patriarchs

It has been seen from an analysis of Genesis 14 that the patriarchs were not only men of the spirit but also of the sword, and diplomats to boot. However, the wars they fought and the treaties they made were not simply matters of bookkeeping but also food for the heroic imagination. Although the biblical writers kept a tight control on this human tendency, they occasionally allowed the heroic free rein. As Gunkel pointed out, nowhere do we see this oscillation more clearly than in the conflicting traditions about Jacob's activities at Shechem, one heroic and warlike, the other timid and apprehensive. According to the canonical narrative preserved in Genesis 33:18–20, Jacob is anything but aggressive; he is only too happy to have arrived at the outskirts of the city unharmed (*shalem*) and to have unobtrusively bought a piece of land for himself. His learning about the violence of his sons throws him into a panic: "You have brought trouble upon me by making me obnoxious to the inhabitants of the land . . . with our ranks so meager, if they unite against me, I shall be wiped out with all my people" (34:30–31). However, Gen 48:22 reads: "As for me, I give you [Joseph] Shechem (more than to one of your brothers), which I captured from the Amorites with my sword and bow." The history of the verse is somewhat as follows: the original form was unequivocally military and did not include *ʾeḥad ʿal ʾaḥeykha*; these words were added by a pious redactor whose intention was to obfuscate the original warlike tone.

This is not the only case where different traditions concerning the patriarchs are preserved. For example, the tradition preserved in Hosea 12 (in spite of a few textual difficulties) is outspokenly critical of Jacob's behavior. We follow the reconstruction of Ginsberg and the version of the NJPS.[58]

> Ephraim surrounds Me with deceit,
> The House of Israel with guile. . . .
> In the womb he tried to supplant his brother;
> Grown to manhood, he strove with a divine being,
> He strove with an angel and prevailed—
> The other [i.e., the angel] had to weep and implore him.
> At Bethel [Jacob] would meet him,
> There to commune with him (Hos 12:1, 4–5).

Furthermore, Jacob's battle with a divine being hardly reflects a timid, non-aggressive type. In fact Skinner, following Gunkel, makes a significant comment on the last part of Gen 32:29, "'You have striven with God *and with men*.' This can hardly refer to the contests with Laban or Esau; it points rather to the existence of a fuller body of legend, in which Jacob figured as a hero of many combats, culminating in this successful struggle with the deity."[59] It is no coincidence that Jacob, who fights with God and men, already displays an heroic prowess when he single-handedly rolls the stone off the well (Genesis 29), an act that ordinarily required the combined strength of "all the herdsmen."

Jacob's warlike spirit seems to have been inherited by some of his sons—note Simeon and Levi's destruction of Shechem. Even a superficial perusal of the last words of Jacob (Genesis 49) and the last words of Moses (Deuteronomy 33) presents us with a whole host of heroic deeds and military attributes. See, for instance, both passages on Dan:

Dan shall be a serpent by the road,
A viper by the path
That bites the horse's heels
So that his rider is thrown backward.
(Gen 49:17)

Dan is a lion's whelp
That leaps forth from Bashan.
(Deut 33:22)

Or the comments on Joseph:

Archers bitterly assailed him
They shot at him and harried him.
Yet his bow stayed taut
And his arms were made firm.
(Gen 49:23–24)

Like a firstling bull in his majesty
He has horns like the horns of a wild-ox;
With them he gores the peoples,
The ends of the earth one and all.
(Deut 33:17)[60]

This military motif can scarcely be disassociated from the divine promise to the patriarchs that kings shall come forth from their loins (Gen 17:6; 35:11); that they shall multiply north, south, east and west (Gen 28:14); that they shall be teeming multitudes; that their descendants shall be as numerous as the stars, so that all nations of the world shall bless themselves by their offspring (Gen 26:4), i.e., that the nations of the world would like to be similar to Israel. Such a sentiment is actually expressed by Balaam:

Who can count the dust of Jacob,
Number the dust-cloud of Israel?
May I die the death of the upright,[61]
May my fate be like theirs!
(Num 23:10, NJPS)

In all probability, this population explosion is envisaged as the prerequisite of military conquest:[62] "May you grow into thousands of myriads, [so that] your offspring may seize the gates of its foes" (Gen 24:60). Another example is found in Gen 22:17–18: "I will . . . make your descendants as numerous as the stars of heaven and the sands on the seashore;

and your descendants shall seize the gates of their foes. All the nations of the earth shall bless themselves by your descendants. . . . "

If the initial reaction of the outside world was a benign desire to be as blessed as Israel, it soon turned into hostile envy, as in Abimelech's reaction to Isaac's success and ever-proliferating numbers (Gen 26:12–16), and finally, changed to apprehension and dread that this divinely contrived population increase would undo them. Because of this fear (*yqṣw*, Exod 1:12), the Egyptians attempted by means of all kinds of devices to stop the population increase. The Moabites experienced the same alarm (*ygr*, Num 22:3) and tried to put a halt to Israel's numbers by hiring Balaam's services.

Is it possible, in these circumstances, that the names of the deities worshipped by the patriarchs may also carry war-like overtones? Is this what is implied by the name *ʾAbbir Yaʿaqob*, "The Powerful One of Jacob"? Could Isaac's numen *Paḥad Yiṣḥaq* mean, "He Who Inspires Fear in the Heart of Isaac's Enemies"? Does God's self-revelation as Abraham's *magen*, "shield," reflect Abraham's weakness or his strength? (Although the actual term *Magen ʾAvraham* appears for the first time in Ben Sirah, it is probably much older.) Unfortunately, except for *ʾAbbir Yaʿaqov*, the epithets are too problematic to make any definitive inference on the subject. In the meantime, see the well-known studies of F. M. Cross and Patrick D. Miller.[63]

Midrashic Echoes

The following few examples are probably excerpts from an ancient genre of heroic poetry that may have constituted the basis of the lost *Book of Ha-Yashar* (2 Sam 1:18) or the *Book of the Wars of the Lord* (Num 21:14). It is possible that some of this archaic material may have been preserved in apocryphal literature and in early and late midrash.[64] Consider the following passage from the *Testament of Judah* 1:6–2:7:

> And it came to pass, when I became a man, that my father blessed me, saying: Thou shalt be a king, prospering in all things.
>
> And the Lord showed me favour in all my works, both in the field and in the house. I know that I raced a hind and caught it, and prepared the meat for my father, and he did eat. And the roes I used to master in the chase, and overtake all that was in the plains. A wild mare I overtook, and caught it and tamed it. I slew a lion and plucked a kid out of its mouth. I took a bear by its paw and hurled it down the cliff, and it was crushed. I outran the wild boar, and seizing it as I ran I tore it in sunder. A leopard in Hebron leaped upon my dog, and I caught it by the tail, and I hurled it on the rocks, and it

> was broken in twain. I found a wild ox feeding in the fields, and seizing it by the horns, and whirling it round and stunning it, I cast it from me and slew it.[65]

The similarity between this passage and certain passages in annals of Assyrian kings is more than striking:

> The gods Ninurta (and) Palil, who love my priesthood, gave to me the wild beasts and commanded me to hunt. I killed 450 strong lions. I killed 390 wild bulls from my . . . chariot with my lordly assault. I slew 200 ostriches like caged birds. I drove 30 elephants into an ambush. I captured alive 50 wild bulls, 140 ostriches, (and) 20 strong lions from the mountains and forests. I received five live elephants as tribute from the governor of the land Suhu and the governor of the land Lubdu (and) they went about with me on my campaign. I formed herds of wild bulls, lions, ostriches, (and) male (and) female apes. I bred herds of them.[66]

We are dealing with an ancient stereotype whose purpose is to glorify the might of the ruler by a description of his prowess in subduing the world of the wild beast. It is almost as if the author of the *Testament of Judah* had some of these ancient *topoi* in front of him (perhaps in Aramaic garb) when he celebrated the prowess of the ancient patriarchs.[67]

The same genre of literature also delights in depicting the military prowess of Jacob and his sons as they wage the wars of the Lord. According to the *Testament of Judah*, Jacob not only fights at Shechem; he also kills his brother Esau in a pitched battle and takes up arms against the Amorites. There is a significant overlap between cities conquered by Jacob and those conquered by the Maccabees. Patriarchal prowess may simply reflect Hasmonean military achievement.[68] A fine example of the depiction of the military prowess of Jacob and his sons is the following, from the *Testament of Judah* 3:1–10:

> And when the two kings of the Canaanites came sheathed in armour against our flocks, and much people with them, single-handed I rushed upon the king of Hazor, and smote him on the greaves and dragged him down, and so I slew him. And the other, the king of Tappuah, as he sat upon his horse, I slew and so I scattered all his people. Achor the king a man of giant stature I found, hurling javelins before and behind as he sat on horseback, and I took up a stone of sixty pounds weight, and hurled it and smote his horse, and killed it. And I fought with (this) other for two hours; and I clave his shield in twain, and I chopped off his feet, and killed him. And as I was stripping off his breastplate, behold nine men his companions began to fight with me. And I wound my garment on my hand; and I slung stones at them, and killed four of them, and the rest fled. And Jacob my father slew Beelesath,

> king of all the kings, a giant in strength, twelve cubits high. And fear fell upon them, and they ceased warring against us. Therefore my father was free from anxiety in the wars when I was with my brethren. For he saw in a vision concerning me that an angel of might followed me everywhere, that I should not be overcome.[69]

Although this glorification of the military might of the patriarchs is found sporadically in the early rabbinic midrash, it is in the later midrash (ca. tenth century C.E.) that we find the theme emphasized. In a collection called *The Wars of the Sons of Jacob* we have a cycle of military legends that is virtually identical in word and spirit with the ancient legends preserved in *The Testaments of the Twelve Patriarchs* and *The Book of Jubilees*.[70] While the exact details of the chains of literary transmission are not adequately known, the common origin of the two cycles is a fact.[71]

Certain sectors of later Jewry were interested in legends, circulated by Eldad Ha-Dani and similar paramilitary types, about the independent existence of a kingdom of Jews living on the other side of the River Sambatyon, and of another in Havilah, the land of gold, near Ethiopia. The latter realm was constantly at war with neighboring tribes and kingdoms. The Ten Tribes often figured in these accounts. Eldad Ha-Dani's aim was probably to

> raise the spirits of Jews by giving them news of tribes of Israel who lived in freedom and by creating an attractive Jewish Utopia. The report of the existence of such Jewish kingdoms undoubtedly encouraged and comforted Eldad's hearers, by contradicting the Christian contention that Jewish independence had ceased after the destruction of the Second Temple. For the Jews his stories obviously had far-reaching messianic implications.[72]

Perhaps it was in such circles that the ancient apocryphal heroic cycles were cultivated and preserved.

New Light on the Habiru Problem

The preceding sections have dealt with the military-heroic aspect of the patriarchs in general and, in particular, with those aspects of Genesis 14 that present Abraham as a noble warrior who carefully observes the niceties of booty-restoration known in his day. It is important to remember that one of the anomalies of the chapter is that Abraham is called a Hebrew (Gen 14:13), a term usually employed by foreigners concerning the Israelites (Gen 39:14) or by Israelites as a self-designation to outsiders (Gen 40:15, 43:32).

Because of the unequivocal military-heroic nature of the patriarchs, and especially of Abraham, the epithet *ʿivri* and the Habiru problem cannot be as lightly disassociated as some modern scholars would have it. Thompson's rejection of a link between the Habiru and the *ʿivri*, although in most cases convincing, collides head-on with the unequivocal overlap between the military activities of Abraham and the Habiru of history.[73] Albright's imaginative connection between Abraham and the Habiru is, however, doubtful.[74] While I greatly admire Thompson's sober critique of the pan-Babylonianism of Speiser, Albright, and others, this remarkable overlap between the activities of Abraham and of the earlier Habiru cannot be ignored as easily as I myself have often wished.

As Speiser noted,[75] the evidence of Genesis 14 accords more closely than that of any other chapter with cuneiform data on the western Habiru; he calls attention to the Alalakh date formula in *AT* 58 (eighteenth/ seventeenth centuries B.C.E.), which mentions a treaty with Habiru warriors, and to the Statue of Idrimi (fifteenth century B.C.E., Alalakh), which tells how the royal fugitives found asylum among Habiru warriors.[76]

To this, a further—although tentative—observation may be added. According to M. B. Rowton, Habiru warriors tended to locate themselves in certain scrub woodlands called "maquis forests" (the French maquis of World War II were called by the name of the forest in which they hid).[77] The maquis forests of Syria-Palestine consisted mostly of evergreen-oak and tamarisk (*ʾelah/ʾelon* and *ʾeshel* in Hebrew). One of the two maquis forests of ancient Palestine lay between Hebron and Shechem. Although Abraham's movements were not exclusively confined to this area, it may be more than a simple coincidence that Abraham the Hebrew happened to live *beʾelone Mamre*, "in the terebinths of Mamre." If Abraham were a type of Habiru, and if Rowton's suggestion is correct that Habiru warriors preferred the maquis forests, then Abraham's association with the terebinth forests of Mamre would make excellent sense. Taking into consideration his military activities (and those of the other patriarchs), the epithet *ʿivri* for Abraham in this context, and in this context alone, leads to the question: Could it be that Abraham the warrior is none other than Abraham the Habiru? These suggestions, however attractive they may seem, are highly speculative and need further corroboration.

Conclusions

In this study, an attempt has been made to illumine the behavior of Abraham in Genesis 14 in the light of the laws of war, and specifically of booty-restoration, as preserved in Hittite and Akkadian international treaties. The patriarch appears as a noble warrior, decisive in battle and wholly magnanimous in victory, who, like Shuppiluliuma before him, relinquishes the victor's rights to the restored booty, taking neither *ḫāmu* nor *ḫuṣābu* (or in West Semitic *miḥuṭ ve-ʿad serokh naʿal*). Furthermore, the recognition that Abraham (according to the simple meaning of the text, even without the parallel from Ras Shamra) functions as a military personage allied by treaty to three local grandees, possesses a private army of over three hundred men, and is concerned about the rations of his troops and the rightful share of the booty for his allies like a good commander—all of this forces us to re-examine significant fragments of evidence concerning the military, or paramilitary, aspects of Isaac and especially of Jacob. As we have seen, they too are requested to enter into peace treaties signed and sealed by local kings and their generals. As in the case of Abraham, much of the treaty-law reflected in the patriarchal narratives has sound Near Eastern treaty parallels. Although these parallels (in Akkadian and Hittite treaties of the late second millennium and the Aramaic treaties from Sefire in the eighth century) attest to the authenticity of the local color of the stories, they do not decisively establish the date when these stories were written down. Nor should our inability to pinpoint the date of reception perturb us too much. The illumination of the structure of an institution, in this case the laws of war, seems to be of greater significance than pure problems of chronology.[78]

NOTES

1. If literary convention demanded that the conquering hero be greeted ceremoniously on his return from battle (so B. Jacob, *Das erste Buch der Tora: Genesis* [Berlin: Schocken, 1934]), the storyteller may have lifted the Melchizedek pericope from an original literary setting and creatively restructured it to suit the demands of his new plot. Although the literary "seams" may still show, the new sequence of events (battle, capture of allies and Lot, plundering of booty, battle, ceremonial welcome, dialogue between Abraham and the king of Sodom) seems natural, especially if we take into consideration the elliptical nature of biblical storytelling, as pointed out by Y. Kaufmann (see, e. g., *Joshua* [Jerusalem: Mosad Bialik, 1955; in Hebrew] 74–76, and *Judges* [Jerusalem: Kiryat Sefer, 1962; in Hebrew] 161ff.). For a contrasting, more atomistic view of Genesis 14, see G. von Rad, *Genesis* (trans. J. H. Marks; 2d ed.; Old Testament Library; Philadelphia: Westminster, 1972).

In this context, it should be noted that the "sudden" reappearance of the king of Sodom is less surprising than is usually thought, since the common view that *va-yippelu shammah* (Gen 14:10) means "they (accidentally) fell there (and perished)" is wrong. Ibn Ezra (followed by Umberto Cassuto, "Bereshit," *Entsiḳlopedyah Miḳra'it. Encyclopædia Biblica* [Jerusalem: Mosad Bialik] vol. 2 [1954], cols. 318–35; A. B. Ehrlich, *Mikrâ ki-Pheschutô* [Berlin: Poppelauer, 1899–1901; rpt. New York: KTAV, 1969]; NJPS; and others) realized that *nafal* can also refer to a voluntary lowering of oneself, as in the common locution *nafal ʿal panav*, "he fell on his face." Ibn Janah (*The Book of Hebrew Roots* [ed. A. Neubauer; Oxford: Clarendon, 1875; rpt. Amsterdam: Philo Press, 1968) lists many other examples of such a voluntary lowering, the most telling being *va-tippol meʿal ha-gamal*, "she lowered herself from her camel" (Gen 24:64). Furthermore, there is the distinct possibility that in our passage the word *nafal* has overtones of "fleeing, taking refuge," as in the expression *nafelu ʾel ha-kasdim*, "they have fled to the Chaldeans" (Jer 38:19). The use of the Akkadian *maqātu*, "to fall," with the secondary meaning "to flee, take refuge," is well attested (cf. *AHw*, s. v. *maqātu* and *maqtu*).

The real artificiality of the story is not the reappearance of the king of Sodom after his supposed demise; the narrator was more subtle than that. Ehrlich suggests that the storyteller needed the king of Sodom for the final scene, where the magnanimity of Abraham is demonstrated. This purpose would have been defeated if the kings of Sodom and Gomorrah had fled to the mountains with their confreres, never to return, as one would have expected. The storyteller thus provided the interlude in the bitumen pits as a way of "naturally" reintroducing the king of Sodom in the final scene—a kind of literary *deus ex machina*. Whether Ehrlich is right on the last point is immaterial. While there can be little doubt that a wide range of sources went into the composition of the chapter, all of them—even the seemingly intrusive Melchizedek pericope—were subordinated by the storyteller (who was more than a redactor) to his literary ends.

2. Hugo Grotius, *Commentary on the Law of Prize and Booty*, trans. G. L. Williams and W. H. Zeydel (Oxford: Clarendon, 1950) 136ff. et passim. As we shall see below, Grotius anticipated aspects of our interpretation of Genesis 14; see at n. 21, below.

3. H. G. Güterbock ("Die historische Tradition und ihre literarische Gestaltung bei Babyloniern und Hethitern," *Zeitschrift für Assyriologie* 42 [1934] 1–91 at 77–79) was among the first to establish the literary character of the *narû* form and was followed by, e.g., E. A. Speiser, "Ancient Mesopotamia," *The Idea of History in the Ancient Near East*, ed. R. C. Dentan (New Haven: Yale University Press, 1955) 35–76, and J. J. Finkelstein, "Mesopotamian Historiography," *Proceedings of the American Philosophical Society* 107 (1963) 461–72.

4. M. C. Astour, "Political and Cosmic Symbolism in Genesis 14 and its Babylonian Sources," *Biblical Motifs—Origins and Transformations* (ed. Alexander Altmann; Philip W. Lown Institute of Advanced Judaic Studies, Brandeis University, Studies and Texts 3; Cambridge: Harvard University Press, 1966) 65–112. The texts were first extensively treated by A. Jeremias, "Die sogenannten Kedorlaomer Texte," *Orientalistische Studien Fritz Hommel . . . beigetragen I* (Mitteilungen der Vorderasiatischen Gesellschaft 21: Leipzig: Hinrichs, 1917) 69–97. W. F. Albright's recognition of their importance for biblical studies, in "A Third Revision of the Early Chronology of Western Asia," *Bulletin of the American Schools of Oriental Research* 88 (1942) 28–36, was forgotten until Astour's work.

5. E. A. Speiser, *Genesis* (Anchor Bible 1; Garden City, New York: Doubleday, 1964) 101, 108.

6. R. de Vaux, *Histoire ancienne d'Israël. Des origines à l'installation en Canaan* (Paris: Gabalda, 1971) 211–12.

7. E. A. Speiser, "A Figurative Equivalent for Totality in Akkadian and West-Semitic," *JAOS* 54 (1934) 200–3.

8. AP, no. 15:15.

9. H. Pick, "Drei neue Veröffentlichungen zu den Privaturkunden aus der Hammurabi-Zeit," *Orientalistische Literaturzeitung* 11 (1908) 315–18 at 317; G. R. Driver, "The Aramaic *Papyri*: Notes on Obscure Passages," *Journal of the Royal Asiatic Society* (1932) 77–90 at 78.

10. Cf. the discussion of the Aramaic phrase and Near Eastern analogues in SALPE, 59 n. 1.

11. E. F. Weidner, *Politische Dokumente aus Kleinasien. Die Staatsverträge in akkadischer Sprache aus dem Archiv von Boghazköi* (Boghazköi Studien 8–9; Leipzig: Hinrichs, 1923) 17 n. 3.

12. The text is RS 17.340, published by J. Nougayrol, *Le Palais royal d'Ugarit IV* (Mission de Ras Shamra 9; Paris: Imprimerie Nationale, 1956) 48–52. In the following, *illakma išpuranna*, "went and sent" (lines 9–10) seems to be a Canaanite construction; cf. *va-yelek va-yishlaḥ* in 2 Kgs 3:7. In both cases "(and) he went" indicates the initiation of an activity rather than an actually going.

13. The word for "ally" or "friend" in Akkadian is usually *šalmu* or *salmu*, not *šalāmu*; as far as I can tell, *šalāmu*, "ally," is only found here. Do we have before us a reflex of a Canaanite *šalāmu* = Hebrew *shalom*, "ally"? Cf. Ps 55:21: *shalaḥ yado bishlomav ḥillel berito*, "He attacked an ally; he violated his covenant."

14. Akkadian *išmēma*, "as soon as he heard" = Hebrew *va-yishmaᶜ*, Gen 14:14.

15. *Šallātu* is used for both possessions and people, and it is often difficult to determine the proper nuance. Cf. Nougayrol, *Le Palais royal d'Ugarit IV*, 49 n. 1.

16. Nougayrol's interpretation of Ras Shamra Akkadian *samāḫu* as "to luxuriate," instead of the sense, well attested at Nuzi and Boghazköy, "to come close, have a share in," has led him astray in a number of cases. (a) In our text he renders *lā summuḫ* as "let themselves be seduced," which does not fit the context; "have/ take a part in [the rebellion]" is the only possible translation. (b) RS 15.146 + 161 (Nougayrol, *Le Palais royal d'Ugarit III* [Mission de Ras Shamra 6; Paris, Imprimerie Nationale, 1955] 58) is a transfer of property; after the statement about the ceding of property, it is said that the seller parted with his property, according to Nougayrol, "pour la raison que (??) dans sa maison, ses terres ne prosperaient (?) pas." This interpretation is both legally and linguistically impossible. The clause is an expression declaring that the seller has no share in the property any more. The following clause, "just as the sun is *zāki*, pure/quit, so the seller is quit," clinches this interpretation; such declarations are quite common in the peripheral areas of cuneiform law (cf. SALPE, 178), e. g., the Nuzi clause, "The sellers *lā iqe(rri)bu ullan eqlētišunu irtēqū*, they shall not lay claim (literally, come near) to their property, they have removed themselves from their fields." A cognate of this *rêqu* reappears in the Elephantine Aramaic clause: *rḥqt min* + buyer/field, "I have removed myself from the buyer/field"; cf. also the Arsacid–Seleucid transfer formula and SALPE, 134 n. 3.

17. For a discussion of the reconfirmation of divine and royal gifts or donations, see Chapter 7 in this volume.

18. Some years ago, I was gratified to learn from a private conversation with my friend Samuel E. Loewenstamm that he had independently reached the same conclusion about the relationship between the biblical and Ugaritic texts. Cf. now his review of L. Fisher, ed., *Ras Shamra Parallels* II, *Biblica* 59 (1978) 100–22 at 111.

19. Cf. G. E. Mendenhall's observation: "The description in Gen. 14:13 implies military obligations of Abraham's allies, but it is not possible to say definitely that this is a parity covenant"; "Covenant," *IDB* 1.714–23 at 716.

20. Unless we assume that the words *mlk šlm* in Gen 14:18 are to be read *melek shelomo*, "a king allied to him," i. e., to Abraham, with W. F. Albright, *Yahweh and the Gods of Canaan* (Garden City, New York: Doubleday, 1968) 231.

21. Grotius, *Law*, 55.

22. Thus Idrimi admits, "I took captives . . . and took . . . valuables and possessions and distributed them to my auxiliaries, kin, and friends. Together with them I took booty." The last phrase may mean, "I took only one share, along with the others." See the edition by E. L. Greenstein and David Marcus, "The Akkadian Inscription of Idrimi," *Journal of the Ancient Near Eastern Society* 8 (1976) 59–96.

23. V. Korošec, *Hethitische Staatsverträge* (Leipzig: Hinrichs, 1931); D. J. McCarthy, *Treaty and Covenant* (Analecta Biblica 21; Rome: Pontifical Biblical Institute Press, 1963; rev. ed., Analecta Biblica 21a, 1978).

24. "Wenn Leute von Hatti Fusstruppen (und) Wagenkämper für Duppi-Tesup abtransportieren und ihnen weil sie in die Städte hinaufziehen, Duppi-Tesup Speise (und) Trank regelmässig liefert"; J. Friedrich, *Staatsverträge des Ḫatti-Reiches, in hethitische Sprache. I* (Mitteilungen der Vorderasiatisch-ägyptischen Gesellschaft 31.1; Leipzig: Hinrichs, 1926) Treaty 12, 17ff.

25. Trans. A. Goetze, *ANET*, 529–30.

26. Weidner, *Politische Dokumente*, 106ff.

27. Weidner, *Politische Dokumente*, 98.

28. Such stipulations are found in other areas of Near Eastern law. In one Aramaic document from Elephantine (AP, no. 5) and in one slightly later, Demotic deed from Egypt, we hear of the following situation: A allows B to use his property or a part of it; lest it be assumed that use of the property invests the user with a putative claim to that property, the deed declares that the property is the owner's nevertheless (cf. SALPE, 26). Similar stipulations in Old Babylonian deeds are discussed by J. G. Lautner, "Rechtverhältnisse an Grenzmauern," *Symbolae ad iura orientis antiqui pertinentes Paulo Koschaker dedicatae* (Studia et documenta ad iura orientis antiqui pertinenta 2; ed. J. Friedrich et al.; Leiden, Brill, 1939) 76–95.

29. A. Kempinski and S. Košak, "Der Išmeriga-Vertrag," *Die Welt des Orients* 5 (1969) 191–217 at 195.

30. SALPE, 12–16, 22 n. 4, et passim.

31. G. E. Mendenhall, "Covenant Forms in Israelite Tradition," *Biblical Archaeologist* 17 (1954) 50–74, rpt. in *The Biblical Archaeologist Reader* 3 (ed. E. F. Campbell and D. N. Freedman; Garden City, New York: Doubleday, 1970) 3–24, and in Mendenhall, *Law and Covenant in Israel and the Ancient Near East* (Pittsburgh: The Biblical Colloquium, 1955).

32. E. J. Bickerman, "'Couper une alliance,'" *Archives d'historie du droit oriental* 5 (1950–51) 133–56; rpt. in *Bickerman's Studies in Jewish and Christian history* (3 vols.; Arbeiten zur Geschichte des antiken Judentums und des Urchristentums 9; Leiden: Brill, 1976–86) 1.1–32 with an important supplement.

33. In M. Weinfeld, *Deuteronomy and the Deuteronomic School* (Oxford: Clarendon, 1972; rpt. Winona Lake, Indiana, 1992), see "Treaty Form and Phraseology," 59–146.

34. R. Frankena, "The Vassal-Treaties of Esarhaddon and the Dating of Deuteronomy," *Oudtestamentische Studiën* 14 (1965) 122–54.

35. My translation; for the text see J. A. Fitzmyer, *The Aramaic Inscriptions from Sefîre* (Biblica et orientalia 19; Rome: Pontifical Biblical Institute Press, 1967) 18 or, more conservatively, KAI 222 B.

36. My translation, following the text of Fitzmyer, *Sefîre*, 19. The meaning of *nś*ʾ (*nš*ʾ) in this context is uncertain. Fitzmyer renders it as "deduct," and Dupont-Sommer as "take away." Whatever the case, the general sense is clear.

37. H. L. Ginsberg, in a private conversation.

38. CAD, A/1, s.v. at 102. For *aniḫ* in the sense of "feudal service," see Nougayrol, *Palais royale d'Ugarit III*, 216; in a Susa text mentioned in CAD, MDP 24.379 (see V. Scheil, *Actes juridiques susiens* [Memoires de la délégation en Perse 22–24; Paris, Leroux, 1930–33]), the term is used to describe the faithful work performed by a wife. M. Weinfeld has noted an Aramaic reflex of *aniḫ* in the term *ʿml* in the Birrakib Inscription, in the line, *wbyt.ʾby.ʿml.mn.kl* (KAI 216:7–8), which he renders, "and my father's house exerted itself more than anybody else" ("The Covenant of Grant in the Bible and the Ancient Near East," *JAOS* 90 [1970]:184–203 at 187). While Birrakib's *ʿml* would be a loan translation, Sefire's *ʾnḥ* would be a loanword. It should be noted that in the Akkadian inscription of Idrimi, the word *mānaḫātu* appears as a synonym of *māmitu* and seems to be equivalent to the combination of *riksu*, "treaty," and *māmitu*, "fealty oath." The etymology of this term has been a source of great confusion for the whole problem; cf. Greenstein and Marcus, "Idrimi," 81ff. Could this term for treaty be related to the Ras Shamra Akkadian *aniḫ*, "to perform a feudal obligation"? The semantic transition from feudal obligation to feudal treaty seems more natural. The problem deserves an independent study. For the continuation of second-millennium terms in later Aramaic usage, see the discussion of Ugaritic and Aramaic *spr*, "deed," in SALPE, 207.

39. A. Musil's *The Manners and Customs of the Rwala Bedouins* (American Geographical Society. Oriental Explorations and Studies 6; New York, 1928) is a mine of illuminating parallels to biblical patterns of warfare and booty disposition. For the distinction between those who actually fight and those who stay behind to watch the baggage: "Old men and small boys must not go on a raid. They are left at home to guard the camp. . . . The commander also decides whether booty is to be divided *ḫišer*, or whether everyone has to seize it on his account" (p. 508). "If the commander of a raid agrees to share the booty obtained by all . . . they begin by counting the participants. If one of the leaders has many and another only a few men with him, the latter is given more so as to equalize the strength of all the troops. The booty is divided equally with as many parts as there are leaders; these take their share and apportion the rest among their men" (p. 510). For a discussion of Davidic procedures of booty division and a possible parallel from Mari, cf. A. Malamat, "The Ban in Mari and in the Bible," *Yehezkel Kaufmann Jubilee Volume: Studies in Bible and Jewish Religion Dedicated to Yehezkel Kaufmann on the Occasion of his Seventieth Birthday* (ed. M. Haran; Jerusalem, Magnes, 1960; in Hebrew) Hebrew section 147–58 at 154f.; cf. also U. Cassuto, "Abraham," *Entsiḳlopedyah Miḳraʾit. Encyclopædia Biblica* (Jerusalem: Mosad Bialik) vol. 1 (1955) 61–67.

40. The entire chapter on the war with the Midianites says little about the war itself but goes into great detail about the *post-bellum* division of spoils. It is almost as if the sole interest of the writer is legal (how does one divide booty?), rather than literary. (My thanks to Rabbi Benjamin Scolnic for this observation.)

41. The parallels between David's recovery of the plundered goods and Abraham's behavior in Genesis 14 are clearly seen by M. Weinfeld, *Genesis* (Tel-Aviv: S. L. Gordon, 1975; in Hebrew) 68.

42. Many scholars have contended that elements in Genesis reflect a Davidic background. This is especially true of the pericope of Melchizedek, king of Salem, which seems to reflect the aspirations of the Jerusalem priesthood (cf. Astour, "Symbolism in Genesis 14," 70). U. Cassuto has pointed out that the strange circular itinerary of the four kings reproduces, in the opposite direction, the route ascribed in Deuteronomy 1–3 to the Israelites traveling to Transjordan under the leadership of Moses (quoted apud Astour, "Symbolism in Genesis 14," 73). As to Genesis 14, Cassuto came to the conclusions already reached by Immanuel Benzinger: the four kings conquered all the regions of Transjordan, Edom, and the Negev, then they victoriously crossed all of Canaan from south to north, and Abraham overtook them and pursued them as far as Dan (the traditional northern border of Israel) and pursued them beyond Damascus; therefore, Abraham inherited all the fruits of their conquests, and everything from Elath to Dan, including even Damascus and south Syria (Greater Canaan), belonged to Abraham and his descendants ("Bereshit," *Entsiḳlopedyah Miḳraʾit. Encyclopædia Biblica*, 2.329). A. B. Ehrlich, in *Randglossen zur hebräischen Bibel: Textkritisches, sprachliches, und sachliches* (Leipzig: Hinrichs, 1908–14; rpt. Hildesheim: Olms, 1968), describes the divine command to "get up and walk through the land" as an ancient method of acquisition, with parallels in Homer and the Jerusalem Talmud; for further, Mesopotamian parallels, cf. SALPE, 24 n. 2. For a clear summary of the Davidic color of the chapter, see Weinfeld's *Genesis*, where he assumes that the boundaries mentioned in Genesis 14 are those of the Davidic monarchy and that many of the modes of warfare used by David are virtually identical with those used by Abraham.

43. *Mereʿehu*, literally "friend," functionally "adviser," cf. 2 Sam 15:37, 16:16, where related terms clearly mean adviser-counselor; see also 1 Chr 27:33, where the *reaʿ* is a member of the king's administrative staff. Paradoxically, in negotiating with the so-called weak and colorless Isaac, Abimelech brings along not merely his general, as he did in negotiating with Abraham, but his counselor as well!

44. Although D. J. McCarthy ("Three Covenants in Genesis," *CBQ* 26 [1964] 179–89) is not interested in the military exploits of the patriarchs, his analysis of the covenants between Abraham and Abimelech, Isaac and Abimelech, and Jacob and Laban makes him one of the few scholars to have treated this small but significant body of material. We have simply put greater stress on the military implications inherent in these covenants.

45. An Alalakh text, AT* 54 (Old Babylonian period), records the sacrifice of a sheep in connection with the sale of a city (cf. A. Draffkorn[-Kilmer], "Was King Abba-AN of Yamḫad a Vizier for the King of Ḫattuša?", *Journal of Cuneiform Studies* 13 [1959] 94–98 at 95 n. 11). The unusual detail that "the neck of a sacrificial animal was cut in the presence of PN the general" is an exact parallel to this element concerning Phicol in our passage.

46. This success is an example of a phenomenon which could be called "the endowment given to the men of special blessing" (cf. Arabic *barakat* and Hebrew *berakah*). Cf. J. Pedersen, *Israel, Its Life and Culture*, I–II (London: Oxford University Press, 1926) 182–212. Those endowed with such a special gift exceed the norm in one or more of the following: (1) strength (Jacob moves the stone off the well with the greatest of ease; Abraham conquers the armies of four major world powers with 318 men); (2) fertility (Isaac has a "green thumb"; Laban attributes the multiplication of his flocks to the presence of Jacob; Potiphar's property was blessed, i. e., multiplied, by Joseph's presence; Egyptian fields produce incredible yields in a year of famine; Israelites in Egypt multiplied from 70 individuals to 600,000 families in four generations); (3) beauty (Sarah was the most beautiful of women; David was outstanding in appearance); (4) health (Moses at 120 is still vigorous); (5) age (the phenomenal lifespan of the antediluvians and the patriarchs); and even in (6) size (Saul was taller than all other men). These passages seem to have a Homeric quality that is exemplified by a hero's lifting of a stone, the raising of which would ordinarily require many men, a theme found throughout the *Iliad* ; cf. Weinfeld, *Genesis*, ad Gen 29:10. The whole phenomenon deserves an independent study.

47. McCarthy points out that it is only in Near Eastern parity treaties that both parties take the oath. In the three secular covenants with individuals in Genesis, although both parties take the oath, the relationship of the parties is hardly one of parity. The patriarchs are clearly the superior parties in the first two cases (e. g., it is Abimelech who asks for the oath in Genesis 21), and Laban is clearly superior in the third. Nevertheless, it is the seemingly stronger party who initiates the oath. McCarthy calls attention to the treaty between Abba-AN of Yamḫad and Yarim-Lim of Alalakh, where Abba-AN—the superior party—takes the oath (cf. Draffkorn [-Kilmer], "Was Abba-AN?"). For the equivalence of "taking an oath" and "cutting a covenant" in these biblical treaties and in the treaty between Abba-AN and Yarim-Lim, see McCarthy, "Three Covenants," 181.

48. McCarthy, *Treaty and Covenant*, 53ff. et passim.

49. Trans. A. Goetze, *ANET*, 206.

50. See n. 47, above.

51. C.-F. Jean, *Archives royales de Mari II* (Textes cunéiformes du Louvre 23; Paris: Imprimerie Nationale, 1941) 37; see McCarthy, *Treaty and Covenant*, 53ff.

52. AT* 54; see n. 45, above.

53. Cf. Sefire I A 40. For a discussion, see McCarthy, *Treaty and Covenant*, 52.

54. See n. 45, above.

55. Cf. Sefire I B 38; III 14, 19, 20 and 27 et passim. The verb is found in two different syntactical settings: (a) *šqr bʿdʾ*, "to be false to the treaty" (I B 38 et passim); (b) *šqr l* PN/DN, "to be false to a person or god" (I A 14 and I B 23). Biblical Hebrew follows a similar pattern. The first usage is reflected in *ve-loʾ shiqqarnu bivritekha*, "we have not been false to Your covenant" (Ps 44:18); the second in *ʾim tishqor li u-lenini u-lenekhdi*, "that you will not deal falsely with me or with my kith and kin (literally, my grandson)" (Gen 21:23). This protection of Abimelech's children and grandchildren (*nin vaneked*) against any future breach of covenant (*š-q-r*) is paralleled by similar provisos in the Sefire treaty (I A 14–35). As far as Hebrew usage is concerned, there seems to be a marked difference between the noun *sheqer*, meaning "falsehood," and *shiqqer*, which in a majority of cases does not seem to signify "to tell a lie" as much as "to deal falsely, break (a covenant)" (Gen 21:23; Ps 44:18; Isa 63:8; and probably also in 1 Sam

15:29). The NJPS translation renders Lev 19:11, *ve-loʾ teshaqqeru ʾish baʿamito*, as, "You shall not deal falsely with one another" (contrast "lie to one another," *The Bible. An American Translation* [2d ed.: Chicago: University of Chicago Press, 1935]). See also the comments of Ibn Janah concerning Onqelos' frequent use of the Aramaic *š-q-r* to render the Hebrew *b-g-d*, "to betray" (*The Book of Hebrew Roots* [ed. A. Neubauer]).

56. The *bethel* steles are mentioned in Sefire II C 2, 7, and 9. McCarthy ("Three Covenants," 187) calls attention to Sefire I B 8–9 ("Let not one of the words of this inscription be silent [*štq*]") as proof that the *bethels* "are not passive objects simply to be read. They are *bty ʾlhyʾ* 'residences of the gods' with an active power to make known the texts inscribed on them." Unfortunately, the personified inscriptions on the stele cannot be automatically identified with the steles themselves, which are considered actual deities elsewhere but not specifically in Sefire itself, as McCarthy suggests. If this identification could be established, we would have an even more striking parallel with the Miṣpah stele of Genesis 31. Further discoveries are bound to shed more light on the problem.

57. Fitzmyer's translation, *Sefire*, 13–14.

58. NJPS and H. L. Ginsberg, "Hosea's Ephraim, More Fool than Knave. A New Interpretation of Hosea 12:1–14," *JBL* 80 (1961) 339–347 at 341.

59. J. Skinner, *Genesis* (International Critical Commentary; Edinburgh: T. & T. Clark, 1910).

60. Following the NJPS renderings of these difficult passages.

61. *Yesharim*, a pun on *Yeshurun* (Deut 32:15), a name for Israel (so the note in NJPS).

62. So also M. Weinfeld, *Genesis*, 123. A full study of the divine command to multiply and thus rule the whole world (as in Gen 1:28) is needed.

63. F. M. Cross, *Canaanite Myth and Hebrew Epic* (Cambridge: Harvard University Press, 1973); P. D. Miller, Jr., *The Divine Warrior in Early Israel* (Harvard Semitic Monographs 5; Cambridge: Harvard University Press, 1973).

64. The survival of much archaic material, both legendary and legal, in comparatively late documents is by now a well-established fact of the legal and literary history of the Bible and the Near East. Thus, for example, much archaic cuneiform legal terminology from Old Akkadian times reappears in the legal formulary of Arsacid–Seleucid times. The Old Babylonian quittance term *libbašu ṭāb*, "his heart is satisfied," although replaced by a variety of synonyms in following eras, suddenly reappears in fifth-century-B.C.E. Aramaic documents from Elephantine with all the peculiarities, grammatical, syntactical, and otherwise, of the Old Babylonian term. (A fact is a fact even though it eludes adequate historical explanation—see SALPE, 201.) The phenomenon is not an isolated one. The revival of early legal material in the documents of cuneiform legal culture may also be compared to the archaizing tendencies in both Egypt and Mesopotamia during the late Neo-Babylonian period. Many biblical scholars have sensed a similar archaizing tendency in the Deuteronomic reformation (cf. G. von Rad's *Der heilige Krieg im alten Israel* [3d ed.; Göttingen: Vandenhoeck und Ruprecht, 1958]). Did dying cultures desperately seek rejuvenation by unearthing archaic traditions and recycling them into their lifeblood? Did social upheavals reintroduce into the mainstream material preserved in isolated cultural islands? We can only surmise.

65. R. H. Charles, *The Apocrypha and Pseudepigrapha of the Old Testament in English* (2 vols.; Oxford: Clarendon, 1913) 2.64; for another translation, see H. C. Kee in *The Old*

Testament Pseudepigrapha. 1. Apocalyptic Literature and Testaments (ed. J. H. Charlesworth; Garden City, New York: Doubleday, 1983) 795–96. See also M. de Jonge, ed., *Studies on the Testaments of the Patriarch: Text and Interpretation* (Studia in Veteris Testamenti Pseudepigrapha 3; Leiden: Brill, 1978), and H. D. Slingerland, *The Testaments of the Twelve Patriarchs* (Society of Biblical Literature Dissertation Series 21; Chico: Scholars Press, 1977).

66. A. K. Grayson, *Assyrian Royal Inscriptions. 2. From Tiglath-pileser I to Ashur-nadin-apli II* (Wiesbaden: Harrassowitz, 1976) 175; there are many other examples.

67. See SALPE and Chapters 7 and 8 in this volume.

68. See L. Ginzberg, *The Legends of the Jews* (Philadelphia: Jewish Publication Society, 1909–38) 5.314–23.

69. Charles, *Apocrypha*, 2.64–65; cf. Kee in *The Old Testament Pseudepigrapha. 1. Apocalyptic Literature and Testaments*, 796.

70. See J. T. Townsend, "Minor Midrashim," *Bibliographical Essays in Medieval Jewish Studies 2* (ed. Y. H. Yerushalmi; New York: Anti-Defamation League of B'nai Brith/KTAV, 1976) 333–92 at 360.

71. See Ginzberg, *Legends*, 5.315, and J. Lauterbach's article "Midrash Va-yiseʿu or the Book of the Wars of the Children of Jacob," *Abhandlungen zur Errinerung Hirsch Perez Chajes* (ed. V. Aptowizer and A. Z. Schwarz; Veröffentlichungen der Alexander Kohut Memorial Foundation 7; Vienna, 1933) 205–22.

72. "Eldad Ha-Dani," *Encyclopaedia Judaica*, 6.576–78.

73. T. L. Thompson, *The Historicity of the Patriarchal Narratives* (Beiheft zur Zeitschrift für Alttestamentliche Wissenschaft 133; Berlin: de Gruyter, 1974) 73–83; see also John Van Seters, *Abraham in History and Tradition* (New Haven: Yale University Press, 1975).

74. Albright, *Yahweh and the Gods of Canaan*, 64–91.

75. Speiser, *Genesis*, 103.

76. See n. 22, above.

77. M. B. Rowton, "The Topological Factor in the Habiru Problem," *Studies in Honor of Benno Landsberger on his Seventy-Fifth Birthday* (ed. H. G. Güterbock and Th. Jacobsen; Assyriological Studies 16; Chicago: The Oriental Institute, The University of Chicago, 1965) 375–87.

78. For the tension between the human and divine elements in biblical historiography, see I. L. Seeligmann, "Menschliches Heldentum und göttliche Hilfe," *Theologische Zeitschrift* 19 (1963) 385–411.

CHAPTER 5

"THE MONEY CAME TO ME": TWO COMPARATIVE LEXICAL STUDIES*

Aramaic ʿl ʿl = *Hebrew* baʾ ʾel *"to receive"*

One of the salient characteristics of ancient Near Eastern legal language is the figurative, rather than abstract, manner by which many key legal concepts are expressed.[1] What looks like poetry is often a technical legal expression. Take but a few examples. In Akkadian, the metaphor of "purity" (*elēlu, ebēbu, zakû*, etc.) expresses the idea of "freedom from" (taxation, slavery, etc.); the metaphor of "satisfaction" (*šabû, libbašu ṭāb*) expresses the idea of "quittance upon the receipt of a consideration"; the metaphor of "removal" (*duppuru, eṭēru*; cf. Aramaic *rḥq*) expresses the "relinquishment of rights."[2] Unfortunately, the specific legal meaning of these ancient locutions has often escaped the attention of modern legal historians, who tend to dismiss them as part of the narrative structure of the deed.[3]

The ancients also had their problems. When Aramaic scribes attempted to transpose Akkadian legal terminology into Aramaic, they were faced with a set of problems known to all translators. First of all, there are few true synonyms. Synonymity—within a language or between two different languages—often involves the intersection of two widely different semantic fields that happen to overlap in one limited area. Furthermore, the linguistic resources of the two languages—the original and the one into which it is being translated—are not necessarily the same.[4] Some languages are richer and some are poorer. Furthermore, it is possible for a concept or a metaphor to function within a given language without the concept having adequate linguistic expression.[5] In

* This article first appeared in *The Journal of the Ancient Near Eastern Society* 5 (1973) 287–98.

such cases, concepts and root metaphors often get hidden and even buried.

A case in point is our subject. While Aramaic can make a clear distinction between "come" (*ʾtʾ*) and "enter" (*ʿll*), Biblical Hebrew *baʾ* does double duty: while it usually means "come," it often means "enter" (like the later Hebrew *nikhnas*).[6] The native speaker may feel the distinctions intuitively, but it is the translator who is really confronted with the problem. Take, for example, the Old Babylonian receipt clause, *apil/maḫir libbašu ṭāb*, "(the rightholder) is paid/has received (the money), his heart is satisfied." The Aramaic scribes had little difficulty with the last term, which they rendered as *ṭyb lbby*, "my heart is satisfied."[7] The other elements in this clause presented greater difficulties. In the Aramaic papyri from Elephantine, the receipt clause for a bride price (*mohar*) is *ʿl ʿly/k wṭyb lbby/k bgw*, "I/you have received the money and my/your heart is satisfied therewith."[8] While *ʿl ʿl* is the functional equivalent of the Akkadian *apil/maḫir*, "paid/received," in the stereotyped clause "term of receipt + term of satisfaction," it differs from the rather unmetaphoric Akkadian by employing, instead, the metaphor of "entrance" to express the idea of "receipt."[9] So far as I can tell, a comparable Akkadian expression **kaspu ana yâši īrub*, literally, "the money has entered my possession," has not been found.

Not only has the Elephantine usage not been found in earlier Akkadian documents, but it seems to have no reflex in later Aramaic documents. Thus, the Aramaic legal documents of Samaria being edited by F. M. Cross (late fourth century)[10] and the even later deeds of Murabbaʿat express the same idea by the unusual phrase *kspʾ ʾnh mqbl* "I am the receiver of the money."[11] Murabbaʿat occasionally has *qblt* or *ʾtqblt*.[12] All of these are more or less what one could call "normal" modes of expression.

On the surface, then, it would seem that the Elephantine phrase *ʿl ʿl* PN, literally "(the money) has entered (the possession of) PN," is a locution limited to that particular corpus of deeds. However, further investigation indicates that this mode of expressing the idea of "receipt" by the metaphor of "entrance" is not an isolated phenomenon. There is good reason to believe that a similar locution obtained in Biblical Hebrew as well. Unfortunately, this West Semitic mode of expressing the receipt of (full) payment is hidden somewhat by the inability of Biblical Hebrew to distinguish lexically between the ideas of "come" and "enter." Unlike Aramaic, with its contrast between *ʾtʾ*, "to come," and *ʿll*, "to enter," or later Hebrew, with its contrast between *baʾ*, "to come," and *nikhnas*, "to enter," Biblical Hebrew has only one term—*baʾ*—to express the contrasting concepts of "coming" and "entering."[13] However, in spite of this difficulty, most translators of the Hebrew Bible—old and new—did catch the nuance of receipt (of full payment, property, etc.) in two biblical texts in which the expression *baʾ ʾel* PN appears.

The first text is in Genesis 43. Part of the cat-and-mouse game Joseph played with his brothers was to restore to their bags the sale-price of the grain they had already paid out, a tactic that created the expected anxiety. If they were caught, they might be put to death as thieves. After much consternation, they returned to Egypt with two separate sums of money: the old sale-price and the new one. There they were met by one of Joseph's men and were promptly brought to his palace. Their reaction was quite natural: "It must be . . . because of the money replaced in our bags . . . that we have been brought inside, as a pretext to attack us and seize us as slaves" (v 18, NJPS). However, at the moment of their greatest apprehension, Joseph's agent assures them: "Be at ease, do not be afraid! It must have been your God, the God of your fathers, who put treasure in your sacks for you" (v 23). The capstone of the whole discussion is the statement *kaspekhem baʾ ʾelay*, which ends the verse.

At first glance, one might translate this statement literally as "Your money has come to me"—a translation which, although not incorrect, does not really convey the specific idea the writer meant to convey. What the agent is really saying is: "Legally, you have nothing to worry about. As far as I (that is, my master Joseph—so Gunkel) am concerned, the money for the first grain-sale has *already* been received in full and I have absolutely no claims against you.[14] As far as the extra money found in your bags, it is simply a gift of God."

Clearly *kaspekhem baʾ ʾelay* is the biblical equivalent of the Aramaic *ʿl ʿly*, "I have received your money"; like the Aramaic term, it may carry the quittance overtones of the Aramaic complement *wṭyb lbby bgw*, "and my heart is satisfied therewith." While most modern translations,[15] commentaries,[16] and lexica[17] realize that in this context *kaspekhem baʾ ʾelay* must mean something like "I have received the money in full," translations such as "I had/have your money" hardly make much sense.[18] Even those translators who correctly render the clause with "I received your money" or the like indicate by their lack of comment that they are unaware of the exact legal nuance of the term and its dramatic significance in the story.[19] The various Aramaic targums[20]—with the possible exception of the Peshitta and the Samaritan Targum[21]—are not very illuminating on this point, and neither are the midrashim and medieval Jewish commentators, Saadya being a notable exception.[22]

On the other hand, the Septuagint's *to argurion humōn eudokimoun apechō*, whether rendered as "I *have enough* of your good money" or "I *have received* your good money," in keeping with the usage of the verb *apechō* in contemporary Greek deeds of receipt from Egypt, expresses the terminological nuance of the phrase quite clearly.[23] Furthermore, the close relationship between the ideas of receipt, satisfaction, and quittance that is so common in Aramaic and cuneiform legal documents was seen with great insight by the translator of Bagster's English version of the Septuagint, who glossed the verse under discussion in the following manner: "I am satisfied with the money you have given me, both as to quality and quantity."[24] Among moderns, only Ehrlich and BDB spelled out the legal nuances and implications of the term with adequate precision.[25]

To sum up: Joseph's steward is simply consoling the brothers in the legal language of contemporary West Semitic traders by insisting that no claims were outstanding against them and that since the sale price had been received in full, they were in no trouble. Unless the specific terminological nature of the expression is recognized, the passage loses much of its vividness and meaning.

The second passage where *baʾ ʾel* is a technical term of receipt and the exact equivalent of Aramaic *ʿl ʿl* is Num 32:19. The tribes of Reuben and Gad, and half of the tribe of Manasseh come before Moses and outrage him with their request to settle in the territory they had already conquered in Transjordan—an area evidently not included in the original divine landgrant to the Children of Israel.[26] The altercation is successfully resolved (a) when Moses grants them permission to settle in Transjordan in return for their solemn promise that "we will hasten as shock-troops in the van of the Israelites until we have established them in their home" (v 17, NJPS); and (b) when they promise that "we will not have a share with them in the territory beyond the Jordan, *ki baʾah naḥalatenu ʾelenu meʿever ha-yarden mizraḥah*" (v 19). The rather weak rendering of the American Translation, "because our heritage has *fallen to us* on the other side of the Jordan,"[27] although not incorrect, does not convey the specific juridical connotations of the expression *ki naḥalatenu baʾah ʾelenu*, namely, that since they have already *received* their legitimate share in Transjordan and are satisfied therewith, they formally renounce any claim on territory they might conquer on the other side of the Jordan, while fighting in concert with the other tribes. Once again, the realization of the formal receipt-quittance nature of this term is crucial for the proper understanding of the whole transaction. Contrast the more correct rendering of the NJPS: "having received our share on the east side of the Jordan." Among the medievals it was Saadya who captured the legal nuance most correctly[28]; the same can be said for the Septuagint[29] and most of the Aramaic translations.[30]

Certainly none of the ancients, nor any of the moderns who worked after the discovery of the papyri, associated the expression with its unmistakable terminological reflex *ʿl ʿl* in the Aramaic legal documents of Elephantine.

From the point of view of biblical studies, the Elephantine evidence clearly vindicates the translators who rendered the idiom as an expression of receipt and translated, "we received," according to sense, rather than by "it fell to us," according to form. It also establishes the expression *baʾ ʾel* as one more of a growing list of legal terms used *en passant* in Pentateuchal narratives.[31]

From the vantage point of the comparative legal historian, this expression, together with its clear Aramaic counterpart, adds to the small, but ever-expanding body of evidence that the Aramaic legal formulary of Elephantine and its West Semitic analogues did not always slavishly translate from the Akkadian, but that at least in certain cases, local West Semitic usage[32]—here the metaphor of "entry" as an expression of "receipt"—did exercise its influence on the basically Akkadian structure of the Elephantine formulary.

Finally, a few words concerning the implications of the biblical material for the dating of the Aramaic idiom. It is obvious that the Elephantine formulary of the fifth century B.C.E. did not spring into existence overnight.[33] Yaron was certainly correct in pointing out its affinities with the legal traditions of second-millennium Syria (Ras Shamra, Alalakh, etc.).[34] In searching for the *proximate* models of the formulary, I pointed out in SALPE the strong Neo-Assyrian element in it. Kutscher made the important observation that the syntactical orientation of the legal documents was essentially West Semitic.[35] In his review of recent studies in Old Aramaic, Kutscher agreed with my tentative attempt to make historical sense out of these various legal and philological observations.[36] In SALPE, I suggested that "the indigenous legal traditions of second-millennium Syria-Palestine . . . were taken over by the first-millennium Aramean dynasties of the West."[37] These kingdoms with their expanding mercantile and administrative activities could not have functioned without some sort of formulary written in the Old Aramaic of the West, which was subsequently heavily Assyrianized when the Assyrians moved into Syria. This Aramaic formulary was later introduced into

Egypt, even before the conquest of Sargon, by Assyria's strong mercantile interest in that country.

I would now suggest—with all due reservation—that it was not only the Old Aramean states which took over the legal traditions of second-millennium Syria, but the Davidic-Solomonic empire with its wide-ranging trade activities as well.[38] The same holds true for the Israelite kingdom, which, as we know from the Book of Kings, had strong economic ties with the Arameans of the north: reciprocal trade facilities were often an integral part of the various peace settlements between the two countries.[39] It therefore seems reasonable to assume that there existed Judean and Israelite counterparts to the Old Aramaic formulary we have theoretically posited. Since actual evidence concerning the existence of an Old Aramaic formulary is quite sparse, and that concerning the hypothetical Old Hebrew one virtually nonexistent, any bit of new information is of more than peripheral importance.

In our philological investigations concerning the western nature of the receipt expression, *ʿl ʿly*, and its equivalence with the Hebrew *baʾ ʾelay*, it was the Aramaic that helped to illuminate the specific legal background of the Hebrew term. Now, let us reverse the process. According to classical source-critical theory, Gen 43:23 belongs to the J or JE stratum, which all authorities date sometime during the early centuries of the monarchy.[40] Historically, this would mean that the Hebrew terminological equivalent of the Aramaic *ʿl ʿly* was operative in the literary and, I would assume, in the legal parlance of the Solomonic court as well—many centuries before the occurrence of the term in fifth-century Elephantine. It is not inconceivable to suggest—with due care—that Solomon's trade receipts may quite possibly have used the term *baʾ ʾelay*. Nor would it be unreasonable to assume that Ben-Hadad of Aram in dealing with Israelite merchants may have used the Aramaic *ʿl ʿly*.

Now, the passage in Numbers is usually attributed to P, whose date is the subject of lively scholarly debate.[41] If it is from the time of the First Temple, we have found another piece of evidence for the antiquity of the term. If, however, P is actually post-exilic, then it is roughly contemporary with the Elephantine papyri, a fact that would hardly surprise any modern scholar. However, it was probably not later than the Samaria papyri, since these documents regularly use the formula *kspʾ ʾnh mqbl*, "I am the receiver of the money."[42] The term, however, may have survived sporadically in the Aramaic of the Peshitta and the Samaritan Targum, either as a reflex of contemporary legal language—which I doubt—or as an archaism, which is more probable.[43] In any case, our philological discussion is not without historical implications, however theoretical.

Hebrew ʿoz *= Akkadian* ezzu, *"anger"*

In SALPE I had occasion to discuss a pair of Akkadian idioms, *ḫadiš naplusu*, "to look at (someone) joyfully/to be well disposed toward," and its antonym, *ezziš nekelmû*, "to look at (someone) with anger/punitive wrath."[44] In spite of their seemingly poetic or figurative nature, these two expressions are used in royal donations and in *kudurru* documents with specific legal meanings. The first idiom—*ḫadiš naplusu*—is often accompanied by a series of complements, *ina būnīšu namrūti zīmēšu ruššûti damqāti īnāšu* "(the donor looked at the donee) with his bright gaze, shining countenance and sparkling eyes."[45] The legal import of this rather baroque cluster is quite simple: it indicates the kind and generous intentions of a donor, usually a deity or a king. The joyful look of the deity expresses the eternal and unalterable intention with which he bestows kingship upon his elect. Similarly, the joyful look of the king expresses the firm and unalterable intention with which he bestows some grant or perquisite upon a courtier or priest.[46]

The antonym of the idiom is *ezziš nekelmû*, "to look at (someone) with anger/wrath." In the *kudurru* documents, it expresses the punitive wrath the deity metes out to whoever would dare undo a grant given with the "joyful look" of the divine or royal donor.[47]

The metaphorical use of Akkadian terms of joy (*ḫadû, ṭābu*) as expressions of uncoerced willingness and the parallel use of certain Hebrew terms of joy, especially in early rabbinic sources, is the subject of Chapters 7–8 in this volume. Some of the functional equivalents and literary echoes of the clause *ḫadiš naplusu* in the Aramaic papyri from Elephantine[48] and in royal and divine grants in the Bible have already been discussed by the author and by M. Weinfeld.[49]

If both the word *ḫadiš* and the clause *ḫadiš naplusu* have clear reflexes in later Aramaic and Hebrew sources, it is possible to ask whether the antonyms of these clauses—*ezziš* and *ezziš nekelmû*—may also be reflected in similar Hebrew sources. In general, it is not wise to start off with a particular Akkadian term in mind and attempt to force difficult Hebrew expressions into artificial Akkadian matrices. Similar attempts to interpret Hebrew cruxes in the light of Arabic[50] or Ugaritic[51] lexica have contributed to the bad name comparative Semitic lexicography has incurred—often deservedly—in some very respectable circles.[52] Only after new meanings emerge naturally from the context of one language should comparative material be brought into the picture.

A good case in point is Ginsberg's discovery that the word *ʿoz* in Qoh 8:1 can only mean one thing in its context—namely, "anger."[53] Let us follow his arguments. The second half of the verse reads *ḥokhmat ʾadam taʾir pana(y)v ve-ʿoz pana(y)v yeshunneʾ*. The verse is usually translated something like "A man's wisdom illumines his face and his hard face is changed."[54] Working within the immediate context of Qoheleth and the closely related Ben Sirah, Ginsberg makes the following observations. (1) The idea the author is trying to convey does not come through the text as presently preserved, since wisdom does not make the face shine: it is joy that does that. However, even if we accept the reading in stich a, poetic structure would seem to demand that the shining face of stich a be paralleled by a dark and gloomy face in stich b. (2) Furthermore, in the closely related Ben Sirah literature, we often find that a happy face is an expression of inner joy, while a sad or dark face is the expression of inner grief and anger.[55] This parallelism may provide the key for the proper understanding of the passage in Qoheleth. (3) Jerome read *pana(y)v yeshanneʾ*—instead of *yeshunneʾ*—which is a perfectly good Hebrew idiom for "make the face sad/dark,"[56] an idiom which nicely parallels *taʾir pana(y)v*, "makes his face shine/glad" in stich a. (4) Taking a hint from Ben Sira that it is sadness or anger that makes the face gloomy, the natural conclusion is that the subject of the sentence *pana(y)v yeshanneʾ* is *ʿoz*, which in that case can mean nothing other than "anger." The verse, therefore, should be translated: "and anger is what makes a man's face gloomy." For further confirmation of this new meaning of *ʿoz*, Ginsberg cites Ezra 8:22: *ve-ʿuzzo ve-ʾappo ʿal kol-ʿozeva(y)v*, which should be rendered "and his anger and wrath are upon all who leave Him."

It is at this point, after the new meaning has been worked out inner-biblically, that it is appropriate to remark that this rare meaning of the Hebrew *ʿoz* is clearly related to the common Akkadian *ezzu*, "anger, wrath."[57] Whether or not there is any historical significance to the fact that the two examples of *ʿoz*, "anger" come from books written in post-exilic Hebrew, a dialect strongly influenced by Aramaic (and ultimately by Akkadian), cannot be answered at this point.[58]

So far we have demonstrated that Ginsberg's inner-biblical investigations concerning the meaning of *ʿoz*, "anger," are nicely supported by parallel Akkadian usage. One may well ask if parallels to this usage may be adduced from later Hebrew sources.

In the Jerusalem Talmud, *Yoma* 6:1, 43b, in a discussion concerning the proper behavior of a judge vis-à-vis the parties before him, we read the following statement:

> (Equal treatment means) that one party shall not stand while the other sits; that one has to be silent while the other can speak; that one can speak all he needs to, while the other party is told by the judge, "Make your statement short!", that the judge should not look graciously/favorably (*masbir panim*) at one of the parties, while he is *meʿez pana(y)v* at the other.

Clearly, the two idioms *masbir panim* and *meʿez panim* are antonyms. The first is a well-known idiom meaning "to look at/receive (someone) with a smiling/gracious disposition." In function it is quite similar to the Akkadian *ḫadiš naplusu ina būnīšu namrūtim.* The other idiom, *meʿez panim*, is at least as common. However, in all other contexts, it means "to be fresh or insolent toward"—usually said of a rebellious child or of an underling to a superior. In this context, however, the usual meaning of "insolence" does not fit. As the antonym of *masbir panim*, "to look at with a smiling disposition," *meʿez panim* can only mean "to look at with an angry disposition." In fact, *masbir panim* is to the Akkadian *ḫadiš naplusu* as the Hebrew *meʿez panim* is to the Akkadian *ezziš nekelmû*. Thus, we are comparing not isolated words where comparisons are often fortuitous, but complexes of syntax and idiom—something that lends greater credence to the comparison. Furthermore, while it is perfectly reasonable to reject comparisons of words and phrases that share a common etymon (in this case the stem *ʿzz*) but differ radically in meaning and function, the presence of the shared etymon in functionally identical expressions provides added confirmation of their semantic affinity.

Lexically, this passage with its clear juxtaposition of *masbir panim* and *meʿez panim* certainly establishes "anger" as a legitimate meaning of the Hebrew *ʿoz*, even for those who may not fully accept Ginsberg's interpretation of the verse in Qoheleth. However, the fact that *ʿoz* is found in late Hebrew and its cognate and functional equivalent *ezzu* in pre-Qoheleth Akkadian certainly adds credence to Ginsberg's intuitive reconstruction of the verse under investigation. It is clear that he did not attribute a meaning to *ʿoz* that it did not have at that period.

NOTES

1. SALPE, 27 n. 3; see also SALPE, index s. v. "Metaphors, legal."
2. Consult the glosssaries of SALPE.

3. Cf. SALPE, 27 n. 3, for an example.

4. A. Bendavid, *Biblical Hebrew and Mishnaic Hebrew* (2 vols.; Tel-Aviv: Dvir, 1967–71; in Hebrew).

5. We are all acquainted with the story of the French bourgeois who was pleasantly surprised to discover that he had been speaking in "prose" all his life without knowing it. Or take a West Semitic example: according to S. Lieberman (*Hellenism in Jewish Palestine* [New York: The Jewish Theological Seminary of America, 1950] 83 n. 3), the Hebrew term *halaka*, "law," was borrowed from Aramaic (and ultimately from Akkadian), where it was used with the meaning "fixed tax." If so, the concept "law" was probably operative before the word for it was borrowed by the rabbis. Furthermore, Lieberman claims that many basic exegetical methods of the rabbis were not borrowed from the Greeks, as is usually alleged; rather these were ancient and universal laws of logic; what was borrowed were names for these methods. Even those who might reject his interpretation of the exegetical norm *gezera shava* (inference from analogy) must admit that the exegetical method *qal va-ḥomer* (inference *a fortiori*) was widely employed in the Bible in the form *hinneh . . . af ki*, "behold . . . even"; cf. S. Lieberman, *Hellenism*, 61, and, for the biblical usage, H. L. Ginsberg, "Notes on the Minor Prophets," *Eretz Israel* 3 (M. D. U. Cassuto Volume, 1954) 83–84 (in Hebrew). For another relevant example, see SALPE, 40 n. 1.

6. Bendavid, *Biblical Hebrew*, 1:118.

7. See SALPE in the glossaries under the individual terms, *apālu*, *maḫāru*, *ṭyb*.

8. See SALPE, 51–62. The texts are AP, no. 15, and BP, no. 15.

9. For the uneven historical process by which Mesopotamian terms of receipt shift from metaphorical to unmetaphorical and back to metaphorical modes of expression, cf. SALPE, 108–15.

10. My deepest thanks go to Professor Cross, the editor of the deeds, for giving me the opportunity to examine them and cite material from them. For preliminary discussions of these texts, cf. F. M. Cross, "The Discovery of the Samaria Papyri," *Biblical Archaeologist* 26 (1963) 110–21; Cross, "Papyri of the Fourth Century B.C. from Dâliyeh," *New Directions in Biblical Archaeology* (ed. D. N. Freedman and J. C. Greenfield; Garden City, New York: Doubleday, 1969) 41-62.

11. Cf. P. Benoît, J. T. Milik, and R. de Vaux, *Les grottes de Murabbaʿât* (Discoveries in the Judaean Desert 2; Oxford, Clarendon, 1961) 135, no. 25, recto line 5. Cf. also Milik, "Deux documents inédits du désert de Juda," *Biblica* 38 (1957) 245–68 at 259, line 8. The participial forms are to be compared with similar Neo-Babylonian uses of forms such as *mittaḫḫuru*, "receiver," instead of the older *maḫir*, "he has received"; cf., e. g., L. W. King, *Babylonian Boundary-Stones and Memorial-Tablets in the British Museum* (London: British Museum, 1912) 40, no. 7, col. 1, line 30.

12. Cf. the Aramaic signature in the Greek documents from the Dead Sea area edited by H. J. Polotsky, "Three Greek Documents from the Family Archive of Babtha," *Eretz Israel* 8 (1967) 46–51 at 50, line 11; cf. Polotsky, "The Greek Documents from the 'Cave of the Letters,'" *Yediʿot Beḥaqirat Eretz-Yisrael ve-ʿAtiqoteha* 26 (1962) 237–41.

13. Cf. n. 6, above.

14. On Joseph and his agent, see H. Gunkel, *Genesis* (4th ed.; Handkommentar zum Alten Testament; Göttingen: Vandenhoeck und Ruprecht, 1917) ad loc. For the close association of the concepts of "receipt" with those of "quittance" and "no contest," cf. SALPE, 43–50.

15. Without being exhaustive, we may note the following: "I got your payment" (NJPS); "I received your money" (*The Bible. An American Translation* [Chicago, University of Chicago Press, 1935]); "I did receive the silver" (New English Bible). Much less clear is the Jerusalem Bible's version: "your money has reached me safely"; "safely" seems to be a (mis)translation of the Vulgate's *probatam* (*nam pecuniam quam dedistis mihi probatam ego habeo*), where *probatam* seems to be based on the Septuagint's usage *eudokimoun* (*to argurion humōn eudokimoun apechō*); but here *eudokimeō*, "to be approved/ recognized/ genuine" (so H. G. Liddell and R. Scott, *A Greek-English Lexicon* [Oxford: Clarendon, 1968]), refers to the quality of the money received, not to the conditions of receipt.

16. E. g., E. A. Speiser has "I got your payment" (*Genesis* [Anchor Bible 1; Garden City, New York: Doubleday, 1964]); the English version of G. von Rad's commentary gives "I received your money" (*Genesis* [Old Testament Library; Philadelphia: Westminster, 1972]); from an earlier generation, S. D. Luzzatto gives "vostro denaro è stato da me ricevuto" (*Il Pentateuco volgarizzato e commentato* [Padua: Sachetto, 1874; rpt. Tel Aviv: Dvir, 1965; in Hebrew and Italian]); Gunkel's "euer Gelt ist mir zugekommen" (*Genesis*, 405) is less satisfactory. A. B. Ehrlich saw the correct interpretation in his Hebrew commentary on Genesis, in *Mikra ki-Pheschuto* (3 vols.; Berlin: Poppelauer, 1899–1901; rpt., New York: KTAV, 1969; in Hebrew), but for some reason he omitted it from his great German work (*Randglossen zur hebräischen Bibel: Textkritisches, sprachliches, und sachliches* [Leipzig: Hinrichs, 1908–14; rpt., Hildesheim: Olms, 1968]). Cf. also J. Skinner's "Your money came to me" (*Genesis* [International Critical Commentary; Edinburgh: T. & T. Clark, 1910]) and S. R. Driver's "I had your money" (*The Book of Genesis* [Westminster Commentaries; London: Methuen, 1904])—the last a slavish reproduction of older English translations that contrasts with the idiomatic translation in BDB.

17. With typical clarity, BDB s. v. *bwʾ* 2, defines the idiom in Genesis as "*your money came unto me* = I received your money." Strangely enough, this clear treatment in a lexicon printed for the first time in 1907 has escaped the authors of more recent lexica.

18. The Authorized Version has "I had your money"; *The Interpreter's Bible* (Nashville: Abingdon, 1952) has "I have your money."

19. Gunkel, Luzzato, Speiser, and many others.

20. Onqelos has *kspkm ʾtʾ lwty*; Pseudo-Jonathan, *kspkm ʾtʾ lwty*.

21. The Peshitta has *kspkwn ʿl lwty*; the Samaritan Targum, *kspkwn ʿl lydy*.

22. No comment in Rashi, the Rashbam, the Radaq, the Ramban, Ibn Ezra, Ibn Janah, etc. On the other hand, Saadya seems to have caught the nuance: *ammā fiḍḍatukum ṣārat ilayya*, "As far as your silver is concerned, it has already come to me/ become my possession." He could have used the literal *jāʾa ilā*, "came to," following the Targum's *ʾtʾ lwty*. The idiom *ṣāra ilā*, on the other hand, indicates a change of status, a "becoming" (something new) rather than simple "coming." In this use of *ṣāra*, Saadya is simply following contemporary Arabic usage. Cf. J. A. Wakin, *The Function of Documents in Islamic Law: The Chapters on Sales from Ṭaḥāwi's Kitāb al-Shurūṭ al-Kabīr* (Albany: University of New York Press, 1972), 54 n. 4, where she glosses *ṣāra fī yadihī* as "the property itself 'moves' as it were into his [the buyer's] hand by virtue of the purchase." The usage is common in the texts in A. Grohmann, *Arabic Papyri in the Egyptian Library*, vol. 1 (Cairo: The Egyptian Library Press, 1934), e. g., text 54, line 7, *wa-ṣārat mālan min mālihī*, "and it [the house and fields] has become property of his property." (For Saadya's use of *qad* with the meaning "hereby," cf. W. Wright, *A*

Grammar of the Arabic Language [Cambridge: Cambridge University Press, 1896-98] 2:3–4.)

23. According to Liddell–Scott, *A Greek-English Lexicon*, the verb *echō* in the present tense can mean "to have received"; *apechō* has the meaning "to receive in full," as well as an impersonal meaning, "it sufficeth, it is enough." A first-person form can hardly be impersonal, therefore the translation "I have received" seems more fitting; though the verb is present in form, it is present-perfect in meaning. For the use of *apechō* in legal documents, see A. S. Hunt and C. C. Edgar, *Select Papyri with an English Translation. 2. Official Documents* (Loeb Classical Library; London: William Heinemann, 1934), no. 370:9 ("Receipt concerning a consignment of alum"), no. 372:4 ("Receipt for money paid for the transport of government corn"). Note also Matt 6:2, *apechousin ton misthon autōn*, "They have already been paid *in full*."

24. *The Septuagint Version of the Old Testament with an English Translation* (New York: Samuel Bagster and Sons, no date); the names of translator(s) and annotator(s) are not given in most printings; L. C. L. Brenton did the work in 1851.

25. Cf. Ehrlich, *Mikra*, 119; note also the discussion of H. Orlinsky in the prolegomenon to the KTAV reprint, p. xxvi.

26. Following Y. Kaufmann, *The Religion of Israel: From Its Beginnings to the Babylonian Exile* (Chicago: University of Chicago Press, 1960) 202, 210, 258, 445.

27. Cf. "because our patrimony has already been allotted to us" (New English Bible); less clear is "Since our inheritance has fallen to us" (Jerusalem Bible), substantially the same as the Authorized Version.

28. *Idh qabaḍnā niḥlatanā*, "since we have received our inheritance." For the use of *qabaḍa* as a technical term for "receiving/taking possession of property," cf. Grohmann, *Arabic Papyri*, vol. 1, passim, e. g., text 162, line 12.

29. *Hoti apechomen tous klērous hemōn*, "since we have received our inheritance." Cf. discussion above, n. 23.

30. *The Samaritan Targum* (ed. A. Tal; Tel-Aviv: Tel Aviv University Press, 1981) 289, preserves the old metaphor of "entering": *hlʾ ʿlt plgtnn lydnn*. Most of the other translations render the idiom correctly according to context as "receive": Onqelos, *ʾry qblnʾ ʾḥsntʾnʾ lnʾ*; Neofiti, *ʾrwm qbln ʾḥsntn lwwtn*; Peshitta, *mṭwl dqbln yrtwtn*. Pseudo-Jonathan employs the metaphor of "arriving" (*mṭʾ*) to express the transfer of ownership: *ʾrwm mṭt ʾḥsntnʾ lnʾ*. Such a usage is found in Elephantine inheritance documents, e. g., *znh ḥlqʾ zy mṭʾk bḥlq*, "This is the share that comes to you as a share" (AP, no. 1:4, 28:3; cf. 28:7, 9, 10, 12).

31. Cf. SALPE, index s. v. "Biblical law." Cf., with reservation, D. Daube, "Law in the Narratives," *Studies in Biblical Law* (Cambridge: Cambridge University Press, 1947; rpt. New York: KTAV, 1969) 1–73, and the many valuable observations on this subject in Speiser's commentary on Genesis.

32. SALPE, 187 n. 4.

33. SALPE, 14–16.

34. R. Yaron, *The Law of the Aramaic Papyri* (Oxford: Clarendon, 1961) 115; cf. SALPE, 180.

35. E. Y. Kutscher, "Is Biblical Aramaic Eastern or Western Aramaic?", *Leshonenu* 17 (1951) 119–22 (in Hebrew).

36. E. Y. Kutscher, "Aramaic," *Current Trends in Linguistics. 6. Linguistics in South West Asia and North Africa* (ed. T. A. Sebeok et al.; The Hague: Mouton, 1971) 347–412

at 353–64; rpt. in Kutscher, *Hebrew and Aramaic Studies* (ed. Z. Ben Ḥayyim et al.; Jerusalem: Magnes Press, 1977) 90–115.

37. SALPE, 196.

38. Cf. 1 Kgs 5:15–26 (trade relations between Solomon and Hiram); 1 Kgs 9:26–28 (the combined expedition to Ophir from Elath); 1 Kgs 10:1–13 (possible trade relations with Sheba); 1 Kgs 10:28–29 (trade in horses and chariots).

39. 1 Kgs 20:34: "So Ben-Hadad said to him [Ahab]: 'The cities that my father took from your father I will restore, and you may maintain bazaars (*ḥuṣot*) of your own in Damascus as my father did in Samaria.'" The whole matter was significant enough for it to have been solemnified by a treaty: "'And I,' said Ahab, 'will let you go with this understanding.' So he made a covenant with him and let him go." There are two issues in this event that deserve further examination: (a) the role of trade concessions in war; (b) the details of these concessions.

As far as the first matter is concerned, it is quite clear that wars were fought not simply for booty, but also to forcibly open up new markets in the conquered country. This is exactly what Ben-Hadad's father did when he conquered Israel a generation before. At a slightly later date, after his conquest of Rafia, Sargon has the following to say about his achievement: "I opened the sealed [harbo]ur of Egypt. The Assyrians and the Egyptians I mingled together and made them trade [with each other]" (Nimrud Prism, Fragment D, Col. IV); cf. the important study of H. Tadmor, "The Campaigns of Sargon II of Assur," *Journal of Cuneiform Studies* 12 (1958) 22–40, 77–100 at 34. Shades of Admiral Perry!

As far as the second matter is concerned, we know from the Akkadian international documents from Ras Shamra that the legal status of trading posts like those described in 1 Kgs 20:34 was carefully defined by treaty; e. g., in a letter from Hattusilis III of Hatti to Niqmepa of Ugarit, the Hittite king makes a binding agreement (*rikilta*) between the citizens of the town of Ura and those of Ugarit concerning the rights and limitations of the merchants of Ura in their dealings with the citizens of Ugarit (RS 17.130, published by J. Nougayrol, *Le Palais royal d'Ugarit IV* [Mission de Ras Shamra 9; Paris: Imprimerie Nationale, 1956] 103–4). It is first of all stipulated that the merchants of Ura may exercise their trading privileges only during the harvest season (line 11) and must leave during the winter (lines 14–15); the merchants of Ura are also forbidden to acquire land in Ugarit (line 19). It is also agreed that the citizens of each city will indemnify the merchant guild of the other for the slaying of a merchant of the other city in its territory in the event that the murderer is not apprehended. (For a discussion of this last set of provisions, see J. J. Finkelstein, "The Goring Ox," *Temple Law Quarterly* 46 [1973] 169–290 at 278–80.) One cannot say for sure that the agreements between Ben-Hadad and Ahab were identical with those operative between the merchants of Ura and the citizens of Ugarit; however, the documents of Ras Shamra clearly demonstrate the antiquity of the connection between war and the laws of trade.

40. Cf. S. R. Driver, *Genesis*, xvi. The same verdict is offered by virtually all modern source critics, even those who assume that older oral traditions may have been incorporated when the source was put down in writing. Speiser and others consider the author of J to have been a contemporary of the writer of the David and Samuel cycles. E is usually considered somewhat later than J, having been put down in writing in the early part of the eighth century (so Driver). For an investigation of the problem

and a survey of scholarly views, see M. Weinfeld, "Pentateuch," *Encyclopedia Judaica*, 13:231–64, especially p. 243.

41. Cf. Weinfeld, "Pentateuch," especially 243: "It seems that this source is a product of a priestly scholastic circle that was active for hundreds of years. The final crystallization of the work, however, seems to have taken place sometime in the seventh century B.C.E." M. Noth, *The Laws in the Pentateuch and Other Studies* (Philadelphia: Fortress, 1967) 8, dates the "Holiness Code" (Leviticus 17–26) to about the same time as Deuteronomy. Even though many modern scholars will grant the presence of older traditions in P (e. g., Speiser, in his paper "Leviticus and the Critics," *Yehezkel Kaufmann Jubilee Volume: Studies in Bible and Jewish Religion* [ed. M. Haran; Jerusalem: Magnes, 1960] 29–45, and in his introduction to his Genesis commentary), few would concur with Y. Kaufmann (*The Religion of Israel*, 175–208) that all of P is pre-exilic. Cf. the discussion of Otto Eissfeldt, *The Old Testament: An Introduction* (New York: Harper and Row, 1965) 204–8; note especially his observation: "We must assume that P came into being not too long before Chronicles, in the fifth, or perhaps already in the sixth century" (208).

42. Cf. n. 10, above.

43. Cf. nn. 21 and 30.

44. Cf. SALPE, 128–35, especially 132 n. 1.

45. SALPE, 130, 202.

46. SALPE, 135.

47. SALPE, 132 n. 1.

48. SALPE, 130–35.

49. M. Weinfeld, "The Covenant of Grant in the Old Testament and in the Ancient Near East," *JAOS* 90 (1970) 187–88; Weinfeld, "'Bond and Grace'—Covenantal Expressions in the Bible and the Ancient World—A Common Heritage," *Leshonenu* 36 (1971/72) 85–105 at 96–97, 100-1 (in Hebrew).

50. L. Kopf, "Arabische Etymologien und Parallelen zum Bibelwörterbuch," *Vetus Testamentum* 8 (1958) 161–215, 9 (1959) 247–87; rpt. in Kopf, *Studies in Arabic and Hebrew Lexicography* (ed. M. H. Goshen-Gottstein with S. Assif; Jerusalem: Magnes, 1976) 133–228. The critique of J. Barr, in *Comparative Philology and the Text of the Old Testament* (Oxford: Clarendon, 1968; rpt. Winona Lake, Indiana: Eisenbrauns, 1987, with additions), is often quite correct; however, I have a feeling that he sometimes throws out the baby with the wash.

51. Cf. J. C. Greenfield's review of M. Dahood's *Ugaritic-Hebrew Philology* (1965) in *JAOS* 89 (1969) 174–78, and the further critical reviews by M. Pope and A. Rainey mentioned there.

52. This misuse of the comparative method has certainly contributed to the radical purism often encountered in Assyriological circles, where anything having to do with the Bible—or even certain groups of Akkadian texts (e.g., Nuzi, Alalakh, Ras Shamra)—is apriori considered suspect. Unfortunately, a similar attitude—prompted by different considerations—is reflected in the rather indifferent attitude towards the study of Akkadian in certain biblical circles. Cf. F. M. Cross's telling remarks in "W. F. Albright's View of Biblical Archaeology and its Methodology," *Biblical Archaeologist* 36 (1973) 2–5; rpt. in E. F. Campbell and D. N. Freedman, eds., *The Biblical Archaeologist Reader IV* (Sheffield: The Almond Press, 1983) 1-4.

53. Cf. H. L. Ginsberg, *Koheleth* (Tel-Aviv/Jerusalem, 1961; in Hebrew) 104–5.

54. So, for example, *The Bible: An American Translation*. In the NPJS translation, prepared by Ginsberg, the verse is rendered, in accordance with the Masoretic text, "A man's wisdom lights up his face,/ So that his deep discontent is dissembled." Ginsberg's own reconstruction of the first part of the saying is, "A man's joy (read *ḥedvat*) lights up his face"; a discussion of the saying may be found in Ginsberg, *Koheleth*, 104–5.

55. Ginsberg cites Ben Sirah 13:25–26 (slightly emended). Similar ideas are expressed in several other passages, 25:17, 23 and 26:3–4.

56. Citing Job 14:20 and Lam 4:1. Cf. also Dan 5:10, 7:28.

57. Cf. *ezzu* in CAD and *AHw*.

58. Even those who do not accept Ginsberg's thesis that Qoheleth was translated from an Aramaic original agree that the Hebrew of the book shows Aramaic coloring. Translation or not, the Hebrew of the book often contains usages that are identical with, or anticipate, the language of later rabbinic sources, as Ginsberg continually notes; cf., e. g., his discussion of the use of *lavan*, "clean," *Koheleth*, 115 and *shafal*, "slow, lazy," p. 124. On the differences between early Hebrew (of the First Commonwealth) and middle Hebrew, in addition to Bendavid's *Biblical Hebrew and Mishnaic Hebrew*, cited earlier, see E. Y. Kutscher, "Mittelhebräisch und Jüdisch-Aramäisch im neuen Köhler-Baumgartner," *Hebräische Wortforschung: Festschrift zum 80. Geburtstag von Walter Baumgartner* (Supplements to Vetus Testamentum 16; Leiden: Brill, 1967), 158–75; rpt. in his *Hebrew and Aramaic Studies*, 156–73, and A. Hurvitz, *The Transition Period in Biblical Hebrew* (Jerusalem: Mosad Bialik, 1972; in Hebrew). On the interpenetration of Aramaic and Akkadian, see S. A. Kaufman, *The Akkadian Influences on Aramaic* (Assyriological Studies 19; Chicago: The Oriental Institute, 1974); cf. also SALPE, 187 n. 4.

CHAPTER 6

THE PERMITTED AND THE PROHIBITED IN EARLY RABBINIC LITERATURE: THE ROOT *DRK*, "TO BE EMPOWERED"

The equivalence of the term *drkt*, "power," with *mlk*, "kingship, authority," has been a well-established fact of Ugaritic studies from their very inception.[1] While biblical scholars have attempted to apply this new lexical meaning of *drk* to a wide range of biblical texts with varying degrees of success, Saul Lieberman has reclaimed the root *drk*, "to have/delegate power," for the lexicon of Middle Hebrew on the basis of context alone.[2]

In his study of the Ben Sirah fragments from Masada, Lieberman notes that the usual meanings of the term *drk* in Ben Sirah do not suit the context in 42:1e[3]: *ʾl tśʾ pnym wḥṭʾ . . . ʿl ḥšbwn šwtp wdrk wʿl mḥlqt nḥlh wyš*, "Do not exhibit partiality and sin . . . in dealing with a partner and a *drk* and in the division of inheritance and property." Lieberman further notes that the Cairo Geniza B-text and the text from Masada shed significant light on each other. Thus, for Masada's *ʿl ḥšbwn šwtp wdrk*, "in the matter of a partner and a *drk*," the B-text reads *ʿl ḥšbwn ḥwbr wʾdwn*, "in the matter of a partner and a master."[4]

The B-text's *ḥover*, parallel to Masada's *shutaf*, "partner," a loan word from Akkadian, is well attested in early rabbinic literature with the meaning "partner."[5] On the other hand, the term *ʾadon*, literally "master," which is the B-text's equivalent of Masada's *dorekh*, seems to be a loan-translation of Greek *kurios*, which means "master" but is used idiomatically in older Greek legal documents with the meaning of "guardian." The term *ʾadon* is actually used with the same meaning in an Aramaic document dated to ca. 125 C.E. from the Dead Sea region.[6] In a Greek deed of guardianship from the Bavta archive, one of the Aramaic guardians describes himself in his Aramaic signature as *ʾadon Bavta*, a term that is the apparent equivalent of Greek *epitropos*, "guardian," used in the body of the Greek text.[7]

From all this, Lieberman concludes that the term *darakh/darukh*, parallel to *ʾadon, kurios*, and *epitropos*, must be an old Hebrew term for "guardian." It is also possible that the rabbinic deed called *shṭar ʾadrakhta* is virtually identical with the *shṭar harshaʿʾah*, a deed delegating (viz., the courts to seize property).[8] The form *nidrakh* found in the *Sifre* to Deuteronomy simply means "delegated."[9] Finally, our verse in Ben Sirah should be translated: "Do not exhibit partiality and (thus bring about) sin . . . in dealing with a partner or a guardian and in the division of inheritance and property."

Kutscher drew attention to the connection between the Ugaritic and rabbinic usages of the root *drk*. This equation is not without its difficulties. Since the root *drk* has not been decisively shown to exist in Biblical Hebrew, we have before us the skipping of a linguistic generation. Such phenomena are not without parallel.[10] In a later study, Lieberman simplified matters greatly by deriving *drk* not from the exercise of power, but from the metaphor of sending and delegating. Thus *darukh* means "messenger"; *ʾadrakhta* means "delegation."

Now, if Hebrew had the forms *nidrakh*, "delegated," *darakh/darukh*, "empowered/guardian," and *ʾadrakhta*, "empowerment," it stands to reason that Hebrew may also have had *derekh*, "power/right."[11]

Our induction seems to be confirmed by several passages of midrashic literature where no other meaning seems to fit the context. In Numbers 16, at the rebellion of Korah, Moses declares that his administration was not tainted by illicit use of executive privilege, saying: "Pay no attention to an offering from them. Not a single donkey have I taken from them, nor have I done any harm to them" (Num 16:5).[12] Moses' declaration of innocence is paraphrased in the following manner in a midrashic text[13]:

מה שהיה דרכי ליטול לא נטלתי: בנוהג שבעולם אדם שהוא עשה בהקדש נוטל
שכרו מן ההקדש: בשעה שהייתי יורד ממדין למצרים היה דרכי ליטול מהם
חמור שבשביל צרכיהם אני יורד· ולא נטלתי

That which was my *derekh* to take, I did not take from them. Ordinarily, when a person performs some service for the temple, he gets paid from temple funds. But when I was traveling back and forth between Midian and Egypt, I certainly had the *derekh* to commandeer a donkey from them, since I was engaged in their service. Nevertheless, I did not do so.

It is clear from the context that the regular meanings of *drk*, "custom, manner," will just not work. One cannot render the last sentence, "It certainly was my custom to take / commandeer a donkey, but I did not." The only meaning that suits the context is "legal right, prerogative."[14]

A second example of this use of the root *drk* is found in an argument concerning the religious propriety of employing doctors, rather than relying on the omnipotence of the Lord. After he offers his version of the proper prayer to say before going to have one's blood let, R. Aḥa explains that: *sheʾein darkan shel benei-ʾadam lerappʾot ʾella shenahagu*, "People are not allowed to perform healing, but people are nevertheless accustomed to do so."[15] Since *drk* is juxtaposed to "but people are nonetheless accustomed to do so," it is clear that *drk* cannot mean "custom." Context demands something like, "it is not their right/ it is not lawful." This was most clearly seen by Rashi, who paraphrased the expression *sheʾein darkan* by "they should not have gotten involved with cures, but should have sought God's mercy."[16]

While the inner juxtaposition between *drk* and *shenahagu* is quite convincing in itself, the juxtaposition of R. Aḥa's statement with that of Abaye, which immediately follows it, clinches the argument. Abaye's statement that "permission has been given to the physician to heal" is a direct polemic against R. Aḥa's *sheʾein darkan shel benei-ʾadam lerappʾot*, which means, as we have seen, "human beings have no right to heal." Clearly, *drk* is a virtual synonym of *reshut*, "permission."

Obvious though this might be, the current English translation of the text is unclear or misleading on a number of issues.[17] First of all, according to the translation, the prayer does not end at *u-refuʾatekha ʾemet*, "your cure is certain," but actually goes on to include the editorial comment, *sheʾein darkan shel benei-ʾadam lerappʾot*, "human beings have no right to heal." Secondly, although the translator realizes that *derekh*, in direct contrast to *nahagu*, cannot mean "custom," the translation "since men have no power to heal" seems to mean that people lack ability to heal; only God has that ability. The question is not whether they have the ability to cure (R. Aḥa may actually believe that they have) but whether they have the power, namely, the right, to do so. This contrast is spelled out most clearly by Abaye's objection, "From this we learn that *permission* has been given to the physician to heal."[18]

While we have adduced but one example of *derekh* (in Moses' apologia pro sua vita, cited above), it seems that the negative expression, *sheʾein darkan*, with the meaning "it is not their right," is much more common than one might have expected. The phrase *sheʾein darko shel ʾadam la'abbed 'eṣmo lada'at* seems to make better sense translated as "One is not allowed/ has no right to commit suicide" rather than as "It is not common for one to commit suicide."[19] This induction seems to be confirmed by the related statement, *'ein 'adam rashai leḥabbel be'aṣmo*, "One is not (even) allowed to wound oneself."[20] Thus, *'ein darko shel 'adam = 'ein 'adam rashai*. These observations seem to be correct no matter what the etymological relations among the various uses of the term may be.

The phrase found in the Palestinian Talmud, *'ein derekh ha'ishah lihyot yoshevet beṭelah betokh beito*, is hardly to be rendered, "It is not the custom for a wife to sit idle in his (i.e., her husband's) house." More correctly put, "The wife has no right (i.e., it is forbidden) to sit idle in his house."[21]

Philological matters aside, the midrash regarding Moses' declaration of abstinence regarding the use of public property has an almost exact parallel in the letters of Paul.[22] In his first letter to the Corinthians, the apostle seemingly attempts to clear himself of putative charges of misappropriating contributions meant for the Jerusalem Church. In this remarkable passage he borrows the very arguments that Moses and Samuel (cited above, note 13) use in defending themselves against similar charges. It is quite clear that Paul employed our midrash—or an earlier version of it—in a similar situation. Evidently he saw himself in the same predicament. His argument is identical[23]:

> Am I not free? Am I not an apostle? Have I not seen Jesus our Lord? Are you not my work in the Lord? If I am not an apostle to others, at least I am to you; for you are the seal of my apostleship in the Lord. To those who are investigating me this is my defense. Do we not have the right to eat and drink? Do we not have the right to take around a sister as a wife as do the rest of the apostles and the brothers of the Lord and Cephas? Or do only Barnabas and I not have the right of freedom from physical work?
>
> Who ever serves as a soldier and pays his own wages? Who plants a vineyard and does not eat its fruit? Who shepherds a flock and does not partake of the milk of the flock? . . . If others are sharing the right of being supported by you, should not we all the more? We did not, however, use this right. . . . Do you not know that those who perform the temple-rites eat the temple-offerings, and those who serve at the altar share in the altar-sacrifices? So also the Lord directed those who are proclaiming the gospel to live from the gospel. Now I have used none of these rights.

An interesting side effect of the coincidence of *drk*, "road, path, custom" and *drk*, "right, prerogative," is the fact that it can be translated into Aramaic with both meanings intact by a word that linguistically is a translation of *drk*, "road, path" alone: the word *'oraḥ*. The phrase *lav 'oraḥ*

ʾarʿaʾ can thus mean either, "It is not the custom / way / path of the land," or else "It is not permitted in the land." Examples of both meanings abound in the Babylonian Talmud. A concordance will yield all the instances of this phrase.[24] I will only mention three examples that seem to bear the latter, rarer meaning.

1. *b. Tamid* 26b. In response to a suggestion that beds be brought into the Temple on which the priests might sleep, Abaye answers: it is not *ʾoraḥ ʾarʿaʾ* to bring beds into the Temple. Clearly we must understand that this is a prohibition and not a mere custom.

2. *b. Berakhot* 45b. In response to a call for the reason behind Mar Zutra's requirement that ten people be in their places when reciting the grace after meals, the Gemara states: Since it is required to mention God's name, it is not *ʾoraḥ ʾarʿaʾ* that less than ten be there. Here again, we are obviously dealing with a prohibition.

3. *b. Megillah* 23b. For liturgical reasons, it is deemed not to be *ʾoraḥ ʾarʿaʾ* to have fewer than ten present for the *maʿamad* and *moshav* ceremonies connected with funeral processions.

The use of the root *drk* in Ugaritic with the meaning "to exercise authority" is clearly established. The presence of *drk* with the same meaning in biblical literature is a subject of lively discussion in scholarly circles. Whatever the case in Biblical Hebrew, *drk* with this meaning seems to be clearly attested in rabbinic Hebrew.[25] It is hard to deny the relationship between the Ugaritic and early rabbinic uses of the root *drk*.

NOTES

1. J. Aistleitner, *Wörterbuch der Ugaritischen Sprache* (3d ed.; Berichte der Sächsischen Gesellschaft der Wissenschaft, Philologisch-historische Klasse 106 #3; Leipzig, 1967) s. v. *drkt*; W. Baumgartner et al., *Hebräisches und Aramäisches Lexicon zum Alten Testament*, vol. 1 (Leiden: Brill, 1967) s.v. *derekh*; M. Dahood, *Ugaritic-Hebrew Philology* (Biblica et orientalia 17; Rome: Pontifical Biblical Institute, 1965) 17, 55; Dahood, "Ugaritic DRKT and Biblical DEREK," *Theological Studies* 15 (1954) 627–31; [E.] Y. Kutscher, "Marginal Notes to the Biblical Lexicon," *Leshonenu* 32 (1968) 343–46 at 345–46 (in Hebrew); rpt. in Kutscher, *Hebrew and Aramaic Studies* (ed. Z. Ben Ḥayyim et al.; Jerusalem: Magnes Press, 1977) 342–59.

2. S. Lieberman, "Forgotten Teachings," *Leshonenu* 32 (1968) 89–102 (in Hebrew) at 90–92.

3. Y. Yadin, *The Ben Sira Scroll from Masada* (Jerusalem: Israel Exploration Society, 1965), Hebrew Section, 23.

4. The B-text is a Cairo Geniza text of Ben Sirah brought by Solomon Schechter to Cambridge University. See Yadin, *Ben Sira*, English Section, 7–11, for a discussion of the importance of this manuscript. P. W. Skehan's rendering of the key phrase in 42:3

does not take into consideration the discussions of Kutscher and Lieberman: "sharing the expenses of a business or a journey"; Skehan and A. A. Di Lella, *The Wisdom of Ben Sira* (Anchor Bible 39; New York: Doubleday, 1987) 477.

5. E.g., *m. Menaḥot* 9:9 (see Lieberman, "Forgotten Teachings," 91 n. 11); *Sifra, Nedavah* at parashat 2:1 and pereq 17:2; see also the *baraita* in *b. Menaḥot* 94a.

6. Y. Yadin, "Expedition D—Cave of the Letters," *Yediʿot Beḥaqirat Eretz-Israel ve-ʿAtiqoteha* 26 (1962) 204–36 at 223 (in Hebrew).

7. H. J. Polotsky, "Three Greek Documents from the Family Archive of Babtha," *Eretz Israel* 8 (1967) 46–51 at 50; cf. Polotsky, "The Greek Documents from the 'Cave of the Letters,'" *Yediʿot Beḥaqirat Eretz-Israel ve-ʿAtiqoteha* 26 (1962) 237–241 (in Hebrew).

8. The *ʾadrakhta* document is mentioned several times in the Talmud, e. g., *b. Ketubbot* 104b; *b. Bava Qamma* 102b, 112b; *b. Bava Batra* 169a; *b. Bekhorot* 49a. For the medieval text of such a document, see S. J. Halberstam, *Sepher Haschetaroth [of Rabbi Judah b. Barzillai of Barcelona], Dokumentarbuch. Nach der einzigen Handschrift in Oxford (Cat. Neubauer No. 890) zum ersten Male herausgegeben und erläutert* (Berlin: Itzkowski, 1898; in Hebrew) 3.

9. L. Finkelstein, *Sifre Devarim. Siphre ad Deuteronomium* (Breslau, 1935; rpt. New York: The Jewish Theological Seminary of America, 1969; in Hebrew) 343, p. 394, variants to line 6. The form *nidrakh* only appears in the London manuscript. The *editio princeps* (Venice, 1545) has *niskar*, "recalled." The reading *nidrakh* in the London manuscript was contested by M. Mishor, "A Note on Kutscher's Contribution on *drk*," *Leshonenu* 33 (1968) 78, who read *niṣrakh* for *nidrakh*; Lieberman, in the same issue of *Leshonenu*, accepts Mishor's reading but insists that *niṣrakh* is a scribal error for *nidrakh*.

10. For a discussion of Ugaritic words that show up in rabbinic Hebrew but not in Biblical Hebrew, see J. C. Greenfield, "Amurrite, Ugaritic and Canaanite," in *Proceedings of the International Conference on Semitic Studies held in Jerusalem, 19–23 July 1965* (Jerusalem: Israel Academy of Sciences and Humanities, 1969) 92–101; Greenfield outlines the phenomenon but does not seek to explain it.

11. Some have attempted to see *derekh* in the related sense of "government" or "jurisdiction" at Prov 31:3, where it is parallel to *ḥel*, "strength," and at Hos 10:13. Both of these are moot. I might add to the discussion Prov 30:19, where we find the phrase *derekh gever beʿalmah*, "the power (?) of a man over a young girl." The sexual metaphoric range is well-evidenced, e. g., in Syriac, where we find *derūkāʾ*, "concubine," *derūktāʾ*, "progeny," and *madraknūtāʾ*, "reaching the age of puberty"; see s. vv. in R. Payne Smith et al., eds., *Thesaurus syriacus* (2 vols.; Oxford: Clarendon, 1879–1901). It remains unclear whether we are discussing a separate root with a distinct meaning or a metaphorization of Hebrew *derekh*, "road/ path/ custom."

Perhaps there is an underlying metaphoric connection between *drk*, "to exercise power," and *drk*, "road," based on the custom of stepping on something in order to establish ownership of it. In the Nuzi documents, we often find the gesture of the seller lifting his foot from the property and placing the buyer's foot in its place. Perhaps this is suggested in Gen 13:17, when God commands Abraham to acquire the land by walking through it. The idea that land could be acquired by walking through it is also part of rabbinic law; see, e. g., *y. Qiddushin* 1:3, 59d, or *b. Bava Batra* 100a. In this last source, the majority opinion seems to oppose adopting this principle as practical law. Nonetheless, we can point to the extremely interesting comment of Rashbam to *b. Bava Batra* 169a, s. v. *ve-ha-amar Rabbi Naḥman*, where he defines the

ʾadrakhta document as signifying that by its possession the creditor may tread (*drk*) on the debtor's goods in order to acquire them as repayment. A. B. Ehrlich, in his *Mikra ki-Pheschuto* (3 vols.; Berlin: Poppelauer, 1899–1901; rpt. New York: KTAV, 1969; in Hebrew) 35, notes that this principle was also known in Greek tradition; it is evident, e. g., in the prayer of Chryses to Apollo, *Iliad* 1:36–42.

In his *Sifre Zutta* (*The Midrash of Lydda*) (New York: The Jewish Theological Seminary of America, 1968; in Hebrew) 73–74, Lieberman has shown that the phrase *ve-dorekh* (*eḥad le-ṣafon*), found in Version B of *Avot de-Rabbi Natan* (ed. S. Schechter, Solomon; Vienna, 1887; rpt. New York: Feldheim, 1945), chap. 1, p. 3, is parallel to Version A's *meshagro*, "sends/ delegates/ empowers," and thus the phrase yields, linguistically as well as contextually, "he sends (one to the north)."

12. See below for parallel texts.

13. S. Buber, ed., *Midrash Tanḥuma: ein agadischer Commentar zum Pentateuch von Rabbi Tanchuma ben Rabbi Abba* (Vilna, Rom, 1885; rpt. 1946) to Num 16:15, vol. 2, p. 91; cf. M. A. Mirkin, ed., *Bemidbar Rabbah* (Tel Aviv: "Yavneh" Publishing House, 1959) 18:10, p. 199; Mirkin, ed., *Shemot Rabbah* (Tel Aviv: "Yavneh" Publishing House, 1959) 4:1, p. 84; *Yalqut Shimʿoni* 750; Buber, ed., *Midrash Shemuel* (Krakow: Y. Fischer, 1893) Chap. 14, p. 90.

Moses' speech is certainly related to Samuel's disclaimer in 1 Sam 12:3: "Here I am—witness against me before the Lord and before His anointed: Whose ox have I taken? Or whose donkey have I taken? Or whom have I defrauded? Or whom have I oppressed? Or from whose hand have I taken a ransom to blind my eyes therewith? And I will restore it to you." The two speeches are linked by rabbinic exegesis at *b. Nedarim* 38a, cf. *Yalqut Shemuel* 111, 113. The fact that *drk* in Moses' speech means "right" is indicated in the *Yalqut* passage (at 111), where it is glossed in this way by Rabbi Yoḥanan: "From whom should he have taken the donkey, if not from the community? Moses' 'it was my *drk* to take . . .' means the same thing."

Another midrash preserved in the *Tanḥuma* also presents *drk* with the meaning "right, prerogative." In traditional printings of the *Tanḥuma* we find at the beginning of the section on Leviticus the following exegesis of Lev 1:1: "Said the Holy One, Blessed Be He, it is not *din* (i. e., just) that Moses, who made the tabernacle, should stand outside (of it) while I am within. Behold, I will call him to enter. Thus is it written: And He called Moses (Lev 1:1)." In Buber's edition the word *drk* is used instead of *din*, i. e., the text has *drk Moshe*, "the *drk* of Moses," instead of *din sheMoshe*, "(it is not) fitting that Moses . . . ." Our explanation of *drk* obviates the need for such a change. At any rate, *drk* seems to equal *din*, and the only sensible translation remains "it is not his right," that is to say, "it is not fitting."

14. On the difficulties evident in Semitic expressions for the concepts "allowed" and "forbidden," see SALPE, 36–37 n. 2.

15. *B. Berakhot* 60a. Rabbi Aḥa was a Palestinian *ʾamora* who flourished in the fourth generation of *ʾamoraim*.

16. Rashi, ad loc.

17. *The Babylonian Talmud*, ed. I. Epstein, vol. 1 (London: Soncino Press, 1948) 377.

18. The note to the translation seems to suggest just the opposite, that men let their blood even though they know it is a useless act. Why would men open their veins for the sake of a custom and with no expectation of a cure? The ancients clearly expected the cure to take effect, and therefore the apologetic statement of Rabbi Aḥa is appropriate.

19. J. Theodor and Ch. Albeck, *Midrasch Bereschit Rabba mit kritischem Apparat und Kommentar* (Berlin: Itzkowski, 1903–29; rpt. Jerusalem: Wahrmann, 1965) 82:8, p. 985, variants to line 2. This is the text of the *editio princeps* (Venice, 1545), and it is confirmed in a Yemenite manuscript in the Adler collection in London. The associated story is as follows: "At the time of persecution, two students of Rabbi Joshua altered their attire [literally, their headgear; apparently to avoid being recognized as Jews]. A soldier who had become an apostate met them and (recognizing them) said: 'If you are her sons [i. e., of the Torah], then give up your lives for her sake. If, however, you are not her sons, then why get yourselves killed for her sake [in the event that you are discovered—why not leave Judaism completely]?' They replied to him: 'We are her sons, and we (are prepared to) give our lives for her sake. Nonetheless, it is not one's *drk* to commit suicide.'" If the students mean to say that it is not customary to kill oneself, the thrust of the statement is unclear; perhaps the statement is missing from so many sources (see Theodor's notes) because it makes little sense if *drk* is taken as meaning "custom."

20. *B. Bava Qamma* 91b.

21. *Y. Ketubbot* 5:6, 30a. See also Theodor–Albeck, *Bereshit Rabbah* 18:1, p. 161, and 65:4, p. 715; these two latter citations are less definitive. We might add the dictum of Rabbi Aqiba: "Be wary of him who give advice according to his *drk*" (*b. Sanhedrin* 76b). If *drk* means "power," then Rabbi Aqiba is offering his listeners the sage counsel to avoid advisers whose advice is in accord with the limitation of their power. The phrase *biʾah sheloʾ kedarkah*, usually translated "unnatural intercourse," could just as easily refer to forbidden intercourse.

22. See the discussion of H. L. Strack and P. Billerbeck, *Kommentar zum Neuen Testament aus Talmud und Midrasch*, vol. 3 (Munich: Beck, 1926) 400.

23. 1 Cor 9:1–15; translation from W. F. Orr and J. A. Walther, *I Corinthians* (Anchor Bible 32; New York: Doubleday, 1976) 235–37.

24. See, e. g., Ch. J. Kasowski, *Concordance of the Language of the Talmud* (Jerusalem: Ministry of Education and Culture and the Jewish Theological Seminary of America, 1959–80) vol. 6 (1960) 2819ff.

25. As noted earlier, other such philological gaps are not unknown. See, in addition to Greenfield's paper cited above (n. 10), E. Y. Kutscher, "Mittelhebräisch und Jüdische-aramäisch im neuen Koehler-Baumgartner," *Hebräische Wortforschung: Festschrift für 80. Geburtstag von Walter Baumgartner* (Supplements to Vetus Testamentum 16; Leiden: Brill, 1967) 158–75; rpt. in Kutscher, *Essays*, 156–73. My study of the Aramaic papyri from Elephantine, SALPE, discusses similar phenomena. These gaps may result from lacunae in the transmission of texts or quirks in the development of language.

CHAPTER 7

LOVE AND JOY AS METAPHORS OF WILLINGNESS AND SPONTANEITY IN CUNEIFORM, ANCIENT HEBREW, AND RELATED LITERATURES:

PART I: DIVINE INVESTITURES IN THE MIDRASH IN THE LIGHT OF NEO-BABYLONIAN ROYAL GRANTS*

It has been clear for a long time that rabbinic literature can be properly understood only against the background of contemporary Greek and Roman civilization.[1] Less commonly appreciated is the importance of ancient Near Eastern traditions and patterns of thought for the illumination of many difficult passages in postbiblical Hebrew literature, especially the Talmud.[2]

In my *Studies in the Aramaic Legal Papyri from Elephantine* (SALPE), I attempted to demonstrate the continuity of legal terminology and metaphor in ancient Near Eastern legal documents beginning with those written in Sumerian and Akkadian (of the late third and second millennia B.C.E.), continuing with the crucial transformation of late Neo-Babylonian and Neo-Assyrian cuneiform documents into an Aramaic formulary that reworked these ancient materials according to its own spirit.[3] This Aramaic formulary, in turn, exercised a profound influence on legal documents in the West (Demotic, Greek, Coptic, and probably Arabic as well),[4] in Syria (the Aramaic documents from Samaria, the Nabatean, Hebrew and Aramaic deeds from the Dead Sea area)[5] and quite possibly on Persian law in the East.[6] Each new excavation in these areas fills in some missing link in this process of transmission. Thus, the scepticism of a scholar of rabbinic law of the stature of A. Gulak concerning the dangers of using ancient Near Eastern material for the illumination of rabbinic law, although quite legitimate and understandable forty years ago, is entirely out of place today.[7] In any case, as Saul Lieberman

* This article first appeared in *Christianity, Judaism and Other Greco-Roman Cults. Studies for Morton Smith at Sixty. Part Three. Judaism Before 70* (ed. J. Neusner; Studies in Judaism in Late Antiquity; Leiden: Brill, 1975) 1–36.

has often pointed out, much that is called Hellenistic is simply ancient oriental.[8] E. A. Speiser's observation that Near Eastern culture is by nature a palimpsest through which all previous layers of tradition transpire is entirely to the point.[9] Furthermore, the pivotal role of Aramaic in this process of cultural transformation can hardly be underestimated: rooted in cuneiform culture, its offshoots are found in almost all areas of late antiquity.

In one of the chapters of SALPE, I attempted to demonstrate that in Akkadian and Aramaic seemingly metaphorical expressions such as love (*nar'amātu/rēmūtu*)[10] and joy (*ṭūb libbi/ḫūd libbi*),[11] when used in legal contexts, convey the specific legal idea of free and uncoerced willingness, i.e., the will that motivates the giving of a gift or the selling of property, etc. That which was only adumbrated in SALPE in an Akkadian–Aramaic context will be applied here to biblical and especially rabbinic sources and will constitute the subject of the present essay. Although the method used here is basically philological, the aim is conceptual and cultural. How did the ancients, living in the ambience of Near Eastern culture, express (a) the free and gracious will that underpins a divine grant to kings or priests; (b) the spontaneity with which man accepts divine grace or the free resignation with which he accepts divine chastisement; and (c) the willing and joyful alacrity with which man reciprocates the divine gifts and blessings with his sacrifices, tithes, and offerings?

Not only are the volitional metaphors of love and joy found in a wide range of legal situations, but their distribution in seemingly non-legal contexts is much wider than the traditional legalist would ever expect: not only Deuteronomy and Chronicles, but Ben Sirah and Philo, the sermons of Paul, early and late rabbinic midrash and *piyyuṭ*, Jewish and Christian liturgy, Samaritan marriage documents and early Arabic deeds of sale.[12]

Nor should this distribution pattern surprise us too much. Students of cuneiform law, such as Benno Landsberger, have been pointing out for years that the famous Mesopotamian "codes," with their idealizing tendencies, often provide us with a less correct picture of law as it was lived than the less famous legal documents, which in many ways contradict the ideal norms presented by the "codes."[13]

Similarly, Lieberman has said that if one wants to learn how the law was actually practiced during the rabbinic period, one should rely not only on the formal legal corpora (the Mishnah, the Toseftah, etc.), which were less interested in what people did than in what they should have done, but also on the midrash, where actual legal practice is often described *en passant* as part of a story or homily.[14] It goes without saying that the common law, reflected in the Greek papyri, in the Aramaic deeds of the Dead Sea area, in the fragments of legal formulae preserved haphazardly in the Talmuds, and more systematically, in Gaonic formulary handbooks, in many ways more accurately reflects the living law of the times than the idealistic norms of the formal talmudic corpora. In the light of these observations, the wide distribution of the legal use of Hebrew *besimḥah*, "in joy, willingly," and *beʾahavah*, "in love, willingly, with a full heart," in seemingly non-legal contexts would appear to add dramatic support to this significant but neglected observation.

One final comment before discussing the texts themselves. Without a doubt, Aramaic and Akkadian parallels throw much light on many an obscure passage in the Talmud. Although many of these parallel passages may be related historically, in many other cases the similarity may indicate a common, but independent, mental and cultural set of mind. In such cases, the parallel is useful heuristically, but has no necessary historical implications. Let it be made clear at the outset that it is not our intention to institute a new form of Pan-Babylonianism. However, while similarity of one or two details does not prove historical dependence, clusters of similarities are quite different. Such clusters, frequently, are not accidental or fortuitous, especially in contiguous civilizations, but, more often than not, suggest the presence of what one may call "cultures in contact."

The Linguistic Evidence

As we have noted above, the two Akkadian terms for joy used in legal documents with the particular meaning of volition are *ḫūd* (*libbišu*), cognate of Hebrew *ḥedvah*, and *ṭūb* (*libbišu*)/*ṭūbāti*, cognate of Hebrew *ṭov*(*ah*). Hebrew *ṭov*(*ah*), like its Akkadian equivalent, is a well-attested expression of joy both in biblical and in later Hebrew.[15] Just as Akkadian *ḫūd* and *ṭūb* are used together idiomatically, as in the expression *ina ṭūb libbi ina ḫūd šēri*, "in joy of heart/mind (and) gladness of flesh/body," so Hebrew idiom joins *sameaḥ* with *ṭov*, as in the expressions *semeḥim ve-ṭove lev*, "happy and of a glad heart" (1 Kgs 8:66),[16] and "Go, eat your bread in gladness *(besimḥah)* and drink your wine in joy (*lev ṭov*)" (Qoh 9:7). Furthermore, just as *ṭov* is used idiomatically as a synonym of *sameaḥ*, so its antonym *raʿ*/*roaʿ* (*lev*) is used as a synonym of *kaʿas* "care," as in Qoheleth's classic statement, "Banish care (*kaʿas*) from your mind and pluck sorrow (*raʿah*) out of your flesh" (11:10).[17]

Finally, it should be noted that these inner states of mind are dramatically externalized in facial expressions: a joyful mood is reflected in a happy or shining face, while a sorrowful mood is reflected in a sad or dark and gloomy face. As the king says to Nehemiah: "Why is your countenance sad (*panekha raᶜim*), since you are not ill? This is nothing else but sorrow of heart (*roaᶜ lev*)" (Neh 2:2). Or, in a more positive vein, see Ben Sirah's comment on the effect of a good wife on her husband's mood: "Whether rich or poor, his heart is cheerful (*libbo ṭov*) and his face shines (*ʾorim*, literally, lit up) at all times" (26:4).[18]

What is less evident, however, is that the Hebrew terms for joy also function as terms of volition—exactly like their Akkadian equivalents—as, for example, in the common rabbinic expressions *beṭovato*: *birṣono*//*shelo*ʾ *beṭovato*: *beᶜal korḥo*, "gladly: willingly//not gladly: unwillingly." The term *beṭovato* comes to mean "gladly" as a natural extension of its basic meaning "joyfully." Exactly the same situation obtains in Arabic.[19] Furthermore, this equation should shed some light on the meaning of the antonym *beᶜal korḥo*: if *ṭovah* means "joy"—and by extension "willingness"—the basic meaning of *koraḥ* should be "sadness/pain," used by extension as an expression of "unwillingness." The inference that *koraḥ* means "pain" is supported by the common Syriac *kurhono* "pain/sickness,"[20] while the extended use of "pain/sickness" to convey the idea of "unwillingness" is confirmed by the Arabic expression *ᶜala karāhiyatihī*, "against his will; literally, against his feeling of discomfort" (from *kariha*, "to feel disgust").[21]

Babylonian Royal Grants

So far, the comparisons between the cuneiform and Aramaic rabbinic traditions have been purely linguistic: both employ similar metaphorical expressions to convey the idea of volition and willingness. However, both the Akkadian and rabbinic traditions employ these terms of volition in narrative contexts—especially those describing the gifts of gods and kings—that are remarkably similar in their overall literary structure as well.

In many of the so-called *kudurru* documents (phallus-shaped monuments of stone usually covered with divine symbols),[22] in which kings granted land to courtiers, or kings or gods[23] granted revenues to priests, in order to insure the finality of the donation the outer physical manifestations of the joy/volition of the donor are described in some detail. One such baroque description of the donor's joy reads as follows:

(35) *ina ūmišu* (36) *ša Nabū-apla-iddina* (37) *š[ar] Bābili* (38) *libbašu iḫdūma* (39) *immerū zīmūšu* (40) *eli Nabū-nādin-šum* (41) *šangū Sippar bārū* (42) *irtuṣa būnīšu* (43) *ina būnīšu namrūti* (44) *zīmēšu ruššūti* (45) *damqāti īnāšu ḫadiš* (46) *ippalissuma*

At that time, the heart of Nabu-apla-iddina, the k[ing] of Babylon, rejoiced. His countenance became bright. He turned his gaze (i.e., his attention) upon Nabu-nadin-shum, the priest of Sippar, the *baru*. With his bright gaze, shining countenance, and sparkling (literally, good) eyes, he looked upon him joyfully [and granted him the priestly revenues].[24]

In another of these *kudurru* donations, the following appeal is recorded.[25] A certain Mushezib-Marduk was dispossessed of his lands during the anarchy that preceded Esarhaddon's conquest of Babylon. On the restoration of order he was reinstated by the king, who, unfortunately, omitted to give him the property under seal. In the meanwhile, both Esarhaddon and Mushezib-Marduk died, and the property was taken from the latter's heir, Adad-ibni, who now comes before the present king, Shamash-shum-ukin, in order to regain title to his ancestral property. After investigating the case, the king confirms Adad-ibni's right to the property. This time, however, a written document was drawn up and sealed by the king before witnesses; it was probably registered in the royal archive. Significantly, the reconfirmation of the grant came to its successful conclusion when the king looked at the claimant "with his face that shines like Shamash"—i.e., with a firm resolve, expressed by the joy of his countenance. In spite of its literary formulation, the clause is less a matter of poetry than of specific legal function: the desire to insure the donation against all further claims and contests.[26]

Before turning our attention to a rabbinic parallel to this Akkadian deed, we should notice that exactly the same legal structure and volitional terminology are used whether a god bestows revenues on a priest, or a king grants land to a courtier: kings, priests and courtiers all receive their incontestable grants through the "joy" of their masters, human or divine.

The Gift of the Terumot

Now for the rabbinic parallel. Like good literary critics, the rabbis, in their analysis of Scripture, searched for the underlying logical or literary principles that bound the various sections of a narrative into a coherent whole.[27] When such coherence seemed to be lacking, it was usually supplied by a midrashic creation. A good case in point is associated with the narrative recorded in Numbers 17–18: the first chapter deals with the end of Korah's rebellion, while the second interrupts the continuity of the narrative by recording the divine investiture of Aaron and his sons with the priestly revenues (*terumot*). The literary unity of the two chapters is provided by the following comment, recorded in the *Sifre*:

> כרת הכתוב ברית עם אהרן על כל קדשי הקדשים לגזור דין ולכרות להם ברית לפי שבא קרח כנגד אהרן וערער על הכהונה משל למה הדבר דומה למלך בשר ודם שהיה לו בן בית ונתן לו שדה אחת במתנה ולא כתב ולא חתם ולא העלה לו בערכיים בא אחד וערער כנגדו על השדה אמר לו המלך כל מי שירצה יבוא ויערער כנגדך על השדה בוא ואני כותב ואני חותם ואני מעלה לך בערכיים כך בא קרח וערער על הכהונה כנגדו אמר לו המקום כל מי שירצה יבא ויערער כנגדך על הכהונה בוא ואני כותב ואני חותם ואני מעלה לך בערכיים לכך נאמרה פרשה זו סמוך לקרח

> Scripture made a covenant[28] with Aaron [and his sons] concerning the most holy sacrifices, by establishing a definitive charter on their behalf. This was necessary because Korah opposed Aaron by contesting the priesthood. By analogy, the situation can be compared to a human king who had a steward,[29] to whom he granted a field as an [outright] gift, without, however, having [the gift] written down, sealed, and recorded in the archive. [Then] someone appeared who raised claims concerning the field against [the steward]. The king said to the steward: "Since anyone who wants can come and raise claims against you concerning the field, for your benefit, I hereby deed it [to you] in writing; I hereby seal it and register it in the archive!"
>
> Similarly, after Korah opposed Aaron by contesting the priesthood, God said to him: "Since anyone who wants can raise claims against you concerning the priesthood, I hereby deed it [to you] in writing; I hereby seal it and record it in the archive!" It is for this reason that this section (dealing with the donation of the priestly revenues) immediately follows that of Korah.[30]

Notice the structural and substantive identity of the Akkadian and rabbinic traditions: both contain the same story of a royal grant, insufficiently protected against contestation, that was reconfirmed by the king to his courtier. Both sources know the structural analogy between the donation of priestly offerings by the gods and the donation of land by kings. It is only in respect to the specific use of joy as the volition that establishes the fact that the two traditions seem to part company. In the Akkadian tradition, the king gives the gift in the joy of his heart, while in the Jewish tradition, the Lord simply says: *va-ʾani hinne natatti*. As we shall see, this difference is more apparent than real.

Let us re-examine the clause of donation as it is recorded in the Bible.

וידבר ה׳ אל־אהרן ואני הנה נתתי לך את־משמרת תרומתי לכל־קדשי בני־ישראל לך נתתים למשחה ולבניך לחק־עולם

The Lord spoke further to Aaron: I hereby give you charge of My gifts, all the sacred donations of the Israelites; I grant them to you and your sons as a perquisite, a due for all time (Num 18:8, NJPS).

As Rashi (to Gen 14:22) and the Rashbam (to Gen 23:11) clearly recognized, in certain solemn contexts—especially in formal declarations such as donations and oaths—first-person forms such as *natatti* are to be translated not as simple perfects ("I gave") but as present forms or present-perfects ("I give" or "I have given") and often contain the nuance "I, myself, the donor, hereby have given." Notice, for example, how the Rashbam renders *ha-sade natatti lak* in Gen 23:11—*noten ʾani ʾoto ʿakhshav leka*. Furthermore, when the verb form is preceded by *ʾani hinne*, this volitional nuance is brought out explicitly. *ʾAni hinne* thus stresses the person of the donor, his awareness of what he is doing, and the heightened solemnity of the act that follows.[31]

Now Rabbi Ishmael, who held that *ʾen miqra yoṣeʾ mide peshuṭo*, "Scripture must always be interpreted (philologically) according to its simple meaning,"[32] was not unaware of the volitional implications of the words *va-ʾani hinne* in the biblical clause of donation. He paraphrases them in the following manner: *va-ʾani—beraṣon*:: *hinne—besimḥah*, "I"—"with (full) volition":: "hereby"—"with joy."[33]

In this legal context, *besimḥah* "joyfully/gladly," is used with the specific legal meaning of "willingly" and is the synonym of *beraṣon*, "with volition," exactly as the expression *beṭovato*, "joyfully/of his own free will," is the complement of *birṣono* in more common contexts. Furthermore, this equation cuts across linguistic boundaries: Akkadian *ina ḫūd libbišu* is to Hebrew *besimḥah* as Akkadian *ina ṭūbātišu* is to Hebrew *beṭovato.*

Furthermore, I have the feeling that when Rabbi Ishmael paraphrased the biblical verse of donation *va-ʾani hinne* by *beraṣon u-vsimḥah* what he actually was doing was to render the sense of the biblical verse in contemporary legal language, which was itself but a reflex of older cuneiform usage. Many Murabbaʿat conveyances of property begin with the Hebrew clause *ʾani mirṣoni*, "I, of my own free will . . . " or with the Aramaic *ana merʿuti*.[34] In some of the documents from the Genizah edited by Assaf we read the following declarations of volition: *ʾana min daʿati u-min reʿuti u-min ṭivuti*, "I, of my own volition/knowledge, of my own free will, and gladly. . . . "[35] The last two terms are the Aramaic equivalents of the Hebrew *mirṣoni u-vsimḥati.*

These positive terms of volition are explicated by their opposites: "I have given of my own free will, without having been forced, without having been coerced." After the usual terms of coercion—*la ʾanis ve-la mukhraḥ*—one deed continues with a series of terms which in this context can only be construed as the expression of inner psychological reservation: *ve-la kaʿis ve-la raʿiṣ ve-la ʿaṣiv*, "[Nor did I give the property] when I was angry, depressed, or sad."[36] These three terms in this context, when juxtaposed to *beṭivuti*, "gladly/willingly," do not convey sadness in general, but more specifically inner reservation, reluctance and absence of any real desire to part with the property.

To sum up: just as the Babylonian king reconfirms the contested donation by his declaration of joy/willingness, so the divine King reconfirms the priestly portions *beraṣon u-vsimḥah*. The legal situations recorded in the *kudurru* and the *Sifre*, as well as the specific volitional terminology used in them, are so close that some historical relationship must have existed between the two traditions.

The Gift of the Maʿasrot

The *terumot* of the priests were given *beraṣon u-vsimḥah* and thus became the incontestable property of the sons of Aaron. The legal status of the levitical tithe (*maʿaser*), however, was not as clear. According to Rabbi Jonathan, "Just as God made a covenant with priests [concerning the grant of the perquisites], so did He do with the Levites." The *Sifre Zutta* paraphrases the donation formula, "And to the Levites I hereby give all the tithes in Israel as their share in return for the service they perform . . . " (Num 18:21), in almost the same way as Rabbi Ishmael paraphrased the priestly donation formula discussed above.[37] The *Sifre Zutta* reads:

> אין הנה **אלא** שמחה. שמחה היתה לפני המקום שנתן מעשרות ללוים כדרך שהיה
> שמחה לפניו כשנתן מתנות לכהן כך היתה שמחה לפניו כשנתן מעשרות ללוים.

Hinne means nothing other than *joy*: Just as the Lord rejoiced [literally, there was joy before *ha-Maqom*] when he granted the "gifts"/ perquisites to the priest(s), so he rejoiced when he granted the *maʿasrot* to the Levites.[38]

The opinion of the *Sifre Zutta* and of Rabbi Jonathan in the *Sifre* is opposed by another tradition that reflects a less positive attitude on the legal status of the *maᶜasrot* to the Levites. According to this tradition, it was God's original intent to give the *maᶜasrot* to the priests. However, after the latter sinned during the incident of the Golden Calf, the Lord was forced into giving the *maᶜasrot* to the loyal Levites, not as an outright perquisite—an expression of His love and affection—but as a wage for services performed. On the biblical verse, "And to the Levites I hereby give all tithes in Israel as their share in return for the service that they perform . . . " (Num 18:21), Rabbi Joshiah comments:

כל מצות כהונה קנאן השם ונתנן לכהונה וזו חלף עבודתם

> The Lord gave as an absolute grant to the priests [meaning the clergy in general] all priestly perquisites. But this one [namely, the *maᶜasrot*, was given] in return for their services.[39]

With the contrasting view of Rabbi Jonathan, Rabbi Joshiah restates his case in a slightly different, but parallel, formulation:

כל מצות כהונה נאמרה בשמחה מהר סיני וזו בתחלה נאמרה

> All priestly perquisites were proclaimed with joy from Mount Sinai, but this one [concerning the *maᶜasrot*] was proclaimed *btḥlh*.

It is quite clear that *qanah ve-natan*, "to give as final property," is parallel to *natan besimḥah* "to give joyfully."[40] Joy in this donation context is the feeling of kindness and willingness that motivates a donor to part with his property: God gave the priests their portions in joy; therefore, they are final and eternal property. God did not give the Levites their portions in joy—at least according to some—therefore, these portions are liable to cancellation.

The word *tḥlh* seems to be used in this context as an antonym of *simḥah.* Louis Finkelstein has suggested that the word means something like "sadness, inner reservation."[41] In other words, God gave the *maᶜasrot* with inner reservation, not with complete willingness. If this interpretation is correct, *tḥlh* would be functionally equivalent to *kaᶜis* and *ᶜaṣiv* of the Genizah deeds and to *beᶜal korḥo*—if the latter term means "at his discomfort." Could the word somehow be related to the common term *ḥil*, "pain," used here with the specific nuance of "begrudgingly, with mental reservation"?[42]

The Torah as God's Gift to Israel

The *terumot* were the gift given in joy—namely, with full volition—to the priests. In a similar manner, the Torah itself is the gift given in joy to the People of Israel:

> מדת בשר ודם אדם מוכר חפץ לחברו מוכר עצב לוקח שמח אבל הקב״ה אינו כן נתן להם תורה לישראל ושמח שנא׳ כי לקח טוב נתתי לכם תורתי אל תעזבו
>
> It is the way of human beings that when a man sells a valuable object to his fellow, the seller grieves and the buyer is happy. The Holy One, Blessed Be He, however, is different. He gave the Torah to Israel and rejoiced: "For I give you My Torah; forsake not my teaching."[43]

The sadness with which the seller parts with his property is, in this legal context, the indication of a certain mental reservation against the transaction: in all probability, the seller was coerced into the transaction by economic necessity and even though his acceptance of the price indicates formal agreement to the transaction, his inner being is hardly in accord with it.[44] Thus, even though *ʿaṣvut* and *kaʿas* were not formal halakhic impediments against the deal, the Genizah deeds stress that the transaction took place when the seller was neither sad nor depressed. Conversely, I would suggest that the joy in which God parts with his precious possession, the Torah, like the joy with which God gave the *terumot*, is the *simḥah* of volition, of the total absence of any mental reservation: it is just such joy that makes the transaction final and incontestable. Freely paraphrased, the clause reads: Whereas humans part with their goods half-heartedly—even for a price—God parts with his precious possession, the Torah, with complete and eternal willingness.

NOTES

1. H. M. Pineles in his pioneering *Sefer Darkah shel Torah* (Vienna: F. Förster, 1861), 133 and passim, not only initiated a source-critical approach to talmudic literature but was one of the first to recognize the value of the comparative approach. For the next stage in research, see the works of S. Lieberman, e. g., *Greek in Jewish Palestine* (New York: The Jewish Theological Seminary of America, 1942); "Roman Legal Institutions in Early Rabbinics and in the *Acta Martyrum*," *Jewish Quarterly Review* 35 (1944) 1–57; *Hellenism in Jewish Palestine* (New York: The Jewish Theological Seminary of America, 1950); "How Much Greek in Jewish Palestine?", *Biblical and Other Studies* (ed. A. Altman; Lown Institute of Advanced Judaic Studies, Brandeis University, Studies and Texts 1; Cambridge: Harvard University Press, 1963) 123–41. For more recent work, see the essays of H. A. Fischel, e. g., "Studies in Cynicism and the An-

cient Near East: the Transformation of a *Chria*," *Religions in Antiquity: Essays . . . Goodenough* (ed. J. Neusner; Supplements to Numen 14; Leiden: Brill, 1968) 372–411; "Story and History: Observations on Greco-Roman Rhetoric and Pharisaism," *American Oriental Society, Middle West Branch: Semi-Centennial Volume* (ed. D. Sinor; Asian Studies Research Institute, Oriental Series #3; Bloomington: Indiana University Press, 1969) 59–88.

For Greek literary motifs in the midrash, see A. A. Halevi, *The World of the Aggadah* (Tel-Aviv, 1972; in Hebrew). For suggestive parallels between Greek and rabbinic exegetical methods, see I. Heinemann, *The Methods of the Aggadah* (Jerusalem: Magnes, 1949; in Hebrew); R. Yaron, *Gifts in Contemplation of Death in Jewish and Roman Law* (Oxford: Clarendon, 1960); B. Cohen, *Jewish and Roman Law: A Comparative Study* (New York: The Jewish Theological Seminary of America, 1966); E. J. Bickerman, "The Altars of Gentiles: A Note on the Jewish *'ius sacrum,'*" *Revue international des droits de l'antiquité* 3e serié, 5 (1958) 137–64, rpt. in Bickerman, *Studies in Jewish and Christian History* (Arbeiten zur Geschichte des antiken Judentums und des Urchristentums 9; Leiden: Brill, 1976–86) 2.324–46; Bickerman, "The Civic Prayer for Jerusalem," *Harvard Theological Review* 55 (1962) 163–185, rpt. in Bickerman, *Studies,* 2.290–312.

2. See Excursus I, "Ancient Near Eastern and Rabbinic Literature."

3. See Excursus II, "Akkadian and Aramaic."

4. For parallels with Demotic law, cf. SALPE, 150–72. For parallels with Greek law, cf. SALPE, 20 n. 3, 138 n. 3, 150 n. 5, 155–57, 191 n. 4, 192; R. Taubenschlag, "Das babylonische Recht in den griechischen Papyri," *The Journal of Juristic Papyrology* 7/8 (1953–54) 169–85; and, on the influence of cuneiform treaty terminology on the Greek world, M. Weinfeld, "'Bond and Grace'—Covenantal Expressions in the Bible and the Ancient World—A Common Heritage," *Leshonenu* 36 (1971/72) 85–105 (in Hebrew). For parallels with Coptic law, cf. SALPE, 11, 138 n. 3. For parallels and a possible interrelationship between Arabic volition clauses ("This transaction is done willingly and without force . . . ") and similar clauses in Akkadian deeds and Jewish documents in Hebrew and Aramaic from the Dead Sea area, cf. SALPE, 138 n. 3. The possibility that certain elements in early Islamic legal documents were derived from Babylonian sources was raised long ago by J. Schacht, "Vom babylonischen zum islamischen Recht," *Orientalistische Literaturzeitung* 30 (1927) 664–69. See now the excellent study of J. A. Wakin, *The Function of Documents in Islamic Law: The Chapters on Sales from Ṭaḥāwī's Kitāb al-Shurūṭ al-Kabīr* (Albany: State University of New York Press, 1972), where Aramaic and Akkadian parallels are quoted intelligently and in abundance. The interdependence of Arabic and cuneiform law is a subject warranting further study.

5. For all of these, see SALPE, 192–194.

6. See SALPE, 14 n. 1. See also J. Neusner, *A History of the Jews in Babylonia* (Studia Post-Biblica 9; Leiden: Brill) 4 (1969) 40; Wakin, *Documents in Islamic Law,* 3 n. 3; M. San Nicolò, *Beiträge zur Rechtsgeschichte im Bereiche der keilschriftlichen Rechtsquellen* (Oslo: H. Aschehong, 1931) 254.

7. A. Gulak, *Das Urkundenwesen im Talmud im Lichte der griechisch-aegyptischen Papyri und des griechischen und römischen Rechts* (Jerusalem: R. Mass, 1935) 159–60.

8. Orally and in his various writings, cf. especially *Hellenism in Jewish Palestine,* 75ff., where he compares some of the more fanciful norms of aggadic interpretation with those used in contemporary Greek dream interpretation, stressing the fact that

both Jews and Greeks derived these methods from "hoary antiquity," and then immediately cites a Babylonian example.

9. E. A. Speiser, "Cultural Factors in Social Dynamics in the Near East," *Middle East Journal* 7 (1953) 133–52 at 134–35.

10. Since the linguistic evidence concerning the use of the Aramaic terms *yhb/ ntn brḥmn*, "to give in affection (i. e., freely and willingly)," *yhb/ ntn brḥmt/ brḥmh/ rḥmt*, "to give as a gift/ freely/ willingly" and their Akkadian models, *ina narʾamātišu iddin*, "to give in love (i. e., freely and voluntarily)" (Aramaic *yhb brḥmn*) and *rēmūtu rēmu*, "to give as a gift, perform an act of generosity" (Aramaic *lmntn brḥmt/h*), is most complicated, the interested reader is directed to SALPE, 40–50, 132–135, where the etymological complexities of the problem are discussed in great detail. Suffice it to say that while Akkadian distinguishes between (i) *rāmu*, "to love," (ii) *rēmu*, "to be merciful, grant a benefaction (?)," and, according to W. von Soden, (iii) *rīmu*, "to give as a gift" ("*Mirjām*—Maria "(Gottes)geschenk," *Ugarit-Forschungen* 2 [1970] 269–72), Aramaic expresses the meaning of all these Akkadian roots by the root *r-ḥ-m*, which conveys and fuses the ideas of willingness and volition inherent in *rāmu* (and the noun *narʾamātu*, "willingness") with the idea of "gift, benefaction" inherent in *rēmu* (and the postulated *rīmu*). Aramaic *rḥmh/ rḥmt*, "a gift" (Akkadian *rēmu/ rēmūtu*) is that which is given "in love, willingly," *brḥmn* (Akkadian *narʾamātu*).

11. See Excursus III, "Volition Clauses."

12. Only divine gifts to man are covered in this study. The rest of the themes enumerated here and the literature in which they are embodied remain to be studied.

13. On the idealized character of the law found in the various cuneiform "codes," see B. Landsberger, "Die babylonischen termini für Gesetz and Recht," *Symbolae ad iura orientis antiqui pertinentes Paulo Koschaker dedicatae* (ed. J. Friedrich et al.; Studia et documenta ad iura orientis antiqui pertinenta 2; Leiden: Brill, 1939) 219–34; J. J. Finkelstein, "Ammiṣaduqa's Edict and the Babylonian 'Law Codes'" *Journal of Cuneiform Studies* 15 (1961) 91–104; W. F. Leemans, "King Hammurapi as Judge," *Symbolae ivridicae et historicae Martino David dedicatae. 2. Iura orientis antiqui* (ed. J. A. Ankum et al.; Leiden: Brill, 1968) 107–29. Consider a particular law: did the children of a debtor sold by their father to his creditor in payment of debts actually go free after three years, as is stipulated by the Code of Hammurapi (No. 117)? One could make a good case that they did not, that the laws here and elsewhere reflected utopian vision rather than social reality.

14. Lieberman's strongest and most articulated statements on this subject were made in conversation. Nonetheless, his *Greek in Jewish Palestine* is filled with striking examples where the actual law as it was lived is found to have been "buried" in an obscure midrash and can only be brought back to life, so to speak, by an illuminating parallel from contemporary Greek papyri. See, for an example, his "Introduction," 1–14.

15. The classic discussion of figurative expressions of joy and sadness in Akkadian and Hebrew is Édouard Dhorme, *L'Emploi mėtaphorique des noms des parties du corps en Hébreu et en Akkadien* (Paris: Geuthner, 1923); for vocabulary relevant here, see 52ff.; for *ṭov* as an expression of joy, see 54 n. 3 and 116.

For *ṭov lev*, "a happy person," see Prov 15:15; for the verbal expression "when his heart was glad" (*ṭov*), see Judg 16:25 (the leaders of the Philistines); 1 Sam 25:36 (Nabal); 2 Sam 13:28 (Amnon). For the expression (*y*)*yṭb lb*(*b*) (in the imperfect), see Judg 18:20, 19:6, 9 (the Levite from Ephraim); 1 Kgs 21:7 (Jezebel to Ahab); Ruth 3:7

(Boaz); Qoh 7:3. For *hetiv lev*, "to give oneself enjoyment, enjoy oneself," see Judg 19:22 (the man from Benjamin); Qoh 11:9 ("Let your heart lead you to enjoyment," NJPS; see H. L. Ginsberg, *Koheleth* [Tel Aviv–Jerusalem, 1961; in Hebrew] ad loc.). For *ṭovah*, "enjoyment," in Qoheleth (especially with the verb *raʾah* [= *rawah]*, "to be sated"), see Ginsberg, *Koheleth*; note Qoh 3:12–13 ("get enjoyment"); 4:8 ("while denying himself enjoyment," NJPS); 5:17 ("that one should eat and drink and get pleasure from all the gains he makes under the sun," NJPS); 6:6.

In later Hebrew, see Ben Sirah 26:3–4 (*libbo ṭov*, "[he is] happy"); 30:15 (*ruaḥ ṭovah*, "a happy spirit"); 30:16 (*ṭuv levav*, "a happy disposition"). The *lev ṭov* mentioned in *m. Avot* 2:9 may simply be "a good/happy disposition"; cf. E. Z. Melamed, "Comments on the Language of *Avot*," *Leshonenu* 20 (1954) 106–11 (in Hebrew) at 108–9.

16. For similar pairings, see Deut 28:47; Esth 5:9; Qoh 11:9.

17. For *raʿ* with the meaning "sad," see the story of Joseph in jail (Genesis 40), where the *zoʿafim*, "worried," of v 6 corresponds to the *penekhem raʿim*, "gloomy," of v 7. Deut 15:10 warns the Israelite who gives to the poor not to perform the act "sadly, grudgingly" (*ve-loʾ yeraʿ levaveka*). Note also Prov 15:15, "All the days of a poor man are sad (*raʿim*)"; Prov 25:20, "Like one who drops vinegar upon a wound (with the Septuagint) is he who sings songs to a sorrowful heart (*lev raʿ*)"; Qoh 9:3, "Men's hearts are filled with sadness (*raʿ*)"; Ben Sirah 38:18, "Sadness of the heart (*roaʿ levav*) prostrates vigor (so the Septuagint)." The *lev raʿ* of *m. Avot* 2:9 may be a "sad disposition"; cf. Melamed's article cited above. For a fundamental discussion of joy and sadness in Qoheleth and Ben Sirah, see H. L. Ginsberg, *Koheleth*, especially 66, 90, 97, 104–5, 128; see also his *Studies in Koheleth* (New York: The Jewish Theological Seminary of America, 1950) 35, 45–46. Many of the improvements of Ginsberg's commentaries on Qoheleth (and the NJPS translation) over those of his predecessors result from his realization that most of the uses of *ṭov* and *raʿ* have more to do with good and bad luck, and especially with happiness and sadness, than with moral good or evil.

18. For the outward expression of inner feelings, see Dhorme, *L'Emploi*, and SALPE, 130–33. On rabbinic uses of *panim*, "face," see Excursus IV, "The Face and Related Matters in Rabbinic Literature."

19. On Arabic idioms and the interrelationship of all these idioms, see Excursus V, "Volition Idioms in Comparative Semitic and Cultural Perspectives."

20. The derivation of the term *beʿal korḥo* from words denoting sadness or sickness was already seen by Saadya; see N. Allony, *Ha-ʾEgron: Kitāb ʾUṣūl al-Shiʿr al-ʿIbrāni* (Jerusalem, 1969) 398. For similar interpretations by modern lexicographers, see J. Levy and H. L. Fleischer, *Neuhebräisches und chaldäisches Wörterbuch über die Talmudim und Midraschim* (Leipzig: Brockhaus, 1876–89) s. v., and E. Ben-Yehuda et al., *Millon ha-Lashon ha-ʿIvrit ha-Yeshanah ve-ha-Ḥadashah: Thesaurus totius hebraitatis et veteris et recentioris* (Jerusalem, 1911–59; New York: Yoselof, 1960) s. v. The interpretation of *be-ṭovato* as "in his joy, willingness" suggested here only tends to confirm ancient and modern interpretations of *beʿal korḥo*.

21. On *k-r-h/ḥ*, see Excursus VI, "The Roots *k-r-h* and *k-r-ḥ*."

22. See Excursus VII, "Royal *kudurrus* and Questions of Sealing."

23. Cf. F. Thureau-Dangin, "Une acte de donation de Mardouk-zâkir-šumi," *Revue d'Assyriologie* 16 (1919) 117–56 at 141–43. Divine donations are rarer than royal donations, but this is probably due to the hazards of excavations. In spite of the rarity of this type of *kudurru*, it should be noted that the *kudurru*-type expression "The god

looked at the king with a joyful eye" is common in divine investitures of kings and is attested as early as the time of Hammurapi; cf. SALPE, 202, and I. J. Gelb, "A New Clay-nail of Ḫammurabi," *Journal of Near Eastern Studies* 7 (1948) 267–71.

24. L. W. King, *Babylonian Boundary-Stones and Memorial-Tablets in the British Museum* (London: British Museum, 1912), no. 36, vol. IV, 120ff. Nabu-apla-iddina reigned in Babylon ca. 887–855 B.C.E.; cf. J. A. Brinkman, *A Political History of Post-Kassite Babylonia, 1158–722 B.C.* (Analecta Orientalia 43; Rome: Pontifical Biblical Institute, 1968). During the reign of Simbar-Shipak (ca. 1026–1029 B.C.E.), the cult figure of the god Shamash was lost. Even though the king was not able to mend this loss, nevertheless he established a cult enclosure before the god, instituted regular offerings, and settled the priest Ekur-shum-ushabshi there. In the reign of one of the following kings, Eulmash-shakin-shumi (ca. 1005–989 B.C.E.), the same priest complained that due to the unstable political situation, "the temple offerings of Shamash has ceased." The king immediately took care of the situation, reestablishing at the same time the legitimate share of the priest in the temple offerings. Meanwhile, "in the reign of Nabu-apla-iddina, Shamash, who had been angry with Akkad and had averted his neck from his people, had mercy and turned his countenance again." This act of divine grace expressed itself in the discovery of a clay model of Shamash by Nabu-nadin-shum, a descendant of the original priestly incumbent, who had been commanded to fashion anew the cult-figure of the god. The text cited above records the joyful reconsecration of the temple with its new cult-figure—the palpable sign that the deity had taken up his dwelling there once more—the reinvestiture of the priest, and the reconfirmation of his share in the temple-offerings.

25. King, *Babylonian Boundary-Stones*, no. 10, vol. IV, 73.

26. In another document of the same collection (King, *Babylonian Boundary-Stones*, no. 28, vol. IV, 105), the priest mentioned above in note 24 appears again, this time in connection with the reconfirmation of ancestral property. It seems that in a previous document, the priest had made a petition before the king concerning ancestral property that had been taken from him. Once again, the king investigates the case, reimburses the present owner, and "with his bright countenance" looks at the plaintiff and bestows the property on him for all time.

27. Most modern biblical scholars resolve problems of narrative coherence by assuming the composite nature of the biblical narrative. Thus, although different in method, source criticism and certain types of midrash attempt to answer similar problems.

28. The term *berit* in this context expresses a divine gift sealed by a covenant rather than a human obligation sealed by a covenant. The semantic range of this term in rabbinic literature is virtually the same as that found in the Bible. A rather felicitous expression used for the first meaning of *berit*—one that is quite appropriate for our passage in the *Sifre*—is the "covenant of grant," a term employed by M. Weinfeld in his study "The Covenant of Grant in the Old Testament and in the Ancient Near East," *JAOS* 90 (1970) 184–203. This essay creatively applies to the Bible some of my work on the terminology of *kudurrus*, Neo-Assyrian royal grants, and Aramaic analogues. Both my study and his article—later expanded in his excellent book, *Deuteronomy and the Deuteronomic School* (Oxford: Clarendon, 1972; rpt. Winona Lake, Indiana: Eisenbrauns, 1992)—owe much to Arno Poebel's *Das appositionell bestimmte Pronomen der I. Pers. Sing. in den west-semitischen Inschriften und im Alten Testament* (Assyriological Studies 3; Chicago: University of Chicago Press, 1932) 53–70.

29. Although *ben bayit* with the meaning of *major domo* is typically rabbinic, H. L. Ginsberg has pointed out that the expression is found with its later meaning in Gen 15:3, in "Abram's 'Damascene' Steward," *Bulletin of the American Schools of Oriental Research* 200 (1970) 31–32.

30. The text is quoted from H. S. Horovitz, *Siphre d'be Rab. I. Siphre ad Numeros* (Corpus Tannaiticum. III. Continens Veterum Doctorum ad Pentateuchum Interpretationes Halachicas. 3; Leipzig: Fock, 1917; rpt. Jerusalem: Wahrmann, 1966) 134–35, where the relevant parallels are noted. Although this parable follows the discussion of Rabbi Ishmael and Rabbi Nathan concerning the meaning of *hinne* in Num 18:8, "I hereby (*hinne*) give you charge of My gifts, all the sacred donations of the Israelites" in the *Sifre* (p. 134), it is not specifically attributed to either authority. Later, however, the parable, with a slightly different introduction, is clearly attributed to Rabbi Ishmael (p. 143). The significance of this attribution will become clear in the course of the discussion.

31. The various modes of expressing the nuance "I hereby" in Saadya's Arabic translation of the Bible, the Septuagint, Hebrew deeds from the Dead Sea area, and Arabic documents need to be surveyed; for the time being, see SALPE, 32 n. 2.

32. Cf. *b. Shabbat* 63a. Modern scholarship has begun to realize that talmudic scriptural interpretation was not completely midrashic (i. e., fanciful) in nature, and that the rabbis displayed an excellent sense for the simple meaning of words and texts (cf. the important study of this subject in Lieberman's *Hellenism in Jewish Palestine*, 41–62). They often correctly interpreted, even to the satisfaction of our own modern criteria, biblical words and phrases by rendering them into contemporary Mishnaic Hebrew (cf. A. Bendavid's monumental study, *Biblical Hebrew and Mishnaic Hebrew* [2 vols.; Tel-Aviv: Dvir, 1967–71; in Hebrew]). Nevertheless, one should not equate the rabbinic use of the term *peshaṭ* with its medieval and modern definition, i. e., the simple meaning of the text based on linguistic context and cultural and historical realia. As some scholars have pointed out, many a scriptural interpretation described by the rabbis as *peshaṭ* is hardly different from what we would consider *derash* (cf. W. Bacher, *Midrashic Terminology* [trans. A. Z. Rabinowitz; Tel-Aviv, 1922/23; in Hebrew] 269 n. 3; Heinemann, *Methods of the Aggadah*, note 10 to chapter one, citing *b. Ketubbot* 101b).

Furthermore, as S. Lieberman has pointed out to me, for the rabbis the allegorical interpretation of the Song of Songs as a dialogue of love between God and Israel was the only *peshaṭ*. The use of the Song in the local bars of the time, which most moderns might consider much closer to the original intent of the writer, was not *peshaṭ* for the rabbis at all; it was simply so much blasphemy. Now, if the rabbis considered the simple meaning of the Song of Songs to be the dialogue of love between God and Israel, what then was their midrashic interpretation? In all probability it was the esoteric one, which was more concerned with the mystical contemplation of the divine *soma*, than with a dialogue of love between God and His people. For the mystical midrash on the Song of Songs, cf. Gershom Scholem, *Jewish Gnosticism, Merkabah Mysticism, and Talmudic Tradition* (New York: The Jewish Theological Seminary of America, 1965); see especially Lieberman's appendix on the *Mishnat Shir ha-Shirim*, 118ff.

33. Exactly the same type of paraphrase is attributed to Rabbi Ishmael in a commentary on Num 3:12, *va-ʾani hinne laqaḥti ʾet-ha-leviyyim*, "(The Lord spoke to Moses, saying:) 'I hereby take the Levites (from among the Israelites . . . the Levites shall be mine).'" In M. A. Mirkin, ed., *Bemidbar Rabbah* (Tel Aviv: "Yavneh" Publishing House,

1959) at Parasha 3, 4, Rabbi Ishmael spells out the volitional overtones inherent in the divine pronouncement dedicating the Levites to Himself by means of this paraphrase: *va-ʾani* = *beṣimḥah* ("I" = "joyfully"); *hinne* = *beraṣon* ("behold" = "willingly"). Notice that in the paraphrase used in the *Sifre*, the interpretive words *simḥah* and *raṣon* are reversed: there, *beraṣon* renders *ʾani*, while *simḥah* interprets *hinne*. This may be due to faulty textual transmission, but it is more probably because Rabbi Ishmael was concerned with the volitional solemnity of the phrase as a whole and used two interchangeable terms, *simḥah* and *raṣon*, for that purpose.

This method of paraphrase is also found in the *Sifre* to Deut 26:10. The declaration of the pilgrim offering his first fruits, "And now, see (*ve-ʿattah hinne*) I have brought the first of the produce of the soil, that You, O Lord, have given me," is paraphrased thus: *ve-ʿattah* = *miyyad* ("and now" = "immediately"); *hinne* = *besimḥah* ("behold" = "joyfully"); *heveʾti* = *misheli* ("I hereby have brought" = "of my own [goods]"); quoted from L. Finkelstein, *Sifre Devarim. Siphre ad Deuteronomium* (Breslau, 1935; rpt. New York: The Jewish Theological Seminary of America, 1969) 319. Once again, the term *simḥah* in paraphrases of declarations of donation seems to have clear volitional overtones. However, in this context, *besimḥah* is not used as the complement of *raṣon*, "willingness, intent," as it was in the passages studied above, but with *miyyad*, "immediately." This would seem to indicate that the term has an even wider range of meaning than simple volition. In some contexts, *simḥah*, used as the synonym of *raṣon*, indicates the inner state of mind that motivates the donation. In other contexts, *besimḥah*, used as a synonym of *miyyad* or *bizrizut*, "with alacrity," seems to indicate the outward manner in which the intention is translated into deed.

The use of joy as an expression of inner, uncoerced willingness and of alacrity/immediacy as its outer and concrete expression was known to Philo, as can be seen in "The Special Laws": "From all this it is clear that the law invests the priests with the dignity and honours of royalty. Thus, he [the lawgiver Moses] commands that tribute should be given from every part of a man's property as to a ruler, and the way in which the tribute is paid is a complete contrast to the spirit in which the cities of the Gentiles make their payments to their potentates. *The cities pay under compulsion and reluctantly and groan under the burden* . . . and when they discharge the appointed dues and assessments they do so without regard to the time limits allowed. *But our people pay gladly and cheerfully* (*chairontes*). They *anticipate the demand, abridge the time limits. . . . And so at each of the yearly seasons they make their contributions . . . with a zeal and a readiness which needs no prompting*" (1.141–44; Philo Judaeus, *Works* [trans. F. H. Colson and G. H. Whittaker; Loeb Classical Library; London: William Heinemann, 1928–1962] 7.181; my italics).

34. Cf. P. Benoît, J. T. Milik, and R. de Vaux, *Les Grottes de Murabbaʿât* (Discoveries in the Judaean Desert 2; Oxford: Clarendon, 1961) 105, 132.

35. The deed is a Tiberian marriage contract from the year 1035 C.E., published by S. Assaf, "Ancient Deeds from the Genizah from Palestine, Egypt, and North Africa," *Tarbiz* 9 (1938) 11–34, 196–218 at 24.

36. For a comprehensive investigation of these clauses, based on a wide range of unpublished Genizah manuscripts, see M. Friedman, *Jewish Marriage Contracts in Palestine: A Cairo Genizah Study* (New York: The Jewish Theological Seminary of America, 1980–81). Friedman has shown that these terms were common in marriage contracts of the Palestinian scribal tradition. The terms, however, are difficult and

open to a variety of interpretations. Contextually, it is clear that *la ʿaṣiv* can only mean "not coerced" or "without mental reservation."

Friedman connects this use of the root *ʿṣb* with one seemingly found in 1 Kgs 1:6, *ve-loʾ-ʿaṣavo ʾaviv,* where the context demands something like "his father never constrained him." Instead of emending *ʿaṣavo* to *ʿaṣaro* on the basis of the Greek, Friedman posits the existence of a Hebrew root **ʿṣb*, cognate to Arabic *ghaṣaba,* "to constrain," distinct from normal Hebrew *ʿṣb,* cognate of the Arabic *ghaḍiba,* "to be angry, vexed." (A similar interpretation was suggested by G. R. Driver in his study, "Supposed Arabisms in the OT," *JBL* 55 [1936] 101–20 and accepted by J. A. Montgomery, *Kings* [International Critical Commentary; Edinburgh: T. & T. Clark, 1951] 83.) At first glance, this interpretation is compelling. However, further investigation raises several objections. First, while the derivation of the term *ʿaṣiv* from a cognate of the Arabic for "constrain," rather than from the ordinary Hebrew term for "sadness," may seemingly solve the problem of *ʿaṣiv,* it does nothing to solve that of the closely related *raʿiṣ, raṣiṣ,* and *kaʿis.* But it seems artificial to separate *ʿaṣiv* from these other expressions of sadness, especially since the use of the metaphor of sadness as an expression of inner reservation or of lack of full mental agreement is well established. Secondly, while *ʿaṣiv* could be interpreted as a passive form of a transitive root **ʿṣb,* "to constrain," the closely related phrase [*loʾ*] *ʿoṣevet ve-loʾ ʿagumat nefesh,* found in the volition clause of a widow's quitclaim (Assaf, *Tarbiz* 9 [1938] 211, line 40), can only be interpreted as "[not] sad and not doleful of spirit," i. e., without mental reservation and in full control of mental functions. The active form *ʿoṣevet* cannot mean "constraining." Therefore, it seems wiser to assume that *ʿaṣiv* is nothing more than a passive form of the regular verb for sadness, exactly as are its synonyms *kaʿis, raʿiṣ,* and *raṣiṣ,* and conveys the idea of inner reservation and *inner* constraint. Furthermore, virtually the same juxtaposition of expressions of joy/willingness based on the common Semitic root *ṭ-y-b,* with expressions of sadness and especially *anger,* is found both in the Hebrew–Aramaic legal tradition reflected in the Genizah formulary and in the Arabic legal tradition preserved in the famous lexicon the *Taj al-ʿArūs,* where the legal idiom *ṭābat nafsuhu,* "his soul was joyful, he was willing" (= Aramaic *be-ṭivute*) is defined negatively as *ghayr karāha wa-la ghaḍab,* "without disgust and *without anger*" (= Aramaic *la kaʿis,* "without anger"). The use of disgust/sadness and of *anger* as expressions of mental reservation, in similar legal contexts, could hardly be closer. The historical implications of this remarkable correspondence between the Aramaic–Hebrew and Arabic idioms have yet to be investigated.

37. See L. Finkelstein, "On the Phraseology of the Tannaim," *Tarbiz* 20 (1950) 96–106 at 101–2, for a basic discussion of this section, its difficulties, parallel traditions in rabbinic literature, a wide range of traditional interpretations and emendations, and a suggestive solution that was of inestimable heuristic value for our own investigation, not only of this passage, but of the whole subject of *simḥah* and *raṣon.* Rabbi Jonathan *Siphre . . . ad Numeros* (ed. Horovitz), p. 145; *Sifre Zutta* (ed. H. S. Horovitz et al.; Lodz: Masorah, 1929) p. 297.

38. The *Sifre Zutta* uses the more common method of introducing a rabbinic *peshaṭ*: the biblical word is *ʾeno ʾella,* "none other than," the mishnaic word (cf. Lieberman, *Hellenism in Jewish Palestine,* 49). This method is functionally identical with the paraphrase method discussed above. See Lieberman, *Siphre Zutta* (*The Midrash of Lydda*) (New York: The Jewish Theological Seminary of America, 1968) for a discussion of the historical origins of the book and its often distinctive terminology.

39. *Sifre . . . ad Numeros* (ed. Horovitz), p. 145. The meaning of *miṣvah* as a "gift commanded by God to be given to the clergy" was already seen by Ben-Yehuda (s. v.), who cites Neh 13:5, "where formerly they had put the cereal-offerings, incense, vessels, and tithes of grain, wine and oil, *which were given by command to the Levites* (*miṣvat ha-leviyyim*)." The passage in the *Sifre*, however, was overlooked. For an interesting semantic parallel, compare the double meaning of *ḥoq*, "command" and "commanded share." However, caution is still in order; H. L. Ginsberg has pointed out to me the possibility that in Nehemiah the word *miṣvah* may be a scribal error for *manah*, "portion" (cf. Neh 8:10, 12). The meaning "gift" seems clear in the *Sifre*, however, and its presence there certainly lends support to the received reading in Nehemiah.

The word *miṣvah* with the meaning "donation commanded by God" also seems to appear in the *Sifre Zutta* (ed. Horovitz) 293. On the verse in Num 18:8, "The Lord spoke further to Aaron: I hereby give you charge," we find the following comment: *le᾿Aharon ne᾿emrah ha-miṣvah*, "It was to Aaron [and not to Korah?] that this *miṣvah* was said." The word *miṣvah* here is not an obligation, but a grant based on divine command.

40. The rare expression *qanah ve-natan* is most plausibly taken as a hendiadys with the meaning "to grant as final property." Cf. E. Z. Melamed, "Hendiadys in the Bible," *Tarbiz* 16 (1945) 173–89. There is every reason to believe that this syntactical construction was no less frequent in rabbinic literature than in the Bible; the subject deserves a comprehensive study.

41. Finkelstein, "On the Phraseology," 101–2. Finkelstein sensed the opposition between *besimḥah* and *btḥlh* and realized the impossibility of interpreting *btḥlh* as "in the beginning." Simply on the basis of context he appreciated that the term must mean something like "out of sorrow or anger," i. e., not wholeheartedly. In light of the comparative evidence marshaled here concerning the equivalence of joy with willingness, and sadness with mental reservation, Finkelstein's emendation *toholah* (cf. Job 4:18), although ingenious, is not necessary. It was this heuristically most important observation that stimulated our research on the subject.

42. Although etymology is hardly more important than meaning derived from context, nevertheless, if an etymology has to be provided, Speiser's oral suggestion that *btḥlh* may mean something like "in pain" (from *ḥ-y-l*) should be given consideration. It is supported somewhat by the Oxford manuscript of the *Sifre* which reads *btḥylh*, which, one could argue, is derived from the root *ḥ-y-l*.

43. *B. Berakhot* 5a. Did the author of this midrash read: "*ki leqaḥ* = 'that which you received'—(*be*)*ṭov*(*ah*) = 'joyfully/willingly' have I given it to you?"

44. See *b. Bava Batra* 47b and SALPE, 149.

EXCURSUS I.
ANCIENT NEAR EASTERN AND RABBINIC LITERATURE

Significant work on cuneiform-rabbinic interconnections began in the first decades of this century with Moses Schorr; see his *Urkunden des altbabylonischen Zivil- und Prozessrechts* (Vorderasiatische Bibliothek 5; Leipzig: Hinrichs, 1913) 185 (on *zibburit*); 291 (on *ṣon barzel*); 293 (on *nedunya*); and his review of J. Kohler and A. Ungnad, *Assyrische Rechtsurkunden im Umschrift und Übersetzung*, in *Zeitschrift der Deutsche Morgenländische Gesellschaft* 68 (1914) 625–35 at 629. Other early workers include H. Pick (his pamphlet *Assyriches und Talmudisches: Kulturgeschichtliche und lexikalische Notizen* [Berlin: Calvary, 1903] is quoted by D. B. Weisberg, "Some Observations on Late Babylonian Texts and Rabbinic Literature," *HUCA* 39 [1968] 71–80 at 75) and J. Augapfel (*Babylonische Rechtsurkunden aus der Regierungszeit Artaxerxes I. und Darius II.* [Kaiserliche Akademie der Wissenschaften. Philosophisch-historische Klasse. Denkschrift 59.III; Vienna: Hölder, 1917] 2, 20, 23, 28, 34, 48, 51, 88, and passim).

Subsequent generations have witnessed a slow but ever growing preoccupation with the Near Eastern background of rabbinic law and lore. The works of J. J. Rabinowitz are noteworthy: *Jewish Law: Its Influence on the Development of Legal Institutions* (New York: Bloch, 1956) and especially "Jewish Elements in Babylonian Formulas of the Persian Period," *Sefer ʾAssaf* (ed. U. Cassuto et al.; Jerusalem: Mosad Ha-Rav Kook, 1953) 433–43 (in Hebrew). Although the pan-Judaic bias of these works must be discounted, Rabinowitz has correctly pointed out many an important rabbinic-cuneiform parallel. E. Y. Kutscher's work on the Near Eastern background of talmudic and Elephantine legal terms was an important breakthrough in this area (for references, see the bibliography). The same can be said of R. Yaron's various books and monographs on Elephantine law (for references, see the bibliography). Also important is A. Leo Oppenheim, "A Note on *Ṣôn Barzel*," *Israel Exploration Journal* 5 (1955) 89–92. J. J. Finkelstein, in "*Ana bīt emim šasū*," *Revue d'Assyriologie* 61 (1967) 127–36, convincingly demonstrates the light that Assyriology and critical studies of rabbinic literature can shed on each other. Many of the studies of S. E. Loewenstamm contain valuable observations on the relationship between the cuneiform and rabbinic literatures. This is true not merely of his various contributions to the *Encyclopaedia Biblica*.

Entsiklopedyah Mikra'it. Encyclopædia Biblica (Jerusalem: Mosad Bialik, 1954–88; in Hebrew) on biblical topics, but also his important article on the possible Mesopotamian background of certain aspects of rabbinic mysticism, "What is above and what is below, what is before and what is after," *Yehezkel Kaufmann Jubilee Volume: Studies in Bible and Jewish Religion* (ed. M. Haran; Jerusalem: Magnes, 1960) 112–21 (in Hebrew); now translated in Loewenstamm's *Comparative Studies in Biblical and Ancient Oriental Literatures* (Alter Orient und Altes Testament 204; Kevelaer and Neukirchen-Vluyn: Verlag Butzon und Bercker and Neukirchener Verlag, 1980) 122–36; this volume also reprints and translates various of Loewenstamm's articles and provides a full bibliography of his work.

Among younger scholars, the work of S. A. Kaufman is especially valuable. His 1970 Yale doctoral dissertation, published as *The Akkadian Influences on Aramaic and the Development of the Aramaic Dialects* (Assyriological Studies 19; Chicago: The Oriental Institute, 1974), has much useful material on the lexicographical interrelationships between Akkadian and the Talmud. Even more germane is his article "Akkadian and Babylonian Aramaic: New Examples of Mutual Elucidation," *Leshonenu* 36 (1971) 28–33 (in Hebrew). Although S. Greengus's thesis on the Akkadian background of Elephantine marriage law has unfortunately remained unpublished, it is cited extensively by B. Porten in his *Archives from Elephantine* (Berkeley: University of California Press, 1968), viii, 206, 212, 253 n. 39, 254 n. 40, 256 and passim. Greengus's article, "The Old Babylonian Marriage Contract," *JAOS* 89 (1969) 505–32, contains many an illuminating remark on Akkadian-rabbinic interconnections in the realm of marriage law; cf. pp. 517 (concerning positively formulated marriage declarations), 518 (concerning formulas of divorce at Elephantine), 522 (concerning the participation of the wife in the marriage declaration). Note also the paper by D. B. Weisberg mentioned above and B. A. Levine's study "*Mulūgu/ Melûg*: The Origins of a Talmudic Legal Institution," *JAOS* 88 (1968) 271–85.

Although most of Saul J. Lieberman's comparative material was derived from the Greco-Roman world, he often stressed the "hoary antiquity" of this material. See, e. g., *Hellenism in Jewish Palestine* (New York: The Jewish Theological Seminary of America, 1950), 75–76, where he derives the word *halakha* from the Aramaic *halak*, "tax," and ultimately from the Akkadian *ilku*, with the same meaning; or his use of cuneiform literature in "Afterlife in Early Rabbinic Literature," *Harry Austryn Wolfson Jubilee Volume* (ed. S. Lieberman; Jerusalem: American Academy for Jewish Research, 1965) 2.495–532.

If one cannot as yet speak of a school of Assyriologically oriented talmudic studies, it would not be rash to say that such a school is beginning to emerge. The benefits of a comparative approach for both disciples can hardly be exaggerated. Cf. SALPE, 193–94.

EXCURSUS II. AKKADIAN AND ARAMAIC

Some scholars in discussing SALPE suggested that sufficient attention was not paid to the possible influence of Aramaic language, Aramaic legal terminology, and Aramaic-speaking scribes' praxis on Neo-Babylonian and Neo-Assyrian legal documents. So, e.g., R. Yaron, *Revue biblique* 77 (1970) 415–17, and E. Y. Kutscher in his important survey, "Aramaic," *Current Trends in Linguistics. 6. Linguistics in South West Asia and North Africa* (ed. T. A. Sebeok et al.; The Hague, Mouton, 1970) 347–412; reprinted in his *Hebrew and Aramaic studies* (ed. Z. Ben Ḥayyim et al.; Jerusalem: Magnes, 1977) 90–115.

The emphasis in SALPE on Akkadian influence on Aramaic rather than the Aramaic influence on Akkadian was more a matter of method than of oversight: "The cuneiform element [in the Aramaic legal formulary] is much more decisive than Kutscher [in his early studies] assumed. In all probability, the Aramaic formulary is based, on the whole, on actual cuneiform models, many of which still have to be isolated. This is not, however, to deny the creative role of the Aramaic scribes. But before we can speak about indigenous Aramaic legal elements, we must carefully determine whether or not such elements are not actually cuneiform in origin" (SALPE, 9). A similar method underlies the careful study of S. A. Kaufman, *The Akkadian Influences on Aramaic* (discussed above, Excursus I): "It is the belief of the author that the [influence of Aramaic on Akkadian], though of great import, can only be undertaken after the results of the first are known, though indeed the final synthesis must consider both processes together" (p. 2).

Moreover, Aramaic influence on the terminology of late Neo-Babylonian documents is discussed in SALPE (187–88 n. 4), in connection with the terms *yaritu*, "heir," and *murruqu*, "to clear (of a claim)." Further, I suggested that the influence of Aramaic-speaking scribes was not simply limited to the introduction of Aramaic loanwords into Akkadian deeds: one of the unique characteristics of the Elephantine formulary is the freedom with which the scribes creatively bring together Akkadian terms and phrases from disparate contexts and from various periods, fusing them into entirely new patterns. This is clearly seen in the case of the common Elephantine cluster of sale terminology: *ṭyb lbby*, "my heart is satisfied (with the price)"; *rḥqt mnk*, "I (hereby) remove myself from you (i. e., relinquish my rights in your favor)"; *ʾnt šlyṭ b-*, "you are (now) in control/owner of (the property)." The first usage is found only in Old Babylonian deeds (ca. 1800–1700 B.C.E.); the second is known only from Nuzi (ca. 1500 B.C.E.); the third is Neo-Babylonian (ca. 600 B.C.E.). In this particular instance, the fusion of disparate elements may not be of great juridical significance and may simply reflect the tendency of the scribes to inflate their documents with tautologous terms in an often counterproductive attempt to insure the inviolability of the transaction. (Compare the talmudic expression *ʾrkbyh ʾtry rkšy*, "He caused it [the deed] to ride on two horses [going in opposite directions]," *y. Bava Batra* 8:5, 16b [top], *y. Qiddushin* 1:5, 60c [bottom].) Yet, one could argue that the Aramaic-speaking scribes have, in this case, creatively articulated the underlying interdependence of the ideas of payment (*ṭyb lbby*), relinquishment (*rḥqt*), and ownership (*šlyṭ*)—a legal idea inherent in cuneiform law but rarely spelled out clearly (cf. SALPE, 177–79).

In my earlier book I discussed another such case, investigating the process by which the Elephantine scribes fused together a whole series of disparate and negatively formulated cuneiform elements into a positive and extremely clear definition of the concept of ownership, a step the tradition-bound Akkadian scribes were apparently unable to take (SALPE 41 n. 2).

I am now more and more convinced that the Akkadian formulary used during the Seleucid and Arsacid periods—a formulary that differs in so many ways from that used in the Neo-Babylonian and Persian periods (see O. Krückmann, *Babylonische Rechts- und Verwaltungs-Urkunden aus der Zeit Alexanders und der Diadochen* [Weimar: Hof, 1931])—probably reflects the influence of Aramaic-speaking scribes and their praxis. The problem is a complicated one—there are suggestive parallels with the later Jewish deeds of the Dead Sea area—and deserves an independent study. See the end of Excursus III.

Excursus III. Volition Clauses

The earliest examples of expressions of joy to indicate volition come from Old Babylonian deeds from Susa (ca. early 19th century B.C.E.), where the clause *ina ṭūbātišu ina narʾamātišu*, literally "in his joy [Akkadian *ṭūb* = Hebrew *ṭov*], in his love [Akkadian *rāmu* = Hebrew/ Aramaic *rḥm*]," is rendered idiomatically by almost all interpreters as "of his own free will and voluntarily" (so CAD, I/J, 12; *AHw*, 745, gives for *narʾamātu* "Freiwilligkeit"; in his review of some volumes of *Archives royales de Mari* in *Orientalia* 28 [1959] 314–17 at 316, he renders *ṭūbu* "freiwillige Handlung"). This clause introduces most deeds of gift, many deeds of sale, and other transactions as well. For a detailed discussion of the problem, see SALPE, 128–41. The same metaphor of joy/volition, *ina ṭūbi libbim*, appears slightly later in deeds from the northwest Mesopotamian city of Mari (ca. 18th century B.C.E.; cf. SALPE, 137–38).

The metaphoric use of joy as an expression of will appears somewhat later in the north Syrian city of Ugarit (ca. 15th century B.C.E.; cf. SALPE, 129, 202) in the form *ina ḫūd libbi*, literally "in the joy of heart" (cf. Hebrew *beḥedvat libbo*); the phrase is attested once.

After a period of absence spanning centuries, exactly the same idiom, *ina ḫūd libbišu*, surfaces again in many Neo-Babylonian sales of mobilia and in most so-called "dialogue documents." In the very latest cuneiform legal formulary, the one used during the Seleucid and Arsacid periods, the use of the joy/volition clause was extended to all types of transactions, including the sale of mobilia.

The seemingly strange reactivation of archaic terms of volition after a hiatus of centuries is one of the salient characteristics of the Seleucid formulary. Furthermore, the problem is not merely inner-Assyriological but cross-cultural as well. Compare, in form, function, complements, and context, the unmistakable identity of the Elephantine phrase *ṭyb lbby*, "my heart is satisfied" (i.e., "I am quit") and the Old Babylonian legal term *libbašu ṭāb*. The Old Babylonian term does not only disappear—it is replaced by various synonyms in later periods before it reappears in Elephantine documents of the fifth century B.C.E. and in other Egyptian documents as well. For some tentative explanations of the problem, compare the comments of B. A. Levine, "On the Origins of the Aramaic Legal Formulary at Elephantine," *Christianity, Judaism and Other Greco-Roman Cults. Studies for Morton Smith. Part Three. Judaism before 70* (ed.

Jacob Neusner; Leiden: Brill, 1975) 37–54 at 44ff., and my attempt at a solution in SALPE, 201.

In addition to the conscious or unconscious archaizing adduced there, one may suggest, with due reservation, that the later the literature—be it legal, religious, or literary—the greater the stress on inner states of mind, and in legal contexts in particular, the great the constitutive importance of intent and volition. The classic example of this process is the radical rabbinic reinterpretation of the biblical cultic stipulation that certain sacrifices be offered *lirṣonkem*: the original meaning of the phrase is that the sacrifice will be accepted by the Lord "on your behalf," but the rabbis contend that the stipulation rather means that the sacrifice will be accepted only if "*your will*" is present. (Contrast most ancient and modern translations, which follow the older interpretation, with the *Sifra* to Lev 1:3, which takes *raṣon* in its later Hebrew meaning "will.")

The growing popularity of this volition clause during the Seleucid period and the ubiquity of similar clauses in the deeds of Murabbaʿat, deeds that are certainly as old as the Seleucid period (which is to say that they date from sometime during the Maccabean era), is historically quite suggestive. However, since one swallow does not make a spring, it should be noted that in each case (i.e., the Seleucid and Murabbaʿat formularies), the terms of volition (Akkadian *ina ḫūd libbi*; Aramaic *brʿwt npšy*) do not appear in isolation, but in virtually identical clusters or configurations composed of elements found elsewhere in older cuneiform documents, though never in the same complex configuration as in the two formularies under discussion. The elements are: "I sell the field (a) 'be it more or less' (Akkadian *lītir limṭi*, Aramaic *ḥsr ʾw ytyr*); (b) 'of my own free will' (see above); (c) 'at full price' (Akkadian *ana šīm gamir*, Aramaic *dmyn gmryn*); (d) 'for all time' (Akkadian *ana ūm ṣāti*, Aramaic *lʿlm*). See J. T. Milik, "Un contract juif de l'an 134 après Jésus-Christ," *Revue biblique* 61 (1954) 182–91 at 183; and his "Deux documents inédits du désert de Juda," *Biblica* 38 (1957) 245–68 at 258–62. The virtual identity of these configurations is hardly fortuitous and is a strong indicator of some historical interconnection; the whole subject deserves a special investigation.

EXCURSUS IV. THE FACE AND RELATED MATTERS IN RABBINIC LITERATURE

Rabbinic literature employs the concrete expressions of a "smiling face" (i.e., a happy mood) and a "gloomy face" (i.e., a sad or angry mood) to contrast the various emotional tonalities of different types of sacred literature:

פנים של אימה למקרא פנים בינוניות למשנה פנים שוחקות לתלמוד פנים מסבירות לאגדה

The face (i.e., the mood) of Scripture is fearsome; the face of the Mishnah is intermediate (i.e., mild, benign); the face of the Talmud is a smiling one, while the face of the *aggadah* is radiant (*Soferim* 16:3).

Furthermore, not only were contrasting genres of literature characterized by a wide range of facial expressions, but the inner moods of the divine person Himself—His joy and His sadness—were boldly described in a similar fashion. Compare, for example, the following passage from the *Pesiqta Rabbati* (quoted from M. Friedmann, ed., *Midrash Pesiqta Rabbati: Midrasch für den Fest-cyclus und die ausgezeichneten Sabbathe* [Vienna: Kaiser, 1880; rpt. Tel Aviv, 1963] § 21, p. 101):

אמר ר׳ לוי בפנים הרבה נראה להם הקדוש ברוך הוא בסיני: בפנים זעופות בפנים הדופות בפנים מוריקות בפנים שמחות בפנים משחקות בפנים מסבירות. כיצד. בשעה שהיה מראה להם פורענותם של רשעים היה מראה להם בפנים זועפות בפנים הדופות בפנים מוריקות. וכשהיה מראה להם מתן שכרם של צדיקים לעתיד לבא היה מראה להם בפנים שמחות בפנים [משחקות] בפנים מסבירות.

Rabbi Levi said: "The Holy One, Blessed Be He, revealed Himself to them at Sinai with many faces: with an angry face, with a downcast face, with a dour face, with a joyful face, with a smiling face, and with a radiant face. How? When He showed them the punishment (awaiting) the wicked, He did so with an angry, downcast, dour face; but when He showed them the reward (awaiting) the just in the World to Come, it was with a happy, [smiling], radiant face."

See the *Mekhilta de-Rabbi Yishmael* (ed. H. S. Horovitz and I. A. Rabin, Frankfurt am Main: Kauffmann, 1931; rpt. Jerusalem: Bamberger and

Wahrmann, 1960) BeShalaḥ, §2, pp. 162–63, for the related expressions *panim meʾirot* and *panim ḥashekhot*.

In the paper it is argued that the smile that reflects the inner joy of the individual and the frown that expresses his inner sadness have striking legal implications: the smile is a poetic but nonetheless legal expression of willingness, while the frown, as the outward reflection of inner sadness, is a dramatic indication of unwillingness and inner reservation. An understanding of the metaphorical use of the idioms of joy and sadness may help us explain several beautiful but hitherto not satisfactorily explained rabbinic expressions: (a) *ʾamot soḥaqot*, literally "smiling cubits," i.e., "generous cubits," and *ʾamot ʿaṣevot*, literally, "sad/frowning cubits," i.e., "niggardly cubits"; cf. *b. ʿErubin* 3b; (b) *ṭefaḥ ʿaṣev*, literally "a sad handbreadth," i.e., "a niggardly handbreadth," and *ṭefaḥ sameaḥ*, literally "a happy handbreadth," i.e., "a generous handbreadth"; cf. *b. ʿErubin* 3b and *b. Sukkah* 7a. Rabbenu Hananel, in commenting on *ṭefaḥ ʿaṣev* in *b. ʿErubin* 4a, mentions (c) *ʾeṣbaʿot soḥaqot*, literally "smiling fingers," i.e., "generous fingers." I would suggest, with all due reservation, that the inner attributes of generosity or niggardliness expressed by the joy or sadness of the subject were metaphorically transferred to his outer agents, his handbreadth or fingers. Thus, a measure measured with a smile—happily and willingly—engendered the metaphorical expression a "smiling (i. e., generous) measure." Similarly, the generosity expressed by the idiom "smiling fingers" is but a poetic transference of the inner frame of mind of the human subject to his external agents, in this case, his fingers.

EXCURSUS V. VOLITION IDIOMS IN COMPARATIVE SEMITIC AND CULTURAL PERSPECTIVE

Arabic has volition idioms comparable to those discussed in the paper in earlier attested Semitic languages. According to Lane, *Arabic-English Lexicon*, s. v. *ṭ-y-b*, the clause *ṭābat nafsuhu* means "he was happy, cheerful," and, by extension, the expression *ṭābat nafsuhu biʾl-shayʾi* means "he granted/conceded/gave the thing liberally, without constraint and without anger." Here Lane quotes from the famous Arabic lexicon, the *Taj al-ʿArūs*, which reads *ghayr karāha* (literally "without disgust") *wa-la ghaḍab* (literally "without anger"); the significance of the equation between the Arabic *la ghaḍab* and the Aramaic *la kaʿis*, a phrase found in Genizah documents, is discussed in Excursus VI.

The same metaphoric equivalence of joy with willingness and lack of constraint also applies to the Arabic noun *ṭībatu*, "joy": *faʿaltu dhālika bi-ṭībati nafsin*, "I did that of my own free will; willingly; not being constrained by anyone" (Lane). Even more important is the fact that these expressions of joy/willingness are not merely attested to by the lexica, but are found alongside of more common expressions of volition in actual legal documents. Cf. Wakin, *Documents in Islamic Law*, 93, who cites the expression *ṭībatan bi-dhālika anfusahum*, "(they did) this willingly/ liberally"; other examples are given from A. Grohmann, *Arabic Papyri in the Egyptian Museum. I. Protocols and Legal Texts* (Cairo: Egyptian Library Press, 1934) 200, and other sources.

Thus, the Akkadian, Hebrew, Aramaic, and Arabic sources all know and employ in virtually identical legal contexts the metaphor of joy as an expression of uncoerced willingness: Akkadian *ina ṭūb/ḫūd libbišu* = Hebrew *beṭovato* = Aramaic (*min reʿuti*) *u-min ṭivuti*, "(of my own will) and gladly/freely" (cf. S. Assaf, "Ancient Deeds from the Genizah from Palestine, Egypt, and North Africa," *Tarbiz* 9 [1938] 11–34, 196–218, at 24) = Arabic *bi-ṭībati nafsin* / *ṭībatan bi-dhālika anfusahum.*

While the philological data seem incontrovertible, the historical relationship between these various idioms is somewhat more complicated. The secondary nuance of willingness that these various Semitic terms for happiness convey is in all probability a natural and spontaneous development within each language. The same process happened independently in other languages; compare the English idiom "I would be glad/happy (i. e., willing) to help you." While the idiomatic equivalence of joy with willingness may be simply a spontaneous development in each of the Semitic languages studied here, nevertheless the specific use of these idioms as actual legal terms in similarly structured documents is hardly a matter of coincidence, but must be interpreted as a sign of mutual interdependence.

Furthermore, I would agree with J. Schacht (cited in n. 4) that a similar close relationship existed between the Akkadian and Arabic formularies. I would strongly suggest that the Aramaic formulary used by Aramaic-writing, Arabic-speaking Nabateans functioned as one of several bridges between the Neo-Babylonian and pre-Islamic common-law formulary.

Thus, from a linguistic point of view, the interesting equivalences between these roots used in similar, if not identical, formulaic contexts cannot be included under the category of loanwords or under the category of loan-translations, since each language possessed the root as part of its basic linguistic stock. What is borrowed is the specific employment of etymologically and functionally identical idioms within the foreign grid of the legal document—a structure created in the older cuneiform world and borrowed by Arameans, Jews, and Arabs. What is borrowed is *a function and a position within a foreign cultural structure,* but not the root or even its meaning. If the process involves neither loanword nor loan-translation, may we legitimately speak of "loan-function"?

EXCURSUS VI. THE ROOTS *K-R-H* AND *K-R-Ḥ*

Functionally, and even etymologically, there seems to be little doubt concerning the equivalence of Hebrew *beʿal korḥo* with a variety of Arabic idioms, *kurhan, karhan, ʿalā kurhin, ʿalā karāhiyatihī*. All of these are derived from the root *k-r-h*, "to feel disgust," and the noun *karāha*, "hatred, aversion; antipathy, disgust and loathing" (cf. H. Wehr, *A Dictionary of Modern Written Arabic* [3d ed., trans. J Milton Cowan; Ithaca, New York: Spoken Languages Services, 1971] s. v.). The Arabic verb is certainly related to Syriac *kurhono*. The final phoneme of Arabic *krh* (final *heh*), Syriac *krh* (final *heh*), and Hebrew *krḥ* (final *ḥet*) is hard, and the root means "to be sick, feel pain."

This root is to be separated from that found in Biblical Aramaic *itkeriyyat ruḥi*, "my spirit was disturbed" (Dan 7:15) and Syriac *keryat ly*, "it grieved me"; these are derived from final-weak verbs meaning "to be short, pinched" and are thus directly related to the Akkadian *karū*/ *kurru*, "to be short, tight." Akkadian *karū* and Aramaic *kry*, "to be short," only take on the meaning "to be angry, disturbed" when they are used metaphorically in a compound idiom, "my soul/ being/ mood (Akkadian *ikku*; Aramaic *ruaḥ*) is short, pinched" (cf. the discussion in CAD, I/J, p. 50, s.v. *ikku* A).

Confusion of these two roots was inevitable. Several questions remain unanswered.

First, why did Syriac, which has the root *krh* (final hard), express the concept "against one's will" by the expression *baqṭṭiro* instead of using the root *krh/ḥ*? Such questions belong to the mysteries of idiom and probably cannot be answered.

Second, why does the Yemenite *Midrash ha-Gadol* to Exodus (M. Margulies, ed., *Midrash ha-Gadol* [Jerusalem: Mosad Ha-Rav Kook, 1947] 213), write *ʿal korho*, with a *heh* instead of a *ḥet*? The possible influence of Arabic *ʿalā kurhin* on the Yemenite midrash is unlikely; although the midrash is relatively late, it does not seem to be notably influenced by Arabic. In all probability the spelling reflects a phenomenon typical of Babylonian-Gaonic Aramaic, whereby *ḥet* was often weakened to *heh* (cf. J. N. Epstein, *A Grammar of Babylonian Aramaic* [Jerusalem: Magnes, 1960; in Hebrew] 18). This may help clear up some of the confusion of the various talmudic lexica, from the *Aruch* to Jastrow and Levy, who posit the existence of two verbal roots *krh* as well as the rare noun form *kerihuta*, "sickness" (*b. Shabbat* 10a), and the adjectival form *keriha*, "sick" (*b. Shabbat* 21a). Although in *b. Shabbat* 145b we read *keriḥe* in printed texts (one text has *beriḥe*), many old manuscripts read *kerihe* (see Levy s. v. *keriha*). In all probability there was but one root *k-r-ḥ*, and in some areas the original *ḥet* was weakened to a *heh*, a situation later reflected in the *Midrash ha-Gadol* to Exodus. The problem is a complicated one, in need of more thorough investigation.

EXCURSUS VII. ROYAL KUDURRUS AND QUESTIONS OF SEALING

For the oldest royal *kudurrus*, see I. J. Gelb, "On the Alleged Temple and State Economies in Ancient Mesopotamia," *Studi in onore di Eduardo Volterra* (Milan: Giuffrà, 1969) 6.137–54 at 143ff.; and M. San Nicolò, *Beiträge zur Rechtsgeschichte im Bereiche der keilschriftlichen Rechtsquellen* (Oslo: H. Aschehong, 1931) 119–21, with interesting parallels to later Greek documents. The still fundamental study of this important type of document is that of F. X. Steinmetzer, *Die babylonischen Kudurru (Grenzsteine) als Urkundenform untersucht* (Studien zur Geschichte und Kultur des Altertums II.4–5; Paderborn: F. Schöningh, 1922). Also basic is L. W. King, *Babylonian Boundary-Stones and Memorial-Tablets in the British Museum* (London: British Museum, 1912). See also Steinmetzer, "Eine Schenkungsurkunde des Königs Melišichu," *Beiträge zur Assyriologie* 8 #2 (1910) 1–38; W. J. Hinke, *A New Boundary Stone of Nebuchadrezzar I. from Nippur* (The Babylonian Expedition of the University of Pennsylvania, Series D. Researches and Treatises 4; Philadelphia: The University of Pennsylvania, 1907); F. Thureau-Dangin, "Une acte de donation de Mardouk-zâkir-šumi," *Revue d'Assyriologie* 16 (1919) 117–56. For an early juridical investigation of the *kudurrus*, see E. Cuq, *Études sur le droit babylonien, les lois assyriennes et les lois hittites* (Paris: Geuthner, 1929) 67–140. A bibliography of *kudurrus* that is useful to legal historians in spite of its art-historical focus is given by U. Seidl, *Die babylonischen Kudurru Reliefs* (Baghdader Mitteilungen 4; Berlin: Deutsches Archäologische Institut, Abteilung Baghdad, 1968). For a more extended discussion of these texts, their legal terminology, and the light they shed on later, non-Akkadian legal texts, especially the Aramaic deeds from Elephantine, see SALPE, 130–35.

For an important juristic analysis of the *kudurrus* and related deeds from Elam and especially Ugarit and Hatti, with special emphasis on the role of seals in royal donations, see G. Boyer, "La place des textes d'Ugarit dans l'histoire de l'ancien droit oriental," *Le Palais royal d'Ugarit III* (ed. J. Nougayrol; Mission de Ras Shamra 6; Paris: Imprimerie Nationale, 1955) 283–308, esp. 283–93. Boyer places great emphasis on the use of the royal seal in Hittite and north Syrian deeds and, possibly, in archaic deeds from Susa. So constitutive was this sealing in confirming the validity of the donation, and especially in preventing any contestation, that often the seal used on a document was not the seal of the reigning monarch but rather the so-called "dynastic seal," that is, the seal of the founder of the dynasty who in some cases ruled generations before the time of the transaction. This practice invested the transaction with a solemnity of an almost magical quality: it was as if the spirit of the great founder, the very power that underpinned the dynasty itself, acted as a guarantor of the grant.

Boyer mentions the importance of the royal seal in the Kassite and Neo-Babylonian *kudurru* documents. He is careful not to lump the various traditions into one monolithic pattern; for example, he notes that dynastic seals were not used in the *kudurru*s. Nonetheless, he seems to have overlooked another significant difference between the *kudurru*s and the rest of these royal grants with respect to sealing. As far as I know, there is no record of a Ugaritic or Hittite document of donation that was contested for lack of a royal seal. At most, we have one litigation based on the claim that the dynastic seal was forged (see Nougayrol, *Palais royal d'Ugarit III*, xxiv–xxvii).

The role of royal sealing in Kassite and Neo-Babylonian *kudurrus*—at least to judge from King's collection—seems to be quite different. There are several examples of royal donations that seem to have been considered perfectly valid at the time they were issued, in spite of the fact that they were not sealed by the king. They were provided with the royal seal at a much later date, only after they had been contested. At first I assumed that the original omission of the royal seal was a rare occurrence and was simply a matter of royal oversight or bureaucratic negligence. I tacitly assumed that theoretically all *kudurru*s had to be affixed with a royal seal to be valid. In this I was wrong. R. Borger, in "Vier Grenzsteinurkunden Merodachbaladans I. von Babylonien," *Archiv für Orientforschung* 23 (1970) 1–26, especially 18, demonstrates that there is every indication that the phenomenon of royal grants valid without royal seals (exactly as in the case in *Sifre* discussed in the paper) was much more common than one would have expected. In one of the deeds edited by Borger, we read of King A who granted (*irīm*) some land to one of his officers without sealing it (*lā kanik*, lines 18–24). Immediately after this laconic statement comes the observation that a later king, Merodachbaladan, had it sealed. Strangely enough, no mention is made of a litigation that motivated the later royal sealing. May we infer that such a litigation took place? Unfortunately, the text is silent on the subject, and no definitive answer can be given.

I offer the tentative suggestion that the frequent omission of the royal seal in *kudurru* grants is not a phenomenon devoid of specific juridical significance: it is not simply a sporadic oversight of kings. It seems more plausible to assume that we are dealing with a legal tradition in which royal sealing was not considered an absolute necessity. The king's word, and/or the curses and the symbols of the gods that covered the *kudurrus*, may have been considered as sufficiently constitutive. The royal seal, in deeds originally lacking it, was affixed only after litigation.

Whether or not this suggestion is correct, we seem to be in a cultural-legal ambience different from that of north Syria and the Hittites and closer to the legal tradition reflected in the Nuzi and Middle Assyrian deeds. (For the similarity of legal practices, specifically the "publication" of an imminent sale of land reflected in the Kassite *kudurrus* and discussed below, with the practices reflected in the Middle Assyrian laws and in Nuzi texts, see L. Oppenheim, "Ein Beitrag zum Kassitenproblem," *Analecta Orientalia* 12 [1935] 266–74.) In Middle Assyrian and Nuzi society, it seems that a transaction between two parties was considered valid without royal involvement. What was constitutive was the measuring of the field before special witnesses and the performing of certain symbolic actions. (For discussion, see P. Koschaker, *Neue keilschriftliche Rechtsurkunden aus der El-Amarna-Zeit* [Abhandlungen der Sächsischen Akademie der Wissenschaften 39.5; Leipzig: Hirzel, 1928] 67–81; cf. also SALPE, 91 n. 8.) In Middle Assyrian-period sale law, although a transaction was considered binding between two parties without the intervention of the king, it had to be registered in the royal archive (in Assyria) after a formal publication (in Nuzi, Assyria, and Babylon) by a royal herald three times in one month (in Assyria). Was the situation reflected in *kudurru* grants similar to ordinary transfers of property? Was the transfer of land, privileges, and immunities between a king and a courtier binding between the two parties simply because of the power of the king's word and/or the presence of many witnesses at the formal measuring of the field (cf. SALPE, 91 n. 8), and/or the curses and divine representations written on the *kudurru*? Was the royal sealing only necessary to insure the grant from claims and litigations of third parties? At present, no definitive answer can be offered.

EXCURSUS VIII.
SIMḤAH AS VOLITION IN THE *SIFRE*

The meaning of the term *btḥlh/btḥylh* suggested here, "in pain," although plausible, is a matter of conjecture and speculation. However, as far as the use of *simḥah* is concerned, I have little doubt that in our context it does not convey simple jubilation but rather a willingness and readiness unhampered by any inner reservation. This additional nuance of the term *simḥah* is established not merely by the Akkadian material—as I said above, the value of the Akkadian parallels *may* simply be heuristic—but by the immediate contexts in the *Sifre*, especially by the striking parallelism between the phrases *qanah ve-natan*, "he acquired and gave," and *neʾmar besimḥah*, "spoken in joy." The evidence marshalled in this article comes from but a limited range of documents and contexts. However, if the volitional nuance posited here is apt, one would expect to find it used in a wide range of contexts, contrasted with a clearer set of antonyms than the ambiguous *btḥlh*, and positively defined by some unequivocal synonyms and complements. Only then can we say with certainty that our suggestion assumes the status of a linguistic fact (cf. SALPE, especially p. 116). As luck would have it, there are many passages in midrashic and related literatures in which we find an action performed *besimḥah* negatively defined as one not performed *beʾangaria* "under duress/coercion" (cf., for example, *Midrash Tehillim* to Psalm 19, in S. Buber's edition [Vilna: Rom, 1891; rpt. Jerusalem: Wahrmann, 1966] 170; and, in the same collection, to Psalm 112, Buber, p. 468). In other contexts it is the synonym of *belevav shalem*, "with a full mind, with complete intention." In yet other midrashic texts, it is both a synonym and a complement of *miyyad*, "immediately" (cf. the text from the *Sifre* to Deut 26:10, cited above in note 33). All of this linguistic evidence will need to be discussed in greater detail in future studies.

Bearing this positive evidence in mind, attention must be drawn to two passages found in the *Sifre* in conjunction with the phrase *ʾani—beraṣon / hinne—besimḥah* that seem to ignore the volitional interpretation of *simḥah*. One is an *ʾasmakhta* or artificial peg on which to hang a bit of aggadic material. The other is a question raised by students of Rabbi Ishmael based on a comparison of syntactically similar texts: the *ʾani hinne* found in Numbers 18 establishing the rights of the priests and Levites, and the *va-ʾani hineni meviʾ*, "I am hereby about to bring [the flood]" in

Gen 6:17. Although *ʾasmakhtot* are often forced, and students' questions, especially in aggadic passages, are often answered by the *darshan* with less than absolute seriousness, it is unfair to dismiss them out of hand as just so much midrash. As fanciful as some midrashim may seem, Heinemann, Lieberman and Kadushin have taught us that even the *ʾaggadah* has its "ways" and methods.

Let us first turn to the *ʾasmakhta*. While Rabbi Ishmael paraphrases *hinne* in Num 18:8 as *simḥah*, he immediately clarifies the nature of this *simḥah* by paraphrasing *ʾani* as *beraṣon* "willingly," thus unequivocally spelling out the volitional character of this *simḥah*. Unfortunately, several other authorities in their comments to Num 18:8 simply inform us of the equivalence of *hinne* with *simḥah* without adding the paraphrase *ʾani—beraṣon* necessary for the proper understanding of the term *simḥah* in this context. The omission of this extra bit of explication has caused difficulty for virtually all interpreters.

To complicate matters, Rabbi Jonathan (*Sifre*, ed. Finkelstein, p. 145), after following similar methods of "deriving" the equivalence of *hinne—simḥah* from the immediate context in Numbers 18, adds the seemingly incongruous quotation from Exod 4:14, "Behold [*hinne*] even now he [Aaron] is coming out to meet you and . . . will rejoice in his heart [*ve-samaḥ belibbo*]." First of all, the relation between *hinne* in this verse and *ve-samaḥ belibbo* is completely non-organic—one could almost say fortuitous—as is typical of most *ʾasmakhta*-type prooftexts. Secondly, the verb *samaḥ* in this sentence seems to have nothing to do with volition, agreement, or lack of inner reservation. It is simply the joy of reunion—hardly a fitting prooftext for the equivalence of joy with willingness and lack of mental reservation. But once again, we may be asking too much from an *ʾasmakhta*. Rabbi Jonathan, at least, provides us with one legitimate philological prooftext (from Numbers 18), before introducing the passage from Exodus. Less satisfying, at least to our taste, is Rabbi Nathan (*Sifre*, ed. Finkelstein, p. 134) who, to prove the identity of joy with *hinne*, simply quotes the *ʾasmakhta* of Exodus.

After taking Lieberman's remarks (in *Hellenism in Jewish Palestine*, 49) seriously—namely, that the formula *ʾeno ʾella* usually introduces what we could call correct lexical *peshaṭ*, we are a bit disturbed to see the same exegetical formula reduced to a forced prooftext. In this context it is illuminating to quote Lieberman in full:

> It appears that comments formulated אין . . . אלא which are incorporated in the *Halakhic Midrashim* have their origin in a very ancient commentary of the

> Law. Most of these comments undoubtedly provide the plain meaning of the text. In course of time this vigorous assertion (i.e., it is nothing but . . .) was extended even to *Midrashic* exposition, but as such it was almost exclusively limited to the narrative parts of the Bible. [This would apply with equal validity to such paraphrases as discussed above that are functionally identical with the *ʾeno . . . ella* formula. Y.M.] The use of this emphatic formula for a *Midrashic* comment therefore becomes one of the characteristic exaggerations of the *Aggadah;* it degenerates into a mere literary phrase, and the Rabbis themselves will not take a comment introduced by these words more seriously than any other *Midrashic* interpretation in the *Aggadah* (*Hellenism in Jewish Palestine,* 51).

For the complete degeneration of an originally sound exegetical method, compare the various interpretations of Exod 4:14, where not only *hinne* becomes an *ʾasmakhta* for *simḥah,* but for virtually every other word in the sentence as well, cf. M. Kasher, *Torah Shelemah* (New York: American Biblical Encyclopedia Society, 1949), 8.181.

Having dismissed the text from Exod 4:14 as an *ʾasmakhta* rather than a real prooftext, one that has little relation to joy, not to speak of volition, let us reconsider the problem, not from our own vantage point, but from that of the ancients. As noted before (cf. note 32), many a rabbinic interpretation that we moderns dismiss as *derash*—even those not based on wild associative word-plays, but grounded in some psychological or cultural reality—were often considered by the rabbis, and even pre-rabbinic scholars, as the simple meaning of scripture.

Thus, for example, Philo in his non-allegorical description of the life of Moses, without actually quoting Exod 4:14 ("Behold even now he [Aaron] is coming out to meet you and . . . will rejoice in his heart") or Exod 4:27 ("The Lord said to Aaron, 'Go to meet Moses in the wilderness'"), alludes to the two situations reflected in these verses and makes the following comments:

> During the journey he met his brother, to whom he declared the divine message, and persuaded him to accompany him. His brother's soul, in fact, had already, through the watchful working of God, been predisposed to obedience, so without hesitation he assented and readily followed. (Philo, "On The Life of Moses,"1.85–86; trans. F. H. Colson, *Philo* [Loeb Classical Library; London: Heinemann, 1928–62] 6.319–21.

It would seem that, according to Philo, Aaron's agreement to Moses' commission and his acceptance of his secondary role in his younger brother's administration was not a matter that could be taken for granted. God had to use His unique powers of persuasion to overcome

Aaron's natural hesitation rooted most probably in feelings of simple jealousy. As we mentioned above, Philo is probably reflecting in this non-symbolic, non-allegorical exegesis what was considered by his contemporaries as the real and simple meaning of the relationship between God's command to Aaron, "Go to meet Moses" in Exod 4:27 (notice that he had to be commanded to go meet his brother: ergo, some counter-feeling had to be overcome), and Aaron's joyful and willing agreement reflected in verse 14, "and will rejoice in his heart." Philo, who in this section is merely explicating Scripture on its simplest—and for him, its least profound—level never even mentions what we would consider the self-evident meaning of the situation depicted in Exod 4:14: the obvious joy and excitement of the reunion of two brothers long separated from each other. For him, as for the later rabbis, as we shall soon see, the laconic text of Scripture reflected a psychological situation much more complicated than we moderns are ready to posit. For us, *ve-samaḥ belibbo* simply means, "he will be happy to see you."

A much later midrash (Tanḥuma Yashan to Exod 4:27; cf. Kasher, *Torah Shelemah*, 8.205), reflects the same ancient tradition already found in Philo's free-flowing pashtanic narrative. This midrash further develops the complexities of the situation, namely, Moses' reactions and hesitations. Following rabbinic method, it derives its interpretation from the exegesis of specific scriptural passages and words.

את סבור שמא עיכב משה שלא לילך, לא עשה אלא כמכבד לאהרן, אמר משה עד שלא עמדתי היה אהרן מתנבא להם שמונים שנה..., ועכשיו אני בא להם בתחום אחי שיהא מיצר, לכך לא ביקש משה לילך, א״ל הקב״ה אהרן אחיך אינו מיצר בדבר הזה אלא ישמח תדע לך שהוא יוצא לאנפטי..., כיון שאמר לו כך קיבל עליו לילך מיד נגלה הקב״ה על אהרן א״ל צא לקראת משה אחיך, כדי שידע שאתה שמח בדבר לכך נאמר לך לקראת משה המדברה.

[And when Moses said to God: "Please send whomever you will send" (Exod 4:13),] you might think that Moses really did not want to go. The real cause of his delay was his concern for his brother's honor. Said Moses: "Before I was appointed, Aaron served them [the Israelites] as prophet for 80 years.... Shall I now come to them as prophet, encroaching on my brother's territory to his distress?" For this reason, Moses did not want to go. The Lord said: "Your brother Aaron is not at all distressed concerning this matter [i.e., your appointment as prophet and his secondary status]. In fact, he is actually happy [i.e., he is in full agreement with the new division of authority and accepts it gladly and willingly]. Know that even now he is coming forth to give you an official welcome." [Greek *apantē*, "toward"—the midrash's paraphrase of *liqrateka* in Exod 4:14—is sometimes used in Greek papyri with the meaning "to give a formal welcome to a visiting or newly appointed official." Cf. J. H. Moulton,

A Grammar of New Testament Greek (3d ed.; Edinburgh: T. & T. Clark, 1963, 1.14 n.4.] As Scripture says: "Behold even now he is coming out to meet you" (Exod 4:14). . . . As soon as this was told to Moses, he agreed to depart on his mission. Immediately, the Lord revealed himself to Aaron and said to him: "Go out to meet Moses, your brother (Exod 4:27), in order to let him know that you are happy concerning this matter [i.e., that you are in agreement with it]." That is why Scripture [which does not waste words on the obvious] includes the verse: "Go to meet Moses in the wilderness." [Or to talk in Philo's language: "His brother's soul, in fact, had already, through the watchful working of God, been predisposed to obedience."]

What is of vital importance is that in this passage, the verse, "Behold (*hinne*) even now he is coming out to meet you," is used in a clearly volitional context; the concluding words *ve-samaḥ belibbo* express willingness, acceptance and agreement, rather than simple jubilation. The verse *hinne . . . ve-samaḥ belibbo* thus becomes a perfect prooftext for the identity of *simḥah* with *raṣon*, and an old one at that—if one is willing to accept the ancients' unarticulated definition of what the simple meaning of Scripture is. Paradoxically, what originally seemed to be a weak *ʾasmakhta* now appears as a perfectly legitimate prooftext for a rabbinic *peshaṭ*.

This is not the place to discuss the much-debated problem concerning the relationship between Philo and the rabbis. (Cf. the works of Wolfson, Heinemann, Belkin, E. Stein, and before them Azaria de Rossi.) However, the close relationship between the Philonic and midrashic passages discussed above, and the light they shed on each other is not an isolated phenomenon. It is obvious that the last word on the subject is yet to be said.

Our second problem is a question raised by Rabbi Ishmael's students: "[If *ʾani hinne* in first-person declarations often indicates joy,] are we to infer that when the Bible says, 'Behold [*hineni*] I on my part am about to bring the flood,' does God really rejoice?" On the surface, once again, the question seems to assume that the students misunderstood the point made by Rabbi Ishmael, namely that *simḥah* in some contexts does not mean simple joy or jubilation, but has clear overtones of agreement and willingness. Rabbi Ishmael's answer that indeed God rejoices when the wicked are destroyed would seem to heighten our problem.

One would have expected the following question: "If *va-ʾani hinne* expresses *simḥah* and *raṣon*, namely, willingness and lack of inner reservation, is the same psychological situation implicit in the syntactically similar divine declaration *va-ʾani hineni meviʾ*, 'Behold I on my part am about to bring (the flood)'?" In other words, does the Lord bring the deluge without inner reservations, sadness or regret, but with full inner agreement and willingness? Such an induction from the previous lexical remarks of Rabbi Ishmael would have seemed more "logical" to our modern tastes. But the ways of the midrash—at least according to the give and take between the master and his students—do not seem to be our ways, at least on the surface.

One could dismiss this question in a number of ways. One could argue that one of the characteristic traits of the midrash is that the same verse may be interpreted in entirely different, and sometimes contradictory, ways, even by the same interpreter. Thus, while in his own interpretation Rabbi Ishmael brought out the volitional aspect of *simḥah,* he was quite aware that *simḥah* did not lose its normal meaning of joy. Therefore, he seemed quite willing to answer his students' question in a conventional way. Both interpretations—his own and his answer to his students' question—were considered true and legitimate, even if from our point of view they may seem to exclude each other. This is part of what Kadushin calls "the indeterminate" aspect of the rabbinic mind.

On the other hand, the question that we might have expected the students to ask is not simply a product of our own inductive logic, but a very actual one in rabbinic thought. Saul Lieberman in his lectures often depicted the Lord as a tragic figure, torn between His feelings of love, prompting Him to pardon the wicked, and His feelings of righteous indignation, prompting Him to punish them. The inner battle raging in the divine mind is between *middat ha-din,* "the quality of justice," and *middat ha-raḥamim,* "the quality of love and forgiveness." The most dramatic expression of this divine tension and God's basic reluctance to punish is found in the well-known passage in *m. Sanhedrin* 6:5: *qeloni meroshi qeloni mizroᶜi;* this is explained by Lieberman [personal letter, Feb. 20, 1974] as follows: "My disgrace from my head, my disgrace from my arm. Maimonides explains the passage, "When a man (i.e., a sinner) is in sorrow, because he is about to be punished, what does the *Shekhinah* say? 'My disgrace from my head, my disgrace from my arm,' i.e., I will be ashamed if I do not use my head and punish the man, and I will be ashamed if I do not use my arm and pardon the man." This idea is concretized most dramatically in the various midrashim and targumim to the flood story. Rashi, reflecting an older tradition, interprets the verse *loᵓ yadon ruḥi* (Gen 6:3) as "My Being cannot continually be at war with itself whether to destroy or pardon mankind." In Gen 6:6 we read, "And the Lord regretted [biblical *va-yinaḥem* = rabbinic *tahut*] that He had ever made man on earth, and He was grieved to His heart [*va-yitᶜaṣṣev ᵓel libbo*]." Rashi, summarizing ancient material, reads *va-yitᶜaṣṣev ᵓel libbo* as reflecting the terrible battle that waged in God's heart between His justice and His mercy. Note also the ample material cited by Kasher, ad loc. The various targumim are particularly sharp and anthropomorphic on this subject; the so-called Targum Yerushalmi says, *wᶜdyyn ᶜm lbyh,* "He struggled with His heart," and the Targum Neofiti reads *ʾtdyn wʾpyys ᶜm lbh,* "He struggled with His heart and came to an agreement with it." (The printed text has *wʾdyq,* which in the light of the other targumim can only be read *ʾtdyn*; see A. Diéz Macho, *Neophyti I . . . Génesis* [Textos y Estudios 7; Madrid: Consejo Superior de Investigaciones Científicas, 1974].)

According to these traditions, God did not destroy joyfully. At most, one can say that He finally agreed and willed to bring the flood only after the resolution of a deep inner conflict. It was a distasteful act of will, not a capricious outburst of enthusiasm. In his commentary to Genesis 6:17, *va-ʾani hineni meviʾ*, Rashi, once again summarizing ancient tradition (cf. Kasher, *Torah Shelemah* 2.407, n. 196), has the Lord say the following:

הנני מוכן להסכים עם אותם שזרזוני ואמרו לפני כבר מה אנוש כי תזכרנו

> I am *ready to agree* with those [angels] who [when God was about to create the world] urged Me [not to create man by citing the verse in Psalm 8]: "What is man that you consider him! (v 5)."

We argued above that, on the basis of Rabbi Ishmael's volitional interpretation of *ʾani hineni,* his students, in their attempt to apply this principle to Gen 6:17, should not have asked whether God brought the flood joyfully, but should have asked whether He brought the flood willingly, i.e., in agreement with Himself, after the resolution of inner conflicts. As we have just seen, the material for such an answer to our hypothetical question was certainly available in abundance, and it would have been in complete harmony with Rabbi Ishmael's initial observation that, in some contexts, *simḥah* simply means willingness and agreement. In this case, we have an answer to a question that was not asked. Why it was not asked still remains a problem.

EXCURSUS IX. QUESTIONS OF TRANSMISSION

Is the parallelism between Babylonian royal grants and the divine grants recorded in the *Sifre* simply a coincidence or is it an indication of historical dependence? If we accept the dependence thesis, what was the immediate channel of transmission? In dealing with such problems, one or two common features are insufficient to establish historical relationships. Ideally, the two cases being compared should be alike in almost all ways: the greater the number of unique elements that go into the making of two somewhat strange configurations, the greater the probability that this overlap is not simply a matter of chance or parallel development. One of the strongest arguments in favor of some sort of dependence is the strange situation that both the *kudurru*s and the grants in the Sifre share in common, involving the validity of royal grants lacking the royal seal and formal registration in the royal archive and the addition of the seal and registration only after a litigation. Nevertheless, before *definitively* arguing that one is actually derived from the other, one would have to investigate the contemporary Greek material to see whether or not a similar situation obtained in that cultural area. If it did not, then the chances of dependence on Mesopotamia are high. If the same situation did obtain in Greece, the problem is still not definitively solved, since, as we are now becoming more aware, much that is Greek is rooted in oriental soil. Conceivably, a Mesopotamian institution could have penetrated the Greek world and from there made its way into the rabbinic one. In fact, any one of these models may be true.

A few words about another model. If Weinfeld's thesis concerning the dependence of the Israelite institution of covenant of grant on Mesopotamian models is correct—and I agree that it is, in spite of a few reservations—could one further postulate the influence of the biblical covenant grant on the rabbinic? The rabbinic and biblical covenant grants are so radically different from each other, and the particular Babylonian elements borrowed—if borrowed they were—so entirely different, that this thesis can be rejected out of hand. If the material was borrowed, it was (a) from an Aramaic reworking of Akkadian material, (b) from an independent Greek source, or (c) from a Greek source that derived the institution from an Akkadian source found in some Aramaic form; it was not borrowed directly from the Bible.

Furthermore, even the specific use of the term *simḥah* with volitional overtones may or may not be derived from the Akkadian. There are some indications that the usage is biblical (mostly, but not entirely late), and is attested to in the Greek word *charis*, which means both "pleasure/joy" and "boon/gift" (cf. Saul Lieberman, *Greek in Jewish Palestine*, 44). Whether or not the parallel donations or the specific use of joy as a term of volition are derived from the Near East, there can be little doubt concerning the valuable light each source throws on the other. However, in view of the large number of parallelisms, the possibility of interdependence, although not "mathematically" proven, is more than likely. Final judgment will have to wait until all the evidence is in. In the meanwhile, it should be noted that the volitional use of *simḥah* and *ʾahavah* and the specific application to the passage in the *Sifre* has been accepted by Lieberman in his *Tosefta Kifshuṭah*, Part III (New York: Jewish Theological Seminary, 1973), Order *Nashim*, 722. My thanks to Lieberman for his aid and encouragement when I first presented the idea at the annual meeting of the American Academy of Jewish Research in New York in 1954.

CHAPTER 8

LOVE AND JOY AS METAPHORS OF WILLINGNESS AND SPONTANEITY IN CUNEIFORM, ANCIENT HEBREW, AND RELATED LITERATURES: PART II: THE JOY OF GIVING*

To the memory of my teacher and friend, M. Bravmann

The religious life of the ancients—Mesopotamian and Hebrew alike—was less a quest for salvation or union with a metapersonal godhead than an ongoing personal relationship, of different degrees of stability and intimacy, between man and his god(s). Like most personal relationships, the divine–human encounter, once formalized, was often experienced in legal terms, as a covenant: between overlord and vassal; between father and son; or between husband and wife. Furthermore, the religious covenant, exactly like its societal analogue, was created, sustained, and renewed by a continuous exchange of gifts and favors—the tangible signs of the mutual good will and loyalty of the parties. Thus, without denying the importance of divine service and the more numinous aspects of ancient religion, there can be little doubt that the normal everyday intercourse between man and his god(s) was reflected in this ongoing exchange of gifts: the gifts—in religious language, "the blessings"—of life and wealth, healing and assistance bestowed by divinity on everyman; the authority bestowed as a gift to kings, especially in Mesopotamia; and in Israel—at least according to the midrash—the gifts of the land, the Torah, and the Sabbath, granted to the people for all time. In return for these blessings, man reciprocated with his contributions to the temple and with the payment of his vows: in Mesopotamia with his food-offerings to the gods; and in Israel with his tithes, first-fruits and sacrifices, and later, with his prayers. And even if his sacrifices were

* This article first appeared in *Journal of the Ancient Near Eastern Society* 11, *Bravmann Memorial Volume* (1979) 91–111. I would like to thank my student Rabbi Martin Cohen for his assistance in preparing this article.

formally considered as divine demands rather than spontaneous donations, nevertheless—at least according to a rabbinic tradition—if offered with a full heart and with enthusiasm, they were accepted as free-will offerings.[1]

Unlike the sale of an object, where the payment of a consideration effected the transfer of ownership, the validity of ancient Near Eastern donations was dependent to a great degree on the intention and good will of the donor; if his feelings of affection towards the donee happened to change, the legal basis of the transfer was weakened, and the gifts may have been demanded in return. Thus, in order to insure the donation against its inherent instability, counterdonations were often offered by the donee, thereby assimilating the donation to the more stable vehicle of sale.[2] Or, more frequently, the donation was accompanied by the donor's declaration of volition.[3] This was especially true of divine donations to kings and priests, and of royal donations to courtiers, where the declarations of volition were particularly elaborate.

Furthermore, while the Mesopotamian and some biblical traditions seem to place little emphasis on the volition that accompanied donations to the deity, in rabbinic tradition the volition and intention of the human donor—although not crucial from a strictly legal point of view—is afforded greater and greater religious consideration.[4] Finally, it should be noted that not only do donations have to be *given* with the proper spirit, they also—at least ideally—have to be *accepted* in the spirit with which they were given: with thankfulness, if the recipient be human; with "favor," if the recipient be divine. It is as if to say that since all the goods in the world belong to the Divine, the only real contribution man can offer is the willingness with which he gives his contributions, and the alacrity with which he performs the act (cf. 1 Chr 29:14).

In the preceding chapter, I attempted to demonstrate that the metaphors of love and joy were used as terms of volition of action and spontaneity, not only in ancient Near Eastern legal documents, where this usage was fairly well known, but also in a wide range of rabbinic texts. In that study, we saw that the inner joy and love of the donor expressed itself by the radiance of the face and the alacrity with which the action was performed. In this study we will spell out these ideas in greater detail, focusing on a number of passages having to do with donation and gift giving.

Volitional Gifts to Temple and Sanctuary

The use of the term *simḥah* to express this willingness and the alacrity that goes along with it can be seen in a rabbinic homily to Num 7:2, a passage that describes the ceremonies that accompanied the completion of the construction of the tabernacle.

> *And the princes of Israel drew close* (Num 7:2): Why did the princes hasten (*nizdarzu*) to come and sacrifice first, when at the time of the erecting of the tabernacle, they had procrastinated (*nitʿaṣṣelu*) and finally were only (able to bring) onyx and precious stones? Because when Moses had said, *everyone whose heart moves him shall bring a donation for the Lord* (Exod 35:5), toward the building of the tabernacle, they were disturbed because they had not been specifically asked to bring a donation. They said, "Let the people bring whatever they want, and we will fill in the deficit." (However,) the people were so enthusiastic about the construction of the tabernacle that they brought all their donations freely and speedily. . . . After two days, when the princes were just about to bring their donation, they could not, since all that was needed had already been supplied by the *hoi polloi*. Therefore, the princes were very dejected at not having had a share in the construction of the tabernacle.[5]

The rabbis ask, Why were the princes so eager (*nizdarzu*) to contribute to the sanctuary after it was completed, while during its construction they seemed to be in no hurry (*nitʿaṣṣelu*), being the last to contribute (Exod 35:27)? The answer is that the princes, expecting a special invitation to make their donations, felt snubbed by Moses, who included them in the general appeal to the people. In their pride, they decided to wait until the popular contributions were in, then to make the aristocratic gesture of making up the deficit from their own pockets. However, to the princes' chagrin, the people responded so enthusiastically to Moses' appeal, that in their rush to bring contributions, they actually brought more than was needed, thus leaving the princes without a significant share in the holy undertaking. The unstinting enthusiasm of the people and their eagerness to contribute is expressed with the phrase: *sameḥu . . . ve-heviʾu besimḥah kol nedaba u-vizrizut*, "they were enthusiastic . . . and brought all their donations freely and speedily." Clearly, in this context, *simḥa* is more than just simple joy; as the complement of *bizrizut*, "eagerly, with alacrity," it must mean something like "willingness" or perhaps, more specifically, "zeal" or "enthusiasm."

The princes thereupon decided that such an indiscretion was not going to recur. Thus, when the sanctuary was completed, in an attempt to preclude such a debacle, the princes *hiqdimu ve-heviʾu qorban bizrizut*, "without being asked, brought an offering with alacrity," saying, *hare hashshaᶜa shenaqrib qorbanot besimḥah,* "this time, we had better offer (our) sacrifices with joy," that is, immediately, with enthusiasm and thus with even greater alacrity than the *hoi polloi.*

A second illustration of *simḥah* used as a partial synonym of *zerizut* is found in the *Sifra*'s comment to Lev 9:5–6. On the eighth day of the installation of the priests, God commanded the people to bring their sacrifices before the sanctuary, that He might appear in their midst. Still anxious that their past sins may have alienated them from their Lord, the people, overjoyed that there was the possibility of a renewed manifestation of divine favor, immediately rushed forward to bring their offerings with more than normal enthusiasm.

> *And the people brought that which Moses commanded:* with zeal (*bizrizut*). *And the whole community came forward and stood before the Lord*: they all came forth *besimḥah,* "freely," and stood before Him. By way of illustration, (their situation) may be compared to a king, who, in his anger, drove his wife out (of the palace). After some time, however, he made up with her. Just as soon as this happened, with every bone in her body (literally, with girded loins and flexed shoulders), she began to wait on him more than was necessary (*yoter middai*). In a similar manner, as soon as Israel realized that the Lord was now disposed to forgive their sins, they rushed forward *besimḥah,* "overenthusiastically." This is what is reflected in the verse: *And the whole community came forward and stood before the Lord* (Lev 9:5).[6]

The slightly negative overtones of the people's *simḥah* are reflected in the parallel expression *yoter middai,* "more than necessary, too much," applied to the rejected wife, still not secure in her husband's affections. Although the *simḥah* and *zerizut* of the people may have been excessive, nevertheless, their overzealousness—or more correctly, their religious enthusiasm—could lead to fatal indiscretion.

According to one rabbinic tradition, the two sons of Aaron, Nadab and Abihu, did not offer "strange fire" to the Lord (Lev 10:1) because of base motives—as the simple meaning of the verse would seem to indicate—but because of an excess of religious zeal.

> *And the two sons of Aaron each took his fire pan, put fire in it . . . and then offered before the Lord alien fire, which he had not enjoined upon them* (Lev 10:1). They, on their part, acted in their *simḥah.* For as soon as they saw the new fire, they spontaneously felt like adding (their) gift to the (divine) gift (*ᶜamedu lehosif ᵓahavah ᶜal ᵓahavah*).
>
> *Nadab and Abihu:* Although they were the sons of Aaron, nevertheless, they did not show respect for Aaron (by consulting with him first), nor did

> they consult with Moses . . . (in fact), they did not even consult with each other before they rushed forward.[7]

The sons of Aaron, therefore, far from being evil men, were religious enthusiasts who felt that something more was called for than the general exultation (cf. Lev 9:24): the divine gift of fire had to be met with a commensurate human gift. In their *simḥah*—not merely the joy over the theophany, but more specifically, the impetuous zeal and enthusiasm precipitated by it—they rushed forward without a second thought and without consulting the ordained authorities, Moses and Aaron, and placed their gift of strange fire on the altar, only to bring on themselves sudden death and on the people a day of mourning in the midst of holy celebration.[8]

The idea of donations given with a glad heart also comes into focus in another series of midrashic statements relating to the gifts given by the people to the tabernacle. In the Targum Pseudo-Jonathan to Exod 25:2, we find the phrase *ʾasher yiddevenu libbo*, "whosoever is of a willing heart," glossed as follows: *min kol gevar deyitreʿe libbe ve-la beʾalamuta*, "from any man whose heart desires and who is not under any compulsion."[9] This seems to correspond to the midrashic exegesis to that verse found in the *Leqaḥ Ṭov*, where we find:

> (Whosoever is of) a willing heart: (The essence of) a generous person depends on his heart (i.e., attitude), as it is written: *whosoever is of a willing heart* (Exod 35:5), (thus implying the exclusion of the man whose gift is given) under compulsion (*ʾones*).[10]

The reasoning behind this midrash is given in the commentary of Rabbenu Meyuḥas, who wrote:

> It is stated "whosoever is of willing heart," which implies that gifts must be given of free will and not under compulsion, in order to differentiate between another type of contribution which is also called *terumah* in Scripture, i.e., the yearly donation of a half-sheqel (for the upkeep of the Sanctuary), where the principle of free-will is not operative. On the contrary, the rabbis were prepared to put a lien against the property of him who declined to pay it. Thus Scripture finds it necessary to make obvious the fact that this donation must come as a free-will contribution.[11]

The fact that this freewill donation was highly desirable is shown by this later midrash:

> *Whosoever is of a willing heart* (Exod 25:2): The tabernacle, which was built with donations that were wholehearted, was impervious to the evil eye. The Temple, which was built with donations that were collected halfheartedly, was (eventually) destroyed by the enemy's hand.[12]

For the *Sifra*, this willingness to give caused certain problems, the gravity of which led Moses to offer an expiatory sacrifice, to which reference is made in Lev 8:15. The midrashist asks rhetorically what the sin was which this sacrifice was to expiate. He answers:

> Moses said, "From the moment that the Lord of the Universe commanded that contributions be brought to the Sanctuary, each Israelite pushed himself so as to have brought donations without full willingness (*shelo᾿ beṭovatam*)." To preclude the possibility that stolen property be dedicated to the sanctuary—and donations given without full willingness were considered to be stolen goods even if stolen from oneself—this expiation was offered.[13]

So it would seem, according to the *Sifra*, that the contributions were not only less worthy because they were offered under compulsion, but they were, in fact, legally questionable, thus requiring the sacrifice.[14]

The statement in Exod 35:22, "they came, men with women," to contribute to the building of the sanctuary, is formulated in an unusual way, using the preposition *ᶜal* to express "with." This gave several midrashic writers pegs on which to hang their exposition of the problem regarding the free will with which the contributions were supposed to be made. Thus, one text explains:

> *And they came, the men against* [*ᶜal*] *women* (Exod 35:22): What does this teach us? Above it says: (And Aaron said unto them:) *Break off the golden rings, which are in the ears of your wives, sons and daughters, and bring them to me* (Exod 32:2). The Israelites said, "How shall we effect atonement for the sin we committed in breaking the golden rings off our wives, sons and daughters, which we brought in piles in order to fashion golden gods?" Thus, when Moses brought them together in order to solicit contributions of gold and silver for the building of the tabernacle, they all brought donations from their homes and from their pockets, as it is written: *And they came, everyone whose heart stirred him up, and everyone whom his spirit made willing, and brought the Lord's offering* (Exod 35:21). And yet some went after the jewelry of their wives and daughters and took them by force [*bizroaᶜ*], as it is written: *And they came. . . .*[15]

It is just such traditions about the coercion that may have occurred in the presentation of contributions to the tabernacle that are consciously undermined by many of the midrashim cited above. Nonetheless, the dominant midrashic idea is that the donations were brought voluntarily, and this is the idea that underlies even the Sifra passage, where it is shown that this generosity led to certain excesses. One source, *Midrash ha-Gadol*, puts it all together, using the word *simḥah* as the key.

> *And all the congregation of the children of Israel departed from the presence of Moses* (Exod 35:20): Scripture tells us that once the people learned that God had forgiven them for that sin (i.e., the golden calf), and that the Holy One, Blessed Be He, had asked them to construct a tabernacle so that He might cause His *Shekhinah* to dwell amongst them, they rejoiced with great joy (*sameḥu simḥah yeterah*) and all went out with great alacrity (*zerizut*) to bring all their money. This we learn from the verse: And they came, *everyone whose heart stirred him up* (Exod 35:21). And precisely because they contributed with all their heart, and with all their spirit, the Holy One, Blessed Be He, is destined to implant within them a new heart and spirit, and thus is it written: "A new heart also will I give you, and a new spirit will I put within you" (Ezek 36:26).[16]

Functionally, *zerizut* is frequently a free variant of the volitional *simḥah*. This may be inferred from a midrash on the same verse (Exod 35:20), which explains the expressions *simḥah* and *zerizut* in other language:

> ויצאו . . . : יצאו להביא תרומת הנדבות ולא עיכבו.

> *And they departed* (Exod 35:20): they departed to bring their donations without procrastinating.[17]

Yannai

In the first part of this study, we have seen from a wide range of midrashim, all dealing with gifts to the tabernacle, the crucial juristic significance of the inner will of the donors. Furthermore, we have seen that absence of inner joy, whether caused by outward coercion, by lack of inner conviction, or by the overzealousness that causes a man to donate more than he ought—thereby suffering rather than rejoicing in his gift giving, if not actually invalidating the gift—at least greatly depreciates its significance and value.[18]

Now, in spite of the poetic nature of midrashic literature, the midrash is dealing with a crucial legal matter, namely, the role of volition in donations to the Deity. Therefore, it should come as no surprise that actual legal terminology—the *leshon hedyoṭ*, "common-law formulary"—should be used in rabbinic midrashim and in payyetanic amplifications of biblical passages. The close relationship between the midrashic tradition and the poetry of the famous early *payyeṭan* Yannai has been discussed by Saul Lieberman and other scholars.[19] In fact, there is hardly a line of Yannai that does not resonate with echoes of the early midrash. We shall see how important knowledge of the common-law Aramaic legal formulary is for the proper understanding of Yannai's poetry in general and specifically of a fragmentary poem on the subject of the building of the tabernacle and the contributions solicited for its construction.[20]

The text of Yannai's *piyyuṭ* is in very bad shape. Stanzas 7 and 8 are fragmentary. However, at least we can tell that they are juxtaposed against one another: stanza 7 talks about the fact that a gift is not to be brought under *ʾones*, "compulsion or duress," while stanza 8 informs us that it should be offered *beshivvuy* and *beraṣon*, "quickly and willingly."[21]

The two stanzas in question read in Zulay's edition follow; the lines of stanza 7 are shown, but stanza 8 is too fragmentary for the lineation to be certain.

ז	1.	בלי אסון ואונס	בלי ב . . . וב . . .
	2.	ב[לי גו]בה [וג . . .]	בלי דיבה ודופי
	3.	[בלי ה . . . וה . . .]	בלי ואנינה ואנח
	4.	בלי זדון וזע[ם]	[בלי ח . . . וח . . .]
	5.	בלי טענה וט . . .	בלי י . . . וי . . .
	6.	בלי כפיפה וכעס	בלי לב ולב
	7.	. . . .	. . . .
	8.	. . . .	בלי עי . . . ועו[ש]ק
	9.	בלי פשיעה ופרץ	[בלי צ . . . וצ . . .]
	10.	[בלי ק . . .] וקוט . . .	בלי רנ[ינה ור . . .]
	11.	בלי שדידה וש . . .	[בלי ת . . .] ות . . . ות

ח כי אם בתום ובשווי וברצון ו[בק... ובצ... ובפ...] ובעוז [ובס... ובנ... ובמ...] ובליקח
ובכושר יד וביקר ובטוב [ובח... ובז...] ובוודיי ובה...ה [ובד... ובג...] ובביטח ובאהב
קידשו עצמם והי[קדישו]..... כקדושת מעלה כִּכ וקרא

At least six of the terms used here are attested in various early medieval legal documents published by S. Assaf.[22] Based on those documents, and also on the acrostic nature of this poem, I believe that it is possible to reconstruct the text of the *piyyuṭ*, and so I will defer translating the text until the philological problems are put in order. First, let us list the terms from the *piyyuṭ* that have exact or almost exact parallels in the documents:

(1) *beli ʾones*, "without coercion," is almost a *sine qua non* in the medieval documents; see below, no. 7.

(2) *beli dofi*, "without deception," is attested in at least one document, parallel to *loʾ shiqqarti*, "I did not lie, break the contract."[23]

(3) *beli ṭaʿanah*, "without contest/ claim," is a regular and well-attested phrase.

(4) *beli lev va-lev*, "without being of two minds (literally, hearts)," is also found in the medieval texts.[24]

(5) *beli ʿosheq*, "without extortion/ oppression," is also found in the texts.[25]

(6) *beli kefifah va-kaʿas*, "without coercion and anger." Again, a medieval legal formula will help us clarify the meaning of this phrase. One of the volitional formulas common in Palestinian marriage contracts reads: *va-ʾana la ʾanis ve-la kaʿis ve-la raʿiṣ ve-la ʿaṣiv ve-la kafif*, "I am (doing this) not forced, not with anger, a broken spirit, sad or coerced." I have shown elsewhere that the logical opposite of joy, meaning willingness, would be sadness, meaning unwillingness.[26] This is clearly reflected in the phrase *kaʿis . . . kafif*, both of which are rare terms, both in the legal formulary and also in payyetanic tradition. The identity of Yannai's line with the legal usage can hardly be coincidental. It is almost as if the poet utilized a known legal formula to make his point that the relationship between man and God is bound by the same rules that apply to human relationships, in this case, the invalidity of a legal contract entered into under compulsion.

(7) *beli ʾason*. The term *ʾones*, "compulsion," needs no explanation, being found in Jewish documents of virtually every age. Obviously, *ʾason* must be something like *ʾones*. It was Saul Lieberman who, in a private communication, intuitively derived the word *ʾason* from the root *ʿ-ś-y*, with the regular *samek–sin* interchange, and the use of *ʾalef* instead of *ʿayin* because they were used interchangeably in Palestine at that period and here the poet needed an *ʾalef* word to begin his acrostic poem; further, we know from Palestinian rabbinic legal material that a *geṭ meʿusse* (written with *sin*) is a writ of divorce given under compulsion. Therefore it is clear that *ʾones* and *ʾason* are virtual synonyms. After having received Lieberman's suggestion, I happened to come upon the extremely rare expression *ve-loʾ ʿissut* (spelled with *sin)* in a collection of deeds edited by Assaf; the term can only mean "without coercion."[27] Thus Lieberman's insight is confirmed by a document.

(8) *bekosher yad*, a synonym for *zariz*, "with alacrity," or *lev ṭov*, "joyfully."[28]

(9) *beli dibbah* is not actually found in any of the documents published by Assaf; but it must be related to a phrase in the Aramaic formulary from Elephantine, *dyn wdbb*, "a claim and a lawsuit," i.e., "a formal process."[29] This certainly ties in with the Syriac term for enemy, *bel devava*, "litigant (literally, lord of opposition)," and the Mishnaic Hebrew *din u-devarim*, "litigation (literally, judgment and words)," found, for instance, in *m. Ketubbot* 9:1.[30]

10) *beli v'aninah va-'enaḥ* is also not actually found in any of the documents themselves, but we have an interesting parallel from Philo.

> The cities (of the Gentiles) pay under compulsion and reluctantly and groan under the burden (i.e., of their taxes) . . . and when they discharge the appointed dues and assessments they do so without regard to the time limits allowed. But our people pay gladly and cheerfully. They anticipate the demand, abridge the time limits . . . and so at each of the yearly seasons they make their contribution . . . with a zeal and a readiness which needs no prompting.[31]

Philo's statement that the Gentiles pay their taxes "under compulsion and reluctantly" and that they groan under the burden sheds light on the phrase *'enaḥ*, "with groaning." Although he does not say so explicitly, Philo does seem to imply that promptness is more than a matter of etiquette, that the Jewish gift would almost be invalid if it were offered in the spirit in which the other nations offer their duly owed taxes. Yannai can therefore be assumed to be trying to show that the gift to which he is referring in his *piyyuṭ* is not marred by this common defect. Yannai's gift is therefore doubly appropriate: it is given neither by one who is not whole or wholehearted, that is, an *'onen*, nor is it being given in a stingy or niggardly way, that is, *'enaḥ*, "with groaning." We know from the *Sifra* that an *'onen*, "one who has lost a relative but has not yet buried him," lacks the mental clarity to offer a sacrifice.[32]

As I mentioned above, the affinity between the language of the Genizah legal documents and the poem of Yannai leads one to wonder if it might not be possible to reconstruct the terms missing from the poem based on its acrostic character and the presence of pertinently initialed terms for volition in the documents published by Assaf. In this reconstruction of stanza 7, I have supplemented the nine complete half–lines of text with a number of other half–lines, marked with a star. In two cases the Assaf documents suggest two possible readings, and in one case I offer four versions. The restored words are italicized in translation.[33]

ז.

1.	בלי אסון ואונס	בלי ב . . . וב . . .
2.	בלי גובה וג . . .	בלי דיבה ודופי
3.	בלי ה . . . וה . . .	בלי ואנינה ואנח
*4.	בלי זדון וזעם	בלי חולי וחרם
*5.	בלי טענה וטעות	בלי י . . . וי . . .
6.	בלי כפיפה וכעס	בלי לב ולב
*7.	בלי מחלקת ומרע	בלי נ . . . וכ . . .
*8a.	בלי ס . . . וס . . .	בלי עצבות ועושק
*8b.	בלי ס . . . וס . . .	בלי עישות ועושק
9.	בלי פשיעה ופרץ	בלי צ . . . וצ . . .
*10.	בלי קללה וקוט . . .	בלי רנינה ור . . .
*11a.	בלי שדידה ושגגה	בלי תרעמת ותביעה
*11b.	בלי שדידה ושבוש	בלי תהות ותהיה
*11c.	בלי שדידה ושעמום	
*11d.	בלי שדידה ושכרות	

1. With neither compulsion nor duress
   With neither . . . nor . . .
2. With neither pride nor . . .
   With neither litigious nor deceptive words
3. With neither . . . nor . . .
   With neither mourning nor groaning
4. With neither malice nor anger
   With neither *illness* nor *a vow*
5. With neither complaint nor *error*
   With neither . . . nor . . .
6. With neither duress nor anger
   Without ambivalence
7. With neither dissent nor evil
   With neither . . . nor . . .

8a. With neither . . . nor . . .
   With neither *sadness* nor oppression

8b. With neither . . . nor . . .
   With neither *compulsion* nor oppression

9. With neither crime nor lawlessness
   With neither . . . nor . . .

10. With neither *curse* nor . . .
   With neither complaint nor . . .

11a. With neither crime nor *error*
   With neither *complaint* nor *force*

11b. With neither crime nor *mistake*
   With neither *regret* nor *remorse*

11c. With neither crime nor *boredom*
With neither [as above]
11d. With neither crime nor *intoxication*
With neither [as above]

For stanza 8, fewer reconstructions are possible, but progress is, I hope, apparent.[34]

ח כי אם בתום ובשווי וברצון ובקיום ובצילות דעת* (ובצדק*) . . . ובעוז . . . ובנפש
חפצה* . . . ובליקח ובכשר יד וביקר ובטוב ובחלימות גוף* . . . ובוודיי ובהגן
ובדעת שלמה* ובגמר לב* (ובגוף בריא*) ובביטח ובאהב

(Without these things) but rather with innocence and with alacrity and with free will and with *certitude* and with *clearheadedness* (*or* with *honesty*) . . . and with strength . . . with a *willing spirit* . . . and with *leqaḥ* (?) and with sure-handedness and with gravity and with goodness and with a *well body* . . . and with knowledge (*or* with *confession*?) and with *dignity* and with *complete awareness* and with *made-up mind* (*or* with *healthy body*) and with certainty and with love (they sanctified themselves and became holy).

In summation: The cumulative effect of these clusters of legal terms in the poetry of Yannai is most impressive. Law, liturgy, and midrash are more closely interrelated than we might ever have suspected.

There is yet another *piyyuṭ* of Yannai, published by Israel Davidson in his *Maḥzor Yannai*, which nicely orchestrates the various themes discussed above.[35] Building on the verse in Lev 22:17, *ʾasher yaqriv qorbano*, "whosoever offers his sacrifices," and taking for granted the rabbinic doctrine that some sacrifices are invalid if offered without total volition (compare our discussion below of Ben Sirah), the poet can write of *ha-nikelalot birṣon ʾishim*, "(an *ʿola* offering whose performance is only) perfected (if accompanied) by the volition of the person offering (it)" (line 3). Later in the poem, he writes of *teshurat qorban . . . tamim leṣivyonam u-lirṣonam*, "a gift of a sacrifice . . . perfect only with their will and volition" (line 12). Equally striking is the line *ve-yuqrevu shelemim ve-yaqrivu shelamim*, "(Only priests) perfect (in mind and body) shall (be invested to) offer *shelamim*-offerings." This interpretation was first given by Louis Ginzberg in his notes to Davidson's edition of Yannai; Ginzberg quotes the remark of the Sifra we quoted above (note 32). In the same vein, the phrase *tefillah shelemah*, "perfect prayer," is used in the poem to refer to prayer offered with intent.

Furthermore, in the final section of this poem, which is both poorly preserved and poorly understood, we find a concatenation of terms that remind us of some of the rare terminology discussed above.

(1) A sacrifice is not acceptable from one who is *ʾanus*, "forced" (line 29).

(2) One cannot appease God's anger (?) with an offering if the sacrifice is offered *bekhaʿas*, "in anger, sadness" (line 30).

(3) One does not force (*kofefim*) a person to make an offering to Him who raises up the fallen (*zoqef kefufim*) (line 31).

(4) If the sacrifice is offered willingly (*lirṣonam*), the offerers' wish shall be granted them according to their wish (*yeʿase reṣonam kirṣonam*) (lines 32–33). The last phrase sounds like a poetic reworking of the expression *laʿasot reṣoneka kirṣoneka*, "(help us) to perform Your (namely, God's) wish according to Your wish." The first case deals with human wishes, the second with those of God.

(5) The sad are not to make offerings—(*ʿa*)*gum loʾ maʿalim* (line 34).

Here are shades of *la ʾanis*, *la kafif*, and *la kaʿis*, terms that we found both in old Palestinian marriage documents and elsewhere in Yannai, and of the phrase *loʾ keʿusa ve-loʾ ʿoṣevet* found in one of Assaf's documents.[36] For further discussion of this text, one must turn to Ginzberg's notes. The fact that virtually the same seemingly rare terminology is found in more than one of Yannai's compositions is hardly without significance.

Volitional Aspects of Sacrifice and Charity

We have seen above and in Chapter 7 in this volume the widespread use of the metaphor of joy as an expression of the willingness with which the donor presents various gifts, especially those gifts called *terumah*, to the Lord. It has been noted that this metaphor was also the common mode of expressing free and uncoerced volition in Akkadian documents from the Old Babylonian to the Neo-Babylonian period, and even later. It stands to reason, therefore, that we may expect to find a similar usage in the period between the late Neo-Babylonian and the early rabbinic eras. Our induction is amply confirmed by a passage in Ben Sirah (35:10–13).

ובטוב עין כבד ה׳ ואל תמעיט תרומת ידך
בכל מעשיך האר פניך ובששון הקדש מעשר
תן לו כמתנתו לך בטוב עין ובהשגת יד
כי אלוה תשלומות הוא ושבעתים ישיב לך

With a good eye (a joyful spirit) honor the Lord.[37]
And do not stint with the *terumah*-offering of your hands.
In all your deeds let your face shine

And with gladness dedicate your tithe.
Give to Him (God) as He has given to you,
With sparkling eye and as much as you can afford.
For He is a God of requital
And sevenfold He will pay you back.

Some of the major implications of this passage for the understanding of certain rabbinic texts were already seen by Segal.[38] He correctly called attention to the offering of the tithe *beṭov ʿayin*, "generously," and the use of the phrase in rabbinic literature. Furthermore, he pointed out that the rabbinic *simḥah shel miṣvah*, literally "the joy of the commandment," seen in the light of this passage would seem to mean the joyful and spontaneous willingness with which one performs a commandment, rather than the emotion generated by performing the commandment itself.

The expression *behassagat yad* (or perhaps *kehassagat yad*) is difficult, and neither Segal nor Charles[39] has much to say about it. It seems clear that what we have here is a term reflecting the biblical demand that a person should only bring sacrificial offerings within his financial capabilities. This demand is regularly expressed with the verbs *n-g-ʿ* (*ve-ʾim loʾ taggiaʿ yado dei se*, "If his means do not suffice for a sheep," Lev 5:7, NJPS) and *n-s-g* (*ve-ʾim loʾ tassig yado lishtei torim*, "If his means do not suffice for two turtledoves," Lev 5:11, NJPS). In the biblical passage the verbal idiom has not yet crystallized into an abstract substantive, as it appears in Ben Sirah and in early rabbinic literature, for instance, in *m. ʿArakhin* 4:1, where the term used, *hesseg yad*, "reach of the hand," reflects, like Ben Sirah's *hassagat yad*, the biblical use of *n-s-g*. The verb *n-s-g* is a technical term of the Priestly writer. The demand that sacrifices reflect resources is expressed differently in Deuteronomy, with the phrase *kaʾasher yebarekhekha*, "according to that which God has bestowed upon you," as in Deut 16:10 (regarding the sacrifices offered during the Feast of Weeks or Shavuot).[40] The immediately preceding phrase involves a rare term, *missat nidbat yadekha ʾasher titten*, "the sufficiency of the offering of your hand, which you will give"; the term *missat* is understandable in light of the Syriac *missat*, which means "that which is sufficient, enough."

The whole phrase is parallel to Deut 16:17, where it is stated that one ought to observe the Feast of Booths or Sukkot *ʾish kemattenat yado kevirkat YHWH ʾelohekha ʾasher natan-lakh*, "each according to his financial ability, according to the blessing that the Lord has bestowed on you." The NJPS translation of the first phrase, *ʾish kemattenat yado*, "each with his own gift" is misleading; we follow S. R. Driver's clearer view.[41] Driver points out the virtual equivalence of the expression *kaʾasher tassig yadekha*, "according to what he can afford," in Ezek 46:7 with *mattat yado* in Ezek 46:5. There seems to be no reason to render the latter term as "as much as he wishes" (so the NJPS). Thus *mattenat / mattat yado* (D) = *hassagat yad* (the P tradition). This equivalence was seen most clearly by Saadya, who renders D's *ish kemattenat yado* (and so on) by "what his hand can afford according to that which God has bestowed on you," using exactly the same *figura etymologica* as he uses in translating P's term.[42] Let us not forget that the concepts of giving according to one's means and the blessings that accrue to the donor are secondary ideas that cluster around the main idea under discussion: giving joyfully and willingly. This idea is found in the same Deuteronomic context as the other concepts just discussed. In Deut 15:10, we find discussed the proper spirit in which gifts are to be given to a needy person: *loʾ yeraʿ levavekha betittekha lo*, "You shall not be sad in giving to him." As Driver clearly realized, the negative formulation is merely a roundabout way of saying, "You shall give joyfully, without any niggardliness, that is, willingly."

Thus, the concatenation of the three ideas, (a) giving willingly—Ben Sirah's *beṭov ʿayin, besason*, (b) according to one's means—Ben Sirah's *hassagat yad*, and (c) the concomitant blessing—in Ben Sirah, the reference to God as *ʾeloah tashlumot*, "a God of requital," is found as early as Deuteronomy. Moreover, each of these ideas is developed in rabbinic literature.

First, willingness. In *Va-yiqra Rabbah*, we read the following:

> If you have brought me a sacrifice freely (*beraṣon*) and willingly (*beṭovah*), I accept it; but if it was (brought) under compulsion and against your will, I reject it, and I consider it only as so much fire, as it is written: *Command the children of Israel and say to them, "My food which is presented to Me for offerings made by fire . . ."* (Num 28:2). What do we learn from the phrase "by fire"? The Holy One, Blessed Be He, said to them: If you brought it freely and willingly, I accept it, but if under compulsion, then it is (only) so much fire and is not an appropriate offering.[43]

Saul Lieberman suggests reading *shalem* instead of *lashem* in the last line of the text, and our translation reflects this emendation.[44] Since offerings that are not required by law are to be brought "according to your will," it must be the intention of the midrash to point out that even those sacrifices that are obligatory (that is, not voluntary contributions) must be brought freely and with complete willingness. It is *raṣon* that makes an offering acceptable; without proper intention an offering is nothing more than fire on the altar. It is significant that in the parallel recension of this midrash in *Pesiqta Rabbati,* the word *beʾahavah,* "with love," replaces the phrase *beṭovah,* "with goodness," thereby demonstrating with particular clarity their equivalence.[45]

The second idea, giving according to one's means, is common in aggadic sources. It is the basis of a halacha attributed to R. Simeon bar Yoḥai:

> It is stated: *Honor the Lord with thy wealth* (Prov 3:9): With what should you honor Him? With that which He graciously gives to you. Separate your gleanings, your forgotten sheaves, the leftover corners of your fields. Separate *terumah,* first tithe, second tithe, poorman's tithe offering, and *ḥallah* loaf. Make a *sukkah* [booth], a *lulav* [branch], a *shofar* [horn], *tefillin* [phylacteries], and *ṣiṣit* [fringe]. Feed the poor and the hungry, and give drink to the thirsty. If you have the means, you are required to do all these things, but if you do not have the means, then you do not have to do even one of them.[46]

On the surface, this midrash seems to be based on a superficial similarity of *ḥon,* "grace," and *hon,* "sufficiency, wealth"; the interchange of the letters *heh* and *ḥet* is a common feature in Galilean Aramaic. The similarity of sounds stimulates the midrashist to use the verse as a peg on which to hang his homily. However, on further examination, the case may be somewhat different. H. L. Ginsberg has suggested to me that in at least two places in the Book of Proverbs (30:15, 16) the noun *hon* is parallel to *loʾ tisbaʿ* or the like, verbs meaning "it is not enough"; in these cases, *hon* simply means "sufficiency." The probable semantic development of *hon* is as follows: *hon* means *sobaʿ*, "satiety," which easily nuances itself into "riches." The problem deserves an independent study. If this surmise is correct, the midrashic explication of the biblical verse may be less forced than a superficial reading would indicate.

The third point, the idea that God will reward the joyful donor—that is, he who gives according to his ability—by increasing his property and implicitly insuring his ability to grow more, prompted the following comment:

> *Give to him (the needy person) readily and do not be sad in giving to him* (Deut 15:10), so that one should not say, "Today I am going to squander my possessions on others, and tomorrow I will have to depend on them." Thus does it say: that for this thing (the Lord thy God will bless thee) (Deut 15:10).[47]

The Torah does not usually excuse the Israelite from his legal responsibilities even if he suffers because of his observance. Here it is important to reassure the donor that he will not suffer, so that he gives freely and willingly.

Midrashic sources extend this to other, more specific cases. Thus, whereas Deuteronomy only instructs the master to furnish his manumitted slave with sheep, grain, and wine, the rabbinic exegesis of the law reads:

אשר ברכך ה׳ אלהיך תתן לו: הכל לפי הברכה אתה מעניק לו

> *With that which the Lord has blessed you, you shall give him* (Deut 15:14): this implies that you are to give to him (gifts) according to your means (literally, according to your blessing).[48]

Presumably, the master is only instructed to give in accordance with his own wealth so that he will not come to begrudge his charity.

In another place we find this exegesis regarding the command *loʾ teʾammeṣ ʾet-levavekha*, "thou shalt not harden thy heart," stated with respect to giving to the needy in Deut 15:7:

> *Thou shalt not harden . . .* (Deut 15:7): There are men who suffer over the decision whether to give or not to give.[49]

Thus the rabbis assumed that the Torah was specifically referring to the act of giving charity in such a way that one later regrets having done so.

Practically all the terms we have described come together in a particularly poignant section of the apocryphal Book of Tobit. There we read the dying Tobit's last words to his son Tobias:

> And in all your days, my boy, be mindful of the Lord our God and be not desirous to sin and to transgress His commandments. Do acts of righteousness all the days of your life, and tread not the paths of sin. Because those who act in truth shall be successful in all their efforts; (and success comes) for all who do the just deed. Bestow charity of your means; let not your eye be niggardly in the practice of charity: turn not your face away from any poor man, and the face of God shall not be turned away from you. As your resources are, according to their sufficiency give (you) alms of them. For you store up a good credit for yourself against the day of necessity. For alms deliver from death, and allow not descent to Darkness. Indeed, alms are an excellent offering in the sight of the Most High for those who are wont to give them.[50]

This idea is carried through in several passages in the New Testament, most notably in the Second Letter to the Corinthians. There, Paul insists that donations be given *hōs eulogian kai mē hōs pleoneksian*, "not as an exaction, but as a willing gift" (2 Cor 9:5). Paul specifically instructs the people of Corinth that they do not have to behave like the community of Macedonia who "gave not only as much as they could afford, but far more, and quite spontaneously, begging us for the favor of sharing in this service to the saints, and, what was quite unexpected, they offered their own selves first to the Lord and under God, to us" (2 Cor 8:3–5). The result of their over-zealousness is that they remain in "intense poverty." Rather, "each one must do as he has made up his mind, not reluctantly or under compulsion, for God loves a cheerful giver (*hilaron . . . dotēn*). And there is no limit to the blessings that God can send you—you will make sure that you will always have all you need for yourselves in every possible circumstance, and still have something to spare for all sorts of good works" (2 Cor 9:7–8, cf. 8:11). God really only wants that which is offered freely. If you are generous within your means, then God will favor you by seeing to it that you always have enough, even enough to be able always to give charity. The idea that through the giving of charity one will win the blessing of always being well enough off to give more charity is a common Jewish motif, as we have seen before. In this eloquent fundraising sermon, Paul again shows his deep Jewish roots.

Elsewhere, Paul presents the following bit of wisdom to his readers on this subject. He states: "Our gifts differ according to the grace given us . . . let the preachers give sermons, the almsgivers give freely, the officials be diligent, and those who do works of mercy, do them cheerfully" (Rom 12:6, 8). The word used here to indicate cheerfulness (*en hilarotēti*) is traditionally used to translate *raṣon*, that is, "will" or "desire."[51] Here the message is clear: just as the job of the preacher is to preach, so is it the job of the almsgiver to give alms properly, that is, freely, and so is it the job of the doer of good deeds to do them properly, that is, cheerfully.

To sum up: Paul's sermon in 2 Corinthians 8–9 clearly reflects our triple complex of ideas, saying, in effect, "I don't want you to overdo it like your brothers elsewhere. God does not want to impoverish you. You don't have to give under duress and coercion, nor do you have to give more than you have; after all, God loves a joyful giver. And if you give in this spirit, God will provide you with the ability to give more." Some have tried to derive the concept of the joyful giver from Hellenistic sources.[52] That might be plausible if we were dealing with only one element, namely, joy. However, here we are dealing with a complex that is well known from the sources we have been examining. These three elements do not converge to form an organic complex in Greek literature, but do so in Deuteronomy, Ben Sirah, and to various degrees in Tobit and rabbinic literature. Paul's sermon is simply a grand articulation of the older Jewish traditions and but another example of Paul's Jewish background.

This particular complex of ideas concerning the psychology of giving charity also seems to be found in Islam. According to Islamic law, unlike the obligatory *zakāt*, "alms tax," the freely given *ṣadaqat*, "charity donation," can only be given from the *ʿafw*, "superfluity," of a man's goods or from *faḍl*, "surplus."[53] Bravmann has examined the entire matter in his excellent essay "The Surplus of Property."[54] The Quranic terms *ʿafw* and *faḍl* are interpreted by him in the light of the following tradition: "Ibn Saʿd asked him (Ibn ʿAbbās) what taxes are due from the goods of the *ahl aḏ-ḏimma* 'protected people'? Ibn ʿAbbās answered: The *ʿafw*, that is, *al-faḍl* 'the surplus.'" Here *faḍl* is equated with the Quranic *ʿafw*. The whole problem is illumined by the following order from ʿAlī concerning the way in which taxes were to be collected: "In collecting money, do not flog anybody, nor sell anybody's food supply, winter or summer clothes . . . . " The officer charged with the collection of taxes was stunned by this ordinance and replied: "O Commander of the Faithful! If so, I will return to you as I left you!" To which ʿAlī replied: "Even if you return to me as you left me!" Then, quoting the Quran, he continued: "Truly, we were commanded (by God) to take the *ʿafw* from them, that is, the surplus." In other words, taxes were not to be taken by force, but were to be given (a) willingly, (b) from the surplus of a man's goods, according to a man's (c) greatest financial ability (*ʿalā qadr aṭ-ṭāqah*). Although Bravmann may be right in insisting that the concept of the superfluity of goods is another example of a pre-Islamic practice that was incorporated into Islam, the correspondence of this three-fold complex of ideas with that found in Paul's sermon, Ben Sirah, and Deuteronomy is hardly coincidental. The wholehearted acceptance of the doctrine by the Prophet and its centrality in the later *ḥadith* literature was clearly facilitated by its centrality in contemporary Judaism and Christianity.

Volition in the Chronicler

Inner-biblically, the idea of giving cheerfully or willingly becomes even more basic in the work of the Chronicler. The volitional overtones of the verb *samaḥ* were intuitively sensed by S. Japhet in her book *The Ideology of the Book of Chronicles and Its Place in Biblical Thought*.[55]

The words *samaḥ* and *simḥah* are used on three different occasions in the Book of Chronicles in a clearly volitional context, two having to do with the free and generous spirit in which donations were presented to the Temple, and one describing the freedom and wholehearted spontaneity with which the people entered into a covenant with the Lord. The first passage is found in 1 Chr 29:9. In this famous passage, David, after having donated his private resources to the building of the future temple, solicits voluntary contributions from the people, somewhat after the manner of Moses in the Pentateuch. The response is overwhelming: all strata of society bring their free-will offerings. In the language of the Chronicler:

וישמחו העם על התנדבם כי בלב שלם התנדבו לה׳

I would render the verse as follows: "And the people rejoiced in their voluntary giving (reading *ʿal* as though it were the equivalent of *b*), for with a complete mind/intent, they gave to the Lord." Whether or not we follow my interpretation of *ʿal* (a linguistic phenomenon that has been carefully investigated by Yalon for later Hebrew),[56] the close association between *simḥah* and *lev shalem*, "wholeheartedness," is hardly fortuitous.[57] Nor is it an isolated phenomenon in Chronicles.

In the second passage, 2 Chr 24:5–10, we learn that the righteous king Joash, in his desire to restore the Temple, gathered all the priests and Levites and charged them to go out to the cities of Judah and to solicit money for the repair of the Temple. Even though the king's command was most urgent (*ve-ʾattem temaharu laddabar*, "As for you, get to it!"), their response was hardly enthusiastic (*ve-loʾ miharu*, "they didn't hurry").[58] After scolding the high priest for this lack of clerical enthusiasm, the king turns directly to the people themselves. In dramatic contrast to the sacerdotal lethargy of v 5, we read in v 10:

וישמחו כל השרים וכל העם ויביאו וישליכו לארון עד־לכלה

I would translate this as: "All the princes and all the people enthusiastically rushed forward to bring (their donations) and they threw them into the box . . . . " Interestingly enough, many commentators find the use of the term "to rejoice" in this context odd indeed, and they are led to various emendations. However, as we have seen above, we are dealing with a rather well-attested literary cliché rather than with a textual corruption.[59]

The third passage is 2 Chr 15:12–14. During the reign of King Asa, "They then entered into a covenant to seek the Lord, the God of their fathers, with a set mind and with full determination . . . —"

וישמחו כל־יהודה על־השבועה כי בכל־לבבם נשבעו ובכל־רצונם בקשהו וימצא להם . . .

"—and all Judah rejoiced in taking the oath, for they had sworn with all their heart, and sought him with all their will, so that He made Himself available to them." Thus, the association of joy with on the one hand full and complete will, and on the other enthusiasm and spontaneous action is a feature of the Chronicler's style. What is even more important than the purely linguistic evidence is the fact that two literary *topoi* used by the rabbis—the reluctance of one group of people to contribute (in the Bible, the Levites; in the midrash, the whole populace) and the joyous alacrity of another group (the whole people, both in the Bible and the midrash); and the joy of willingness with which the people enter into a covenant with the Lord—and the term *samaḥ* are already present in the oldest of midrashim, the Book of the Chronicler.

Just as the rabbinic midrashim on soliciting contributions for the construction and later for the repair of the Temple are based on biblical *topoi* using the word *samaḥ*, so the Chronicler's description of entering into a covenant willingly with God *besimḥah*, "without compulsion," could have served as the *topos* for the rabbinic tradition that the Jews did not accept the Torah under divine compulsion, as some would have it, but rather *hishvu kullam belev ʾeḥad leqabbel ʿalehem ʿol malkhut shamayim besimḥah*, "they all agreed singleheartedly to accept the yoke of the kingdom of heaven joyfully,"[60] which can only mean that, as one man, they, with one concerted action, accepted the yoke of divine kingship with willingness.

If joy can express willingness, then sadness, as we might guess, can express mental reservation. Now, exactly such juridical sadness is alluded to in Deut 15:10, in which, as we have seen, our ancestors were commanded to bestow gifts on their manumitted slaves. However, they were warned that the outer objective donation was not enough—the *animus donandi* was also important: *ve-loʾ yerʿa levavekha betittekha lo*, "Do not give it to him with a sad heart, with mental reservation or reluctance" (according to the LXX). Put positively, "Give to him willingly, fully, unbegrudgingly," for—to paraphrase Paul's paraphrase of Deuteronomy—

"God loves a cheerful giver"; or in the Hebrew of Proverbs, *ṭov-ʿayin hu yevorakh*, "A generous man is blessed" (Prov 22:9).

To close, we present two texts that discuss the facial expression that must accompany the act of giving, an expression that gives testimony to the lack of niggardliness with which the donation is being given. First, a passage from the *Avot de-Rabbi Natan*:

> And receive all men with a cheerful countenance (*besever panim yafot, m. Avot*, 1:15). How is this to be done? It teaches us that if a man gives to his fellow all the good presents in the world but his face is downcast, then it is as if he had not given him anything. But he who receives his fellow with cheerful countenance even though he give him nothing, it is as if he had given to him all the good presents in the world.[61]

And finally, its Islamic mirror image in a *ḥadith* recorded in the name of Jābir:

> The Messenger of Allah, Peace and Blessings of Allah Be On Him, said: Every good deed is charity, and it is a good deed that thou meet thy brother with a cheerful countenance and that thou pour water from thy bucket into the vessel of thy brother.[62]

Love in the Liturgy

In the Old Babylonian documents from Susa we regularly find the following volition clause: *PN ina narʾamātišu ina ṭubātišu iddin*, "PN, in his love and in his joy, sold/gave . . . ."[63] It is clear that "love" functions as a metaphorical expression of willingness alongside the more common "joy." In Neo-Babylonian texts, instead of *narʾamātu*, we find the term *rēmūtu*, literally "love," with the meaning of "freely-given gift." Its loan-translation is found in the Elephantine term *rḥmn*, and most precisely in the term *rḥmt*, "gift given in love and affection."[64]

In rabbinic literature, we often find the cliché *beʾahavah u-verason*, which in many places can only mean "given freely and willingly." This cliché is most common in the liturgy. In the *Qiddush* we read, *Beʾahavah u-verașon hinḥaltanu*," "You have given us [the Sabbath] as a gift of love given willingly." In the Sabbath *shaḥarit* service we say, *Hanḥilenu . . . beʾahavah u-verașon et-shabbat qodeshekha*, "Please give us the Sabbath as a gift of love given willingly."[65] Other expressions are comparable: *Tefillatam beʾahavah teqabbel berașon*, "The prayers they offer spontaneously accept willingly," in the *Amidah* prayer; *ha-boḥer beʿamo yisrael be'ahavah,* "who chooses His people Israel spontaneously," just before the recitation of the *Shemaᶜ*; and *lebarek et-ᶜammo yisrael be'ahavah,* "to bless His people Israel freely without reservation," in the priestly blessing. In all these contexts, *'ahavah,* "love," seems clearly to have the same semantic range as *rașon,* "will." The most paradoxical example is the expression *lanuaḥ bo be'ahavah kemișvat reșonekha,* "to rest spontaneously [on the Sabbath] according to Your personal command," in the grace after meals. The religious paradox in this phrase is the fact that spontaneity is commanded. For a similar paradox, compare the phrase *laᶜasot reșonekha kirșonekha,* "to do your will according to your will," in the liturgical traditions of ancient Palestine.[66]

Notice also the parallelism between the expressions *yissurin shel 'ahavah,* "calamities accepted with calm resignation," and *sameaḥ beyissurin,* "to accept divine calamities with resignation," literally, with "joy." The rabbinic expression cannot be understood as meaning that calamities were accepted joyfully and happily. The rabbis were not masochists who delighted in calamity, but profound realists who received the divine decree with tacit acceptance.

Notice the usage in the *'Atta 'Eḥad* prayer: *menuḥat 'ahavah u-nedavah,* "(You have given us) the day of rest lovingly/willingly, spontaneously." *Nedavah* is a very important term. In the liturgy of the Dead Sea sect it is the functional equivalent of the volitional *simḥah.*[67] A *nedavah* is a voluntary gift or a spontaneous volitional act. Like all volitional terms, *nedavah* is used two ways. When God is the subject, God gives gifts of the Torah, the Sabbath, and the holidays freely and spontaneously to Israel. When Israel is the subject, Israel gives gifts and offerings freely and spontaneously to God.

In the Genizah liturgy of ancient Palestine we find the following declaration before the recitation of the *Shemaᶜ*: ברוך אתה יי אלהינו מלך העולם אשר קדשנו במצותיו וצונו על מצות קרית שמע להמליכו בלבב שלם וליחדו בלב טוב ולעבדו בנפש חפיצה, "Blessed are you, O Lord our God, King of the Universe, Who has sanctified us with His commandments and Who has commanded us with the obligation to recite the *Shemaᶜ*—to proclaim His Kingship with a full heart and to declare His unity with a joyful [i.e., a willing] spirit and to worship Him with a willing soul."[68] Relevant in this context is the later mystical introduction to certain ritual acts performed *bideḥilu u-rḥimu,* literally "in fear and in love," that is, with deeply-felt obedience.

NOTES

1. Could it be that the exchange of Christmas gifts functions as a type of covenant-renewal ceremony in the Christian world, a ceremony by which weakened social and familial relationships are solemnly re-established? See M. Mauss, *Essai sur le don*, translated as *The Gift: Forms and Functions of Exchange in Archaic Societies* (trans. I. Cunnison; Glencoe, Illinois: Free Press, 1954; rpt. New York: Norton, 1967). In Judg 1:15 *beraka*, "blessing," clearly indicates a "gift" as, e.g., does the cognate Arabic *baraka*, which carries the connotative meaning of endowment; cf., on the meaning of "blessing," J. Pedersen, *Israel: Its Life and Culture*, I–II (London: Oxford University Press, 1926); *Israel: Its Life and Culture*, III–IV (1940); *Der Eid bei den alten Semiten* (Strassburg: Trübner, 1914); B. Landsberger, "Das Gute Wort," *Mitteilungen der Altorientalischen Gesellschaft* 4 (1928–29) 294–321 at 319–21.

2. Cf. SALPE for Aramaic and Akkadian illustrations of the principle. The idea is clearly reflected in the Aramaic declaration in which the donee declares that he will not say, "I gave you the gift in affection and now I want it back"; cf. SALPE, 42 n. 1. The underlying assumption is that the gift depends on affection; if the affection vanishes, the gift could be revoked; consequently, the donee specifically gives up this right.

3. A negative declaration, i. e., one that is not made, is quoted in *y. Nedarim* 3:3, 38a, in the name of Rabbi Hela, who observed, כן אורחא דבר נשא מימור לחבריה כורוסתי בייה "Is it the way of a man to say to his friend [the Greek expression] *kharizesthai bia* 'I give you perforce'?" S. Lieberman explains in *Greek in Jewish Palestine* (New York: The Jewish Theological Seminary of America, 1942) 44, that Rabbi Hela is explaining that "people do not behave this way when they make a present. A gift is offered with the good will of both parties; the one is desirous of giving, the other of accepting."

4. Cf. Chapter 7 in this volume. The statement in the text needs qualification: as we shall see later, volition is increasingly more important in the Deuteronomist, the Chronicler, and Ben Sirah.

5. M. A. Mirkin, ed., *Bemidbar Rabbah* (Tel Aviv: "Yavneh" Publishing House, Ltd., 1959) 12:16, p. 36. According to one tradition there were, all told, ten different *terumot*, "offerings," that were to be offered to God. See A. W. Greenup and C. H. Titterton, ed., *The Commentary of Meyuḥas b. Elijah on the Pentateuch* (London: Palestine House, 1909) to Exod 25:3, p. 94.

6. Sifra, *Shemini*, sec. 1:5. Note the literary composition of the passage: first the biblical verse; then an almost pashtanic gloss in Hebrew, virtually identical in form and function to an early Aramaic targum, like many found in Pseudo-Jonathan; then, finally, a midrashic concretization by way of allegory (*mashal*). A superabundance of any strong emotion, be it too much joy or too much willingness or eagerness, causes a man to forget the proper etiquette required in a given situation. Abraham, Balaam, and others broke with the rules of proper behavior when they forgot their dignity and saddled their own animals, a job normally relegated to servants. This notion is expressed in rabbinic literature by the dictum, *ʾahavah meqalqelet ʾet-ha-shurah*, "Love causes one to ignore the rules of conduct"; see J. Theodor and Ch. Albeck, *Midrasch Bereschit Rabba mit kritischem Apparat und Kommentar* (Berlin: Itzkowski; 1903–29; rpt. Jerusalem: Wahrmann, 1965) 22:3, p. 592.

7. *Sifra, Ṣav Milluʾim*, 1:15.

8. Regarding the translation of *lehosif ʾahavah ʿal ʾahavah*: the rendering of *ʾahavah* as "gift (freely given)" is clearly spelled out in the comment of Rabbi Abraham ibn Daud, ad loc., who says: *she-hosifu tosefet doron ḥadash*, "they wanted to bring an extra gift (Greek *doron*)"; hence the equation *doron* = *ʾahavah*. Furthermore, in this context, Hebrew *ʾahavah* = Elephantine Aramaic *raḥmah*/ *raḥmat*, "gift," which is itself either a reflex or a loan-translation of the Neo-Babylonian Akkadian *rēmūtu*, "gift"; cf. SALPE, 38, 133 n. 5. This use of the word *ʾahavah* as "gift" may shed new light on the phrase in the *Amidah* prayer given variously as *ʾahavat ḥesed* (in the Ashkenazi tradition) or *ʾahavah va-ḥesed* (in Saadya's and other oriental texts). The phrase is parallel to both the trio of *raḥamim*, *ḥayyim*, and *shalom*, "(You have given us) mercy, life, and peace," and to *torat ḥayyim*, "(You have given us) a Torah of life." Clearly the phrase means, "(You have given us) a gift of (Your) *ḥesed*" (Ashkenazi) or "You have given us a gift and a *ḥesed*" (Saadya and other oriental rites); it does not mean, "You have given us (the ability) to love *ḥesed*," as it is often misunderstood.

9. M. Ginsburger, *Pseudo-Jonathan (Thargum Jonathan den Usiël zum Pentateuch)* (Berlin: Calvary, 1903; rpt. Hildesheim: Olms, 1971) to Exod 25:2, p. 143. The phrase used in the Targum for "under compulsion" could easily refer to either physical or emotional compulsion. Some light on this question might be shed by a text of the *Midrash Tanḥuma* published by Jacob Mann in his book, *The Bible as Read and Preached in the Old Synagogue. . . . I. The Palestinian Triennial cycle. Genesis and Exodus* (Cincinnati: Hebrew Union College, 1940; rpt. New York: KTAV, 1971) 121; the relevant passage is as follows: "*And they shall make for me a sanctuary* (Exod 25:8): Moses said to Him: 'My God, Master of the Universe! And from what shall they make it (i.e., the sanctuary)? Shall each one of them give a *katadikē*?' Said the Holy One, Blessed Be He, to him: 'No, but rather let them take for Me donations.'" *Katadikē* is a Greek word meaning "sentence, fine (under force of judgment)"; it is but another synonym for *beʾalamuta*, *beʾones*, etc. See also M. Kasher, *Torah Shelemah* (New York: American Biblical Encyclopedia Society, 1949) 20:6 n. 24.

10. Tobias ben Eliezer, *Midrash Leqaḥ Ṭov* (ed. S. Buber; Vilna, Rom, 1884; rpt. Jerusalem, 1959/60) to Exod 25:2, p. 176. For the form *ʾeno ʾella* to introduce a lexical *peshaṭ*, see the remarks of S. Lieberman quoted in Chapter 7 in this volume, Excursus VIII.

11. Greenup, ed., *Meyuḥas*, to Exod 25:2, p. 94. See also J. Liver, "The Half-Shekel Ransom," in *Yehezkel Kaufmann Jubilee Volume: Studies in Bible and Jewish Religion* (ed. M. Haran; Jerusalem: Magnes, 1960), Hebrew section, 44–57 (in Hebrew); or, in English, "The Half-Shekel Offering in Biblical and Post-Biblical Literature," *Harvard Theological Review* 56 (1963) 173–98.

12. M. Margulies, ed., *Midrash ha-Gadol* (Jerusalem: Mosad Ha-Rav Kook, 1947) to Exod 25:2, 569.

13. *Sifra*, *Shemini*, sec. 1:5. It is well known that *ṭov* and *ṭovah* do not serve merely as expressions of moral rectitude, but often refer to a psychological state of inner joy; cf. H. L. Ginsberg, *Kohelet* (Tel Aviv–Jerusalem, 1961; in Hebrew). If we are correct in our view that joy is often used as a metaphor of willingness, the meanings of the stereotypical rabbinic expressions *beṭovato*, "in his goodness," and *birṣono*, "in his willingness," and their opposites *sheloʾ beṭovato*, "not in his goodness," and *beʿal korḥo*, "in his sadness" (i.e., unwillingly), become clear. Cf. Chapter 7 in this volume, especially Excursus VI.

14. This text was pointed out to me by Saul Lieberman.

15. *Sifra*, *Ṣav Millu>im*, 1:15.

16. Margulies, *Midrash ha-Gadol* to Exod 35:20, p. 743.

17. Tobias ben Eliezer, *Midrash Leqaḥ Ṭov* to Exod 35:22, p. 212, and also S. Buber, ed., *Midrash >Aggadat* (Vilna, 1902; rpt. 1925) to Exod 35:22, p. 188. Cf. the terms *lo> >iḥer*, "do not delay," *lo> nitrashshel*, "do not be lazy," *lo> hitmahmeah*, "do not hold back."

18. The tabernacle donations were legally gifts.

19. S. Lieberman, "Ḥazzanut Yannai," *Sinai* 4 (1939) 221–30 (in Hebrew).

20. M. Zulay, *Piyyuṭe Yannai* (Berlin: Schocken, 1938) 106–7. The poem is based on Exod 25:2, *ve-yiqqeḥu li terumah*, "Let them take offerings for me." The relationship of terminology of the type discussed here to *piyyuṭim* in general, especially the early *ʿAvodah*-service *piyyuṭim* and Samaritan *piyyuṭim*, is worthy of study.

21. *Shave* is a favorite word in *piyyuṭim* for willingness and immediacy, and it was used in that sense by the authors of the Dead Sea documents, as well as by the Samaritans. Lieberman, in *Greek in Jewish Palestine*, 176–77, calls attention to the phrase *yeqabbelun den min den shave*, "they receive permission one from the other immediately," in the famous poem *Aqdamuth*, where the parallelism with *de-la beshashta*, "without delay," clearly indicates that *shave* means "quickly." The term occurs in a letter of Bar Kosiba where he asks that something be sent *shave*, "quickly"; see Y. Yadin, "Expedition D—Cave of the Letters," *Yediʿot he-Ḥevra ha-ʿIvrit le-Ḥaqirat >Eretz-Israel* 25 (1961) 49–64 at 53–54. For the Samaritan usage, cf. Z. Ben-Ḥayyim, *The Literary and Oral Tradition of Hebrew and Aramaic Amongst the Samaritans* (Jerusalem: Academy of the Hebrew Language; in Hebrew) vol. 3, part 2 (1967). The term is found in a Genizah fragment of a midrashic text edited by Mann in *The Bible as Read and Preached . . . I*, Hebrew section, 101.

22. S. Assaf, "Ancient Documents from the Genizah from Palestine, Egypt and North Africa," *Tarbiz* 9 (1938) 11–34, 196–218 (in Hebrew), cited in what follows as Tarbiz; Assaf, "Ancient Documents from Palestine and Egypt," in *Jerusalem: Studies in the Land of Israel* 1 (ed. M. Ish-Shalom et al; Jerusalem, 1953) 104–17 (in Hebrew), cited in what follows as Jerusalem.

23. Assaf, Tarbiz, 211, line 43, reconstructed on the basis of other texts. The relationship between these clauses and the confessional recited in the High Holy Day liturgy is not clear: did the liturgy borrow from the legal formulary or vice versa?

24. Assaf, Tarbiz, 214.

25. Assaf, Tarbiz, 210.

26. Chapter 7 in this volume.

27. Assaf, Jerusalem, 116.

28. For the equivalence of *kasher* and *zariz*, see Lieberman, as quoted in S. Spiegel, "Noah, Danel and Job," *Louis Ginzberg Jubilee Volume*, ed. S. Lieberman et al. (New York: The American Academy for Jewish Research, 1945), English section, 305–55 at 312 n. 5. On the other hand, *kasher* is clearly a synonym of *lev ṭov*, "a willing heart," in a *piyyuṭ* by Rav Hai Gaon published in *Sämtliche Gedichte* (ed. S. J. Halberstam et al.; Lemberg, 1889; in Hebrew) 11. The relevant section reads:

דע כי המעט לתת בלב טוב
לדל טוב מזעף פנים וקטוב
מחסר אשר תתן בכושר
מעט טוב מאושר תתן בעושר.

"Know that giving a little with a willing heart / Is better for a poor man than giving a lot but with an angry face (i.e., with niggardliness) / And even almost nothing, if it is given *bekosher,* / Is better than a rich gift (i.e., an expensive gift, but one not given *bekosher*)." A *piyyuṭ* published by D. Goldschmidt, *Kobez ʿal Yad* 8 (1975) 232, confirms the equation of *kisharon* and *zerizut* / *raṣon*:

נתת ליראיך על מלכותך

ובכשרון ששים ושמחים קבלו תורתך

"You gave to those who fear You the yoke of Your kingdom / And with *kisharon* (alacrity) they received Your Torah with joy and gladness."

29. E. g., [*wlʾ*] *ʾkhl ʾgrnk dn wdbb,* "I [shall not] be able to sue you in a formal process" (BP, no. 1, lines 4–5); see SALPE, 33; for the structure of the phrase and Akkadian analogues, SALPE, 182, 196–97.

30. On Aramaic *dyn wdbb* and Hebrew *din u-devarim,* cf. S. D. Sperling, *Journal of the Ancient Near Eastern Society* 1/1 (1968) 35–40, esp. 37–38.

31. "The Special Laws" 1.141–44, Philo Judaeus, *Works* (trans. F. H. Colson and G. H. Whittaker; Loeb Classical Library; London: William Heinemann, 1928–1962) 7.180. See also Chapter 7, n. 33, in this volume.

32. *Sifra, Nedava,* 16, sec. 13.

33. The sources for the reconstructions in Assaf's work are given with the location of the article followed by the number(s) of the relevant document(s). For line 4, *ḥwly,* Tarbiz #19; *ḥrm,* Jerusalem #5. For line 5, *ṭʿwt,* Tarbiz #12, 23. For line 7, *mḥlqt,* Tarbiz #19; *mrʿ,* Tarbiz #12. For line 8a, *ʿṣbwt,* Tarbiz #19. For line 8b, *ʿyšwt,* Jerusalem #8. For line 10, *qllh,* Jerusalem #5; *qbʿ zymnʾ,* Jerusalem #5. For line 11a, *šggh,* Tarbiz #23. For line 11b, *šbwš,* Jerusalem #5, 8. For line 11c, *šʿmwm,* Jerusalem #8. For line 11d, *škrwt,* Jerusalem #5. The terms *thwt,* "changing one's mind," and *thyh,* "going back on one's promise," are common in the Talmud.

34. The sources for the reconstructions in Assaf's work are given, as in the previous note, with the location of the article followed by the number of the document(s). For *qywm,* Jerusalem #8. For *ṣylwt dʿt,* Jerusalem #8. For *ṣdq,* Tarbiz #23. For *npš ḥpṣh,* Tarbiz #19. For *ḥlymwt gwp,* Jerusalem #8. For *hgn,* Tarbiz #23. For *dʿt šlmh,* Tarbiz #12. For *gmr lb,* Jerusalem #6. For *gyp bryʾ,* Tarbiz #14.

35. I. Davidson with L. Ginzberg, *Maḥzor Yannai: A Liturgical Work of the VIth Century, edited from Genizah Fragments* (New York: The Jewish Theological Seminary of America, 1919) 26–27.

36. S. Assaf, Tarbiz, 211, line 40.

37. For the opposite expression, *raʿ ʿayin,* "evil of eye, greedy," see Prov 23:6, 28:22; Ben Sirah 14:10; see below on Prov 22:9.

38. M. Z. Segal, *The Complete Ben Sirah* (2d ed.; Jerusalem: Mosad Bialik, 1958; in Hebrew) 222–23.

39. R. H. Charles, *The Apocryha and Pseudepigrapha of the Old Testament in English* (Oxford: Clarendon, 1913) 1.438.

40. The same phrase is found in Deut 15:14, reading *kʾšr* for MT's *ʾšr,* as confirmed by the Septuagint's *kata.*

41. S. R. Driver, *Deuteronomy* (Edinburgh: T. & T. Clark, 1895) 199.

42. See, for example, Y. Kappaḥ, ed., *Perushei rabbenu Saʿadya Gaʾon ʿal ha-Torah* (Jerusalem: Mosad Ha-Rav Kook, 1962–63) 143.

43. M. A. Mirkin, ed. *Va-yiqra Rabbah* (Tel Aviv: "Yavneh" Publishing House, 1966) at 27:10, p. 97, and see the note in Margulies, p. 644.

44. Compare *b. Rosh ha-Shana* 18a, where *tefillah shelemah* is rendered by Rashi as "prayer with *kavvana*." Cf. also *b. Berakhot* 14b, where the expression *qabalat ʿol malkhut shamayim shelemah* means the acceptance of the yoke of God's kingdom willingly and with proper intention.

The Numbers midrash is based on Lev 22:27, which refers to newborn animals of a certain age being "acceptable as an offering by fire (*ʾishe*) to the Lord." The exact translation is a bit difficult (cf. the comment of Mirkin, ad loc.), but the intention of the midrashist to underline the greater significance of sacrifices offered willingly is clear enough. Similarly, to the verse at Num 28:2, "Be punctilious in presenting to Me at the stated time the offerings of food due me as offerings of fire (*leʾishay*) of pleasing odor to me," we find that *Va-yiqra Rabbah* says: "What is the meaning of the phrase *leʾishay*? The Holy One, Blessed Be He, said to them: 'If you have brought the sacrifice freely and willingly, I accept it. But if it was brought under compulsion, then I consider it as only so much fire, seeing as how it lacks perfection (of will).'" Another interesting text that sheds light on the meaning of these terms is found in Toseftah *Menaḥot* 7:9, where we find: "When Israel is found pleasing before God (*beraṣon lifne ha-Maqom*), what is said regarding them? (*Your sacrifices are*) *my food offerings due to Me* (Num 28:2), just like children who are supported by their father. However, at a time of rebuke, what is said? *As offerings of fire of pleasing odor to Me* (Num 28:2)—all the sacrifices that you offer are only so much fire" (quoted from M. S. Zuckermandel, ed., with a supplement by S. Lieberman, *Toseftah* [Jerusalem: Wahrmann, 1940] 522).

45. M. Friedmann, ed., *Midrash Pesiqta Rabbati* (Vienna: Kaiser, 1880; rpt. Tel Aviv, 1963) 194.

46. *y. Peʾa* 1:1, 15d; cf. Friedmann, *Pesiqta Rabbati*, 126b–27a.

47. D. Hoffmann, ed., *Midrasch Tannaïm zum Deuteronomium* (Berlin: Itzkowski, 1908–9) to Deut 15:10, 84.

48. L. Finkelstein, ed., *Sifre Devarim. Siphre ad Deuteronomium* (Breslau, 1935; rpt. New York: The Jewish Theological Seminary of America, 1969) 119, p. 178.

49. Hoffmann, *Midrash Tannaim* to Deut 15:7, 81.

50. Tobit 4:5–11; translation from F. Zimmerman, *The Book of the Tobit* (New York: Harper, 1958).

51. See, e. g., the Septuagint of Prov 18:22.

52. E. Bruck, "Ethics vs. Law: St. Paul, the Fathers of the Church and the 'Cheerful Giver' in Roman Law," *Traditio: Studies in Medieval History, Thought, and Religion* 2 (1944) 97–121.

53. Cf. Sura 7:198, 2:216–17 (*ʿafw*); 24:22 (*faḍl*).

54. M. M. Bravmann, "The Surplus of Property," *The Spiritual Background of Early Islam: Studies in Ancient Arab Concepts* (Leiden: Brill, 1972) 229–53.

55. S. Japhet, *The Ideology of the Book of Chronicles and Its Place in Biblical Thought* (Jerusalem: Mosad Bialik, 1977; in Hebrew) 217–18.

56. H. Yalon, *Pirqe Lashon* (Jerusalem, 1971) 343.

57. See above for *shalem* in its sacrifical context.

58. For a similar opposition of "to hurry" (whatever the root used) and "to be lax, lazy," cf. Ps 119:60, *ḥashti ve-loʾ hitmahemahti lishmor miṣvotekha*, "I hurried and did not tarry to perform your commandments." In the Qumran Psalms Scroll we find, *haḥbiru yaḥad lehodiʿa yishʿo ve-ʾal titʿaṣṣelu lehodiʿa ʿuzzo*, "Gather together (corporately) to (willingly) declare His saving power and do not delay in declaring His power" (11QPs^a in J. A. Sanders, *The Psalm Scroll of Qumran Cave 11* (*11QPs^a*) [Discoveries in

the Judaean Desert 4; Oxford: Clarendon, 1965] 39). This device of biblical parallelism, namely, to state a fact positively in stich A and negatively in stich B, is attested to by almost endless examples. In rabbinic texts *ʿasa / qibbel besimḥah*, "to do / receive in joy," is often replaced in parallel recensions with *loʾ ʾiḥer, loʾ nitrashshel, loʾ nitʿaṣṣel, loʾ nitmahameah, loʾ ʿikkev*, and other terms meaning "do not delay." Cf. M. Held, "The Action–Result (Factitive–Passive) Sequence of Identical Verbs in Biblical Hebrew and Ugaritic," *JBL* 84 (1965) 272–82.

59. H. S. Horovitz and I. A. Rabin, ed., *Mechilta d'Rabbi Ismael* (Frankfurt am Main: Kauffmann, 1931; rpt. Jerusalem: Bamberger and Wahrmann, 1960), Yitro 2, p. 209. In this connection, the midrash of R. Eliezer b. Parta, cited there (p. 210), takes on new meaning: "(Moses) said to them (the Israelites): *ʾim meqabbelim ʾattem ʿalekhem ʿonashim besimḥah, hare ʾattem meqabbelim sakar . . . ve-qibbelu*." I would paraphrase this: "I know that you are willing to accept the Torah voluntarily, but I want to know whether you realize that in accepting the Torah with its rights and obligations, you are leaving yourselves open to the punishments concomitant with those laws. Are you willing to accept those punishments freely and without coercion?" Here *simḥah* certainly does not mean "with joy"!

60. Horovitz and Rabin, ed., *Mekhilta*, Yitro, 2, p. 209.

61. S. Schechter, ed., *Avot de-Rabbi Nathan* (Vienna, 1887; rpt. New York: Feldheim, 1945), Version A, Chap. 13, p. 57.

62. M. M. Ali, *A Manual of Hadith* (London: Curzon, 1978) 211.

63. References in SALPE, 139.

64. SALPE, 132–33. For the comprehensive discussion of the etymology of the various *rḥm* roots, called for in SALPE, see S. David Sperling, "Biblical *rḥm* I and *rḥm* II," *Journal of the Ancient Near Eastern Society* 19 (Semitic Studies in Memory of Moshe Held, 1989) 149–59.

65. This nuance was pointed out to me by Saul Lieberman.

66. The so-called *Nusaḥ ʾEreṣ Yisraʾel*, "The Text of the Land of Israel." See Jacob Mann, "Genizah Fragments of the Palestinian Order of Service," *HUCA* 2 (1925) 269–338; rpt. in J. J. Petuchowski, ed. *Contributions to the Scientific Study of Jewish Liturgy* (New York: KTAV, 1970) 379–448; see especially 298 (rpt. 396).

67. See Jacob Licht's study of the root *ndb* in his *The Sect of the Judean Desert and Its Writings* (Jerusalem: The Jewish Agency of Israel, Division of Youth Aliyah, Guidance Unit, 1956/57; in Hebrew).

68. My translation; text from Mann, "Genizah Fragments," *HUCA* 2: 293 (rpt., 403).

BIBLIOGRAPHY

Abravanel, Isaac. 1955–56. *Peirush ʿal Ha-Neviʾim Ha-Rishonim.* 2 vols. Jerusalem: Torah Vedaʿat. In Hebrew.

Abusch, Tzvi. 1986. "Ishtar's Proposal and Gilgamesh's Refusal: An Interpretation of *The Gilgamesh Epic,* Tablet 6, Lines 1–79." *History of Religions* 26: 143–87.

Aistleitner, J. 1967. *Wörterbuch der Ugaritischen Sprache.* 3d ed. Berichte der Sächsischen Gesellschaft der Wissenschaft, Philologisch-historische Klasse 106 #3. Leipzig.

Albright, William Foxwell. 1942. "A Third Revision of the Early Chronology of Western Asia." *Bulletin of the American Schools of Oriental Research* 88: 28–36.

_____. 1957. *From the Stone Age to Christianity: Monotheism and the Historical Process.* 2d ed. Garden City, New York: Doubleday.

_____. 1968. *Yahweh and the Gods of Canaan: A Historical Analysis of Two Contrasting Faiths.* Garden City, New York: Doubleday.

Ali, M. Muhammad. 1978. *A Manual of Hadith.* 3d ed. London: Curzon Press.

Allony, N. 1969. *Ha-ʾEgron: Kitāb ʾUṣūl al-Shiʿr al-ʿIbrāni.* Jerusalem.

Assaf, S. 1938. "Ancient Deeds from the Genizah from Palestine, Egypt, and North Africa." *Tarbiz* 9: 11–34, 196–218. In Hebrew.

_____. 1953. "Ancient Documents from Palestine and Egypt." In *Jerusalem: Studies in the Land of Israel. Volume 1,* ed. Michael Ish-Shalom, 104–17. Jerusalem. In Hebrew.

Astour, Michael C. 1966. "Political and Cosmic Symbolism in Genesis 14 and Its Babylonian Sources." In *Biblical Motifs—Origins and Transformations,* ed. A. Altmann, 65–112. Philip W. Lown Institute of Advanced Judaic Studies, Brandeis University, Studies and Texts 3. Cambridge: Harvard University Press.

Augapfel, Julius. 1917. *Babylonische Rechtsurkunden aus der Regierungszeit Artaxerxes I. und Darius II.* Kaiserliche Akademie der Wissenschaften. Philosophisch-historische Klasse. Denkschrift 59.III. Vienna: Hölder.

Avishur, Yishaq. 1979. *Phoenician Inscriptions and the Bible. Part Two. A Selection of Phoenician Inscriptions.* Jerusalem: A. Rubenstein.

Bacher, Wilhelm. 1905. *Die exegetische Terminologie der jüdischen Traditionsliteratur.* Leipzig: Hinrichs. Translated as Bacher 1922/23.

_____. 1922/23. *Midrashic Terminology.* Tel Aviv. Translation of Bacher 1905.

Baillet, Maurice, J. T. Milik, and Roland de Vaux. 1962. *Les "petites grottes" de Qumrân: Exploration de la falaise, les grottes 2Q, 3Q, 5Q, 6Q, 7Q à 10Q, le rouleau de cuivre.* Discoveries in the Judaean Desert 3. Oxford: Clarendon.

Baltzer, Klaus. 1960. *Die Bundesformular.* Neukirchen: Neukirchener Verlag.

Bamberger, Bernard. 1929. "Fear and Love of God in the Old Testament." *HUCA* 6: 39–53.

Bar-Ilan, Meir. 1988. "Magical Seals on the Body among Jews in the First Centuries C.E." *Tarbiz* 57: 37–50. In Hebrew.

Barr, James. 1968. *Comparative Philology and the Text of the Old Testament.* Oxford: Clarendon; rpt. 1987, Winona Lake, Indiana: Eisenbrauns, with additions.

Baumgartner, Walter, et al. 1967-90. *Hebräisches und aramäisches Lexikon zum Alten Testament.* Leiden: Brill.

Belkin, Samuel. 1940. *Philo and the Oral Law: The Philonic Interpretation of Biblical Law in Relation to the Palestinian Halakhah.* Cambridge: Harvard University Press.

Ben-Ḥayyim, Ze'ev. 1957–77. *The Literary and Oral Tradition of Hebrew and Aramaic amongst the Samaritans.* 5 vols. Jerusalem: Academy of the Hebrew Language.

Ben-Yehudah, Eliezer, et al. 1911–59. *Millon ha-Lashon ha-ʿIvrit ha-Yeshanah ve-ha-Ḥadashah: Thesaurus totius hebraitatis et veteris et recentioris.* 15 vols. Jerusalem; rpt., 1960, New York: Yoselof.

Bendavid, Aba. 1967–1971. *Biblical Hebrew and Mishnaic Hebrew.* 2 vols. Tel Aviv: Dvir. In Hebrew.

Benoît, Pierre, Josef T. Milik, and Roland de Vaux. 1961. *Les grottes de Murabbaʿât.* Discoveries in the Judaean Desert 2. Oxford: Clarendon.

Bible. 1611. *Bible. The Authorized or King James Version* (AV).

_____. 1851. *The Septuagint version of the Old Testament with an English translation* by L. C. L. Brenton. London/New York: Bagster.

_____. 1901. *The Bible. American Revised Version.* New York: Nelson (ARV).

_____. 1935. *The Bible. An American Translation,* by J. M. Powis Smith et al., and Edgar J. Goodspeed. 2d ed. Chicago: University of Chicago Press (AT).

_____. 1966. *The Jerusalem Bible.* Garden City, New York: Doubleday (JB).

_____. 1970. *The New English Bible with the Apocrypha.* Oxford and Cambridge University Presses (NEB).

_____. 1985. *Tanakh: A New Translation of the Holy Scriptures According to the Traditional Hebrew text.* Philadelphia: The Jewish Publication Society of America (NJPS).

Bickerman, Elias J. 1950–51. "'Couper une alliance.'" *Archives d'histoire du droit oriental* 5: 133–56. Rpt. in Bickerman 1976: 1–32 with an important supplement.

_____. 1958. "The Altars of Gentiles: A Note on the Jewish '*ius sacrum*.'" *Revue internationale des droits de l'antiquité* 3e série, 5: 137–64. Rpt. in Bickerman 1980: 324–46.

_____. 1962. "The Civic Prayer for Jerusalem." *Harvard Theological Review* 55: 163–85. Rpt. in Bickerman 1980: 290–312.

_____. 1976–86. *Studies in Jewish and Christian History.* 3 parts. Arbeiten zur Geschichte des Antiken Judentums und des Urchristentums 9. Leiden: Brill. Bickerman 1976 = Part One; 1980 = Part Two.

Borger, R. 1970. "Vier Grenzsteinurkunden Merodachbaladans I. von Babylon." *Archiv für Orientforschung* 23: 1–26.

Boyer, Georges. 1955. "La place des textes d'Ugarit dans l'histoire de l'ancient droit oriental." In *Le Palais royal d'Ugarit III*, ed. Jean Nougayrol, 283–308. Mission de Ras Shamra 6. Paris: Imprimerie Nationale.

Bravmann, M. M. 1972. *The Spiritual Background of Early Islam: Studies in Ancient Arab Concepts.* Leiden: Brill.

Brinkman, J. A. 1968. *A Political History of Post-Kassite Babylonia, 1158–722* B.C. Analecta Orientalia 43. Rome: Pontifical Biblical Institute.

Brockington, L. H. 1973. *The Hebrew Text of the Old Testament. The Readings Adopted by the Translators of the New English Bible.* Oxford University Press and Cambridge University Press.

Brown, Francis, S. R. Driver, and Charles A. Briggs. 1907. *A Hebrew and English Lexicon of the Old Testament.* Oxford: Clarendon. Abbreviated BDB.

Bruck, Eberhard E. 1944. "Ethics vs. Law: St. Paul, the Fathers of the Church and the 'Cheerful Giver' in Roman Law." *Traditio: Studies in Medieval History, Thought, and Religion* 2: 97–121.

Buber, Martin. 1960. *The Prophetic Faith,* trans. Carlyle Witton-David. New York: Harper and Row.

_____. 1963. *Israel and the World.* New York: Schocken Books.

_____. 1968. *On the Bible: Eighteen Studies,* ed. Nahum N. Glatzer. New York: Schocken Books.

Buber, Solomon, ed. 1884. *Tobias ben Eliezer. Midrash Leqaḥ Ṭov, ha-mekhuneh Pesiqta zuṭartah.* 5 vols. Vilna: Rom; rpt. 1921–24, Vilna; 1959/60, Jerusalem.

_____. 1885a. *Midrash Tanḥuma: ein agadischer Commentar zum Pentateuch von Rabbi Tanchuma ben Rabbi Abba.* Vilna: Rom; rpt. 1946.

_____. 1885b. *Midrash Zutta.* Berḷin: Itzkowski.

_____. 1886. *Sifre de-ʾagadeta ʿal megillat ʾEster.* Vilna: Rom; rpt. 1946, Jerusalem.

_____. 1891. *Midrash Tehillim.* Vilna: Rom; rpt. 1966, Jerusalem: Wahrmann.

_____. 1893. *Midrash Shemuel.* Krakow: Y. Fischer.

_____. 1902. *Midrash ʾAggadat Bereshit.* Vilna; rpt. 1925.

Buttrick, George A., et al., eds. 1951–57. *The Interpreter's Bible: The Holy Scriptures in the King James and Revised Standard Versions.* New York: Abingdon-Cokesbury Press.

_____. 1962. *The Interpreter's Dictionary of the Bible.* 4 vols. Nashville: Abingdon.

Campbell, E. F., Jr., and D. N. Freedman, eds. 1970. *The Biblical Archaeologist Reader 3.* Garden City, New York: Doubleday.

_____ and D. N. Freedman, eds. 1983. *The Biblical Archaeologist Reader IV.* Sheffield: The Almond Press.

Cassuto, Umberto/Moses David. 1955. "Abraham." In *Encyclopaedia Biblica. Entsiḳlopedyah Miḳraʾit* 1.61–67.

_____. 1955. "Genesis." In *Encyclopaedia Biblica. Entsiḳlopedyah Miḳraʾit* 2.318–35.

Cassuto, U. M. D., J. Klausner, and J. Gutmann, eds. 1952/53. *Sefer ʾAssaf.* Jerusalem: Mosad ha-Rav Kook.

Charles, R. H., ed. 1913. *The Apocrypha and Pseudepigrapha of the Old Testament in English.* 2 vols. Oxford: Clarendon.

Charlesworth, James H., ed. 1983. *The Old Testament Pseudepigrapha. 1. Apocalyptic Literature and Testaments.* Garden City, New York: Doubleday.

_____. 1985. *The Old Testament Pseudepigrapha. 2 Expansions of the "Old Testament" and Legends, Wisdom and Philosophical Literature, Prayers, Psalms, and Odes, Fragments of Lost Judeo-Hellenistic Works.* Garden City, New York: Doubleday.

Cherbonnier, E. LaB. 1955. *Hardness of Heart: A Contemporary Interpretation of the Doctrine of Sin.* Garden City, New York: Doubleday.

_____. 1962. "The Logic of Biblical Anthropomorphism." *Harvard Theological Review* 55: 187–206.

The [Chicago] Assyrian Dictionary of the Oriental Institute of the University of Chicago. 1956–. Ed. I. J. Gelb, Thorkild Jacobsen, Benno Landsberger, A. Leo Oppenheim, Erica Reiner et al. Locust Valley, New York: J. J. Augustin. Abbreviated CAD.

Cohen, Boaz. 1966. *Jewish and Roman Law: A Comparative Study.* 2 vols. New York: The Jewish Theological Seminary of America.

Cohen, Hermann R. 1971. *Reason and Hope: Selections from the Jewish Writings of Hermann Cohen,* trans. Eva Jospe. New York: Norton.

_____. 1972. *Religion of Reason out of the Sources of Judaism,* trans. S. Kaplan. New York: Ungar.

Cowley, A. 1923. *Aramaic Papyri of the Fifth Century B.C.* Oxford: Clarendon. Abbreviated AP.

Crim, Keith R., et al., eds. 1976. *The Interpreter's Dictionary of the Bible. Supplementary Volume.* Nashville: Abingdon.

Cross, Frank Moore, Jr. 1963. "The Discovery of the Samaria Papyri." *Biblical Archaeologist* 26: 110–21.

_____. 1969. "Papyri of the Fourth Century B.C. from Dâliyeh: A Preliminary Report on Their Discovery and Significance." In *New Directions in Biblical Archaeology,* ed. D. N. Freedman and J. C. Greenfield, 41-62 and figs. 34–49. Garden City, New York: Doubleday.

_____. 1973a. *Canaanite Myth and Hebrew Epic: Essays in the History of the Religion of Israel.* Cambridge: Harvard University Press.

_____. 1973b. "W. F. Albright's View of Biblical Archaeology and Its Methodology." *Biblical Archaeologist* 36: 2–5. Rpt. in Campbell and Freedman 1983: 1–4.

Cross, Frank Moore, Jr., and Shemaryahu Talmon, eds. 1975. *Qumran and the History of the Biblical Text.* Cambridge: Harvard University Press.

Cuq, Édouard. 1929. *Études sur le droit babylonien, les lois assyriennes et les lois hittites.* Paris: Paul Geuthner.

Dahood, Mitchell, S. J. 1954. "Ugaritic DRKT and Biblical DEREK." *Theological Studies* 15: 627–31.

_____. 1965. *Ugaritic-Hebrew Philology: Marginal Notes on Recent Publications.* Biblica et orientalia 17. Rome: Pontifical Biblical Institute.

Daube, David. 1947. *Studies in Biblical Law.* Cambridge: Cambridge University Press; rpt. 1969, New York: KTAV.

Davidson, Israel, with Louis Ginzberg. 1919. *Maḥzor Yannai: A Liturgical Work of the VIth Century, Edited from Genizah Fragments.* Texts and Studies of the Jewish Theological Seminary of America 6. New York: The Jewish Theological Seminary of America. In Hebrew.

de Jonge, M., ed. 1975. *Studies on the Testaments of the Twelve Patriarchs: Text and Interpretation.* Studia in Veteris Testamenti Pseudepigrapha 3. Leiden: Brill.

de Vaux, Roland. 1971. *Histoire ancienne d'Israël. Des origines à l'installation en Canaan.* Paris: Gabalda.

_____. 1973. *Histoire ancienne d'Israël. La période des Juges.* Paris: Gabalda.

_____. 1978. *The Early History of Israel,* trans. David Smith. 2 vols. Philadelphia: Westminster. Translation of de Vaux 1971 and 1973.

Dentan, Robert C., ed. 1955. *The Idea of History in the Ancient Near East.* New Haven: Yale University Press.

Dhorme, Édouard. 1923. *L'Emploi métaphorique des noms des parties du corps en hébreu et en akkadien.* Paris: Paul Geuthner; rpt. 1963.

Diéz Macho, Alejandro. 1968. *Neophyti I. Targum Palestinense MS de la Biblioteca Vaticana. I. Génesis.* Textos y Estudios 7. Madrid: Consejo Superior de Investigaciones Científicas.

_____. 1974. *Neophyti I. Targum Palestinense MS de la Biblioteca Vaticana. IV. Numeros.* Textos y Estudios 10. Madrid: Consejo Superior de Investigaciones Científicas.

Donner, H., and W. Röllig. 1968–71. *Kanaanäische und aramäische Inschriften.* Wiesbaden: Harrassowitz. Abbreviated KAI.

Draffkorn[-Kilmer], Anne. 1959. "Was King Abba-AN of Yamḫad a Vizier for the King of Ḫattuša?" *Journal of Cuneiform Studies* 13: 94–97.

Driver, G. R. 1932. "The Aramaic *Papyri* from Egypt: Notes on Obscure Passages." *Journal of the Royal Asiatic Society* 77–90.

_____. 1936. "Supposed Arabisms in the Old Testament." *JBL* 55: 101–20.

Driver, S. R. 1904. *The Book of Genesis.* 2d ed. Westminster Commentaries. London: Methuen.

_____. 1895. *A Critical and Exegetical Commentary on Deuteronomy.* International Critical Commentary. Edinburgh: T. & T. Clark.

Drower, E. S. 1959. *The Canonical Prayerbook of the Mandaeans.* Leiden: Brill.

Ebeling, Erich, Ernst Weidner, Dietz Otto Edzard, et al., eds. 1932–. *Reallexikon der Assyriologie und vorderasiastischen Archäologie.* Berlin: de Gruyter.

Ehrlich, Arnold Bogumil. 1899–1901. *Miqra ki-Pheschuto.* 3 vols. Berlin: Poppelauer; rpt. 1969, New York: KTAV. In Hebrew.

_____. 1908–14. *Randglossen zur hebräischen Bibel: Textkritisches, sprachliches, und sachliches.* 7 vols. Leipzig: Hinrichs; rpt. 1968, Hildesheim: Olms.

Eisenstein, Jehuda David, ed. 1915. *Ozar Midrashim: A Library of Two Hundred Minor Midrashim.* 2 vols. New York: J. D. Eisenstein. In Hebrew.

Eisler, Robert. 1910. *Weltenmantel und Himmelszelt. Religionsgeschichtliche Untersuchungen zur Urgeschichte des antiken Weltbildes.* Munich: C. H. Beck.

Eissfeldt, Otto. 1965. *The Old Testament: An Introduction,* trans. Peter R. Ackroyd. New York: Harper and Row.

Encyclopaedia Biblica. Entsiḳlopedyah Miḳraʾit: Oṣar ha-Yediʿot al ha-Miḳra u-tekufato. 1954–88. Ed. E. L. Sukenik, U. M. D. Cassuto, B. Mazar, et al. Jerusalem: Mosad Bialik. In Hebrew.

Encyclopaedia Judaica. 1971. Ed. Cecil Roth, Geoffrey Wigoder, Raphael Posner, Louis I. Rabinowitz et al. Jerusalem: Keter.

Epstein, Avraham. 1950–59. *The Writings of Avraham Epstein.* 2 vols. Jerusalem: Mosad ha-Rav Kook. In Hebrew.

Epstein, I., ed. 1935–1952. *The Babylonian Talmud.* London: Soncino Press.

Epstein, Jacob Nahum. 1960. *A Grammar of Babylonian Aramaic.* Jerusalem: Magnes. In Hebrew.

Finkelstein, Jacob J. 1958. "Bible and Babel." *Commentary* 26: 431–44.

_____. 1961. "Ammiṣaduqa's Edict and the Babylonian 'Law Codes.'" *Journal of Cuneiform Studies* 15: 91–104.

_____. 1963. "Mesopotamian Historiography." *Proceedings of the American Philosophical Society* 107: 461–72.

_____. 1967. "*Ana bīt emim šasū.*" *Revue d'Assyriologie* 61: 127–36.

_____. 1973. "The Goring Ox: Some Historical Perspectives on Deodands, Forfeitures, Wrongful Death, and the Western Notion of Sovereignty." *Temple Law Quarterly* 46: 169–290.

_____. 1981. "The Ox that Gored." *Transactions of the American Philosophical Society* 71(#2): 1–89.

Finkelstein, Louis. 1950. "On the Phraseology of the Tannaim." *Tarbiz* 20: 96–106.

Finkelstein, Louis, ed. 1935. *Sifre Devarim. Siphre ad Deuteronomium.* Breslau; rpt., 1969, New York: The Jewish Theological Seminary of America. In Hebrew.

Fischel, H. A. 1968. "Studies in Cynicism and the Ancient Near East: The Transformation of a *chria.*" In *Religions in Antiquity: Essays in Memory of Erwin Ramsdell Goodenough*, ed. Jacob Neusner, 372–411. Supplements to Numen 14. Leiden: Brill.

_____. 1969. "Story and History: Observations on Greco-Roman Rhetoric and Pharisaism." In *American Oriental Society, Middle West Branch, Semi-Centennial Volume*, ed. Denis Sinor, 59–88. Asian Studies Research Institute Oriental Series 3. Bloomington: Indiana University Press.

Fisher, Loren R., et al. 1975. *Ras Shamra Parallels. The Texts from Ugarit and the Hebrew Bible. Vol. II.* Analecta Orientalia 50. Rome: Pontifical Biblical Institute.

Fitzmyer, Joseph A., S. J. 1967. *The Aramaic Inscriptions from Sefîre.* Biblica et orientalia 19. Rome: Pontifical Biblical Institute Press.

Frankena, R. 1965. "The Vassal-Treaties of Esarhaddon and the Dating of Deuteronomy." *Oudtestamentische Studiën* 14: 122–54.

Frankfort, Henri, H. A. Frankfort, John A. Wilson, Thorkild Jacobsen, and William A. Irwin. 1946. *The Intellectual Adventure of Ancient Man: An Essay on Speculative Thought in the Ancient Near East.* Chicago: University of Chicago Press.

Frankfort, Henri, H. A. Frankfort, John A. Wilson, and Thorkild Jacobsen. 1949. *Before Philosophy: The Intellectual Adventure of Ancient Man. An Essay on Speculative Thought in the Ancient Near East.* Baltimore: Penguin.

Friedman, Mordechai. 1980. "Israel's Response to Hosea 2: 17b: 'You are my Husband.'" *JBL* 99: 199–204.

_____. 1980–81. *Jewish Marriage in Palestine: A Cairo Genizah Study.* 2 vols. New York: The Jewish Theological Seminary of America.

Friedmann (Ish-Shalom), Meir, ed. 1880. *Midrash Pesiqta Rabbati: Midrasch für den Festcyclus und die ausgezeichneten Sabbathe.* Vienna: Kaiser; rpt. 1963, Tel Aviv.

Friedrich, Johannes. 1926. *Staatsverträge des Ḫatti-Reiches in hethitische Sprache. I.* Mitteilungen der Vorderasiatisch-ägyptischen Gesellschaft 31.1. Leipzig: Hinrichs.

Friedrich, Johannes, J. G. Lautner, J. Miles, with Th. Folkers, eds. 1939. *Symbolae ad iura orientis antiqui pertinentes Paulo Koschaker dedicatae.* Studia et documenta ad iura orientis antiqui pertinenta 2. Leiden: Brill.

Gaster, Moses. 1925–28. *Studies and Texts in Folklore, Magic, Medieval Romance, Hebrew Apocrypha and Samaritan Archaeology.* 3 vols. London: Maggs Brothers; rpt. 1971, New York: KTAV.

Gelb, I. J. 1948. "A New Clay-nail of Ḫammurabi." *Journal of Near Eastern Studies* 7: 267–71.

_____. 1969. "On the Alleged Temple and State Economies in Ancient Mesopotamia." In *Studi in onore di Edoardo Volterra*, vol. 6, pp. 137–54. Pubblicazioni della Facoltà di giurisprudenze dell Università di Roma. Milan: Giuffrà.

Ginsberg, H. L. 1950. *Studies in Koheleth.* New York: The Jewish Theological Seminary of America.

_____. 1954. "Notes on the Minor Prophets." *Eretz Israel* 3 (M. D. U. Cassuto Volume) 83–84.

_____. 1961a. "Hosea's Ephraim, More Fool than Knave. A New Interpretation of Hosea 12: 1–14." *JBL* 80: 339–347.

_____. 1961b. *Koheleth*. Tel Aviv–Jerusalem. In Hebrew.

_____. 1963. "The Quintessence of Koheleth." In *Biblical and Other Studies*, ed. Alexander Altmann, 47–59. Philip W. Lown Institute of Advanced Judaic Studies, Brandeis University, Studies and Texts 1. Cambridge: Harvard University Press.

_____. 1969. "A Strand in the Cord of Hebrew Hymnody." *Eretz Israel* 9 (W. F. Albright Volume) 45–50.

_____. 1970. "Abram's 'Damascene' Steward." *Bulletin of the American Schools of Oriental Research* 200: 31–32.

_____. 1971. "Book of Hosea." *Encyclopaedia Judaica* 8.1012–25.

Ginsburger, Moshe. 1903. *Pseudo-Jonathan (Thargum Jonathan den Usiël zum Pentateuch)*. Berlin: Calvary; rpt. 1971, Hildesheim: Georg Olms.

Ginzberg, Louis. 1909–38. *The Legends of the Jews*, trans. from the German manuscript by Henrietta Szold and Paul Radin. 7 vols. Philadelphia: The Jewish Publication Society of America.

Goetze, Albrecht. 1969. "Hittite Treaties." In *Ancient Near Eastern Texts Relating to the Old Testament*, ed. J. B. Pritchard, 201–6, 529–30. Princeton: Princeton University Press.

Goldschmidt, Daniel. 1975. "Two Liturgical Poems for the Evening of Rosh ha-Shana." *Kobez ʿal-Yad: Minora Manuscripta Hebraica* 8: 227–34.

Grayson, A. Kirk. 1976. *Assyrian Royal Inscriptions. 2. From Tiglath-pileser I to Ashurnadin-apli II*. Wiesbaden: Harrassowitz.

Greenfield, Jonas C. 1969a. "Amurrite, Ugaritic and Canaanite." In *Proceedings of the International Conference on Semitic Studies held in Jerusalem 19–23 July 1965*, 92–101. Jerusalem: Israel Academy of Sciences and Humanities.

_____. 1969b. "Review of Dahood 1965." *JAOS* 89: 174–78.

Greengus, Samuel. 1969. "The Old Babylonian Marriage Contract." *JAOS* 89: 505–32.

Greenstein, Edward L., and David Marcus. 1976. "The Akkadian Inscription of Idrimi." *Journal of the Ancient Near Eastern Society* 8: 59–96.

Greenup, A. W., and C. H. Titterton, ed. 1909. *The Commentary of Meyuḥas b. Elijah on the Pentateuch*. London: Palestine House.

Grohmann, Adolf. 1934. *Arabic Papyri in the Egyptian Library. I. Protocols and Legal Texts*. Cairo: Egyptian Library Press.

Grotius, Hugo. 1950. *Commentary on the Law of Prize and Booty*, trans. G. L. Williams and W. H. Zeydel. Oxford: Clarendon.

Gulak, A. 1935. *Das Urkundenwesen im Talmud im Lichte der griechisch-aegyptischen Papyri und des griechischen und römischen Rechts*. Jerusalem: R. Mass.

Gunkel, Hermann. 1917. *Genesis*. 4th ed. Handkommenar zum Alten Testament. Göttingen: Vandenhoeck und Ruprecht.

Güterbock, Hans Gustav. 1934. "Die historische Tradition und ihre literarische Gestaltung bei Babyloniern und Hethitern." *Zeitschrift für Assyriologie* 42: 1–91.

Ḥakham, Amos. 1984. *The Book of Isaiah. Chapters 33–66*. Daʿat Mikra. Jerusalem: Mosad ha-Rav Kook. In Hebrew.

Halberstam, Solomon Joachim, ed. 1898. *Sepher Haschetaroth [of R. Judah b. Barzillai of Barcelona], Dokumentarbuch. Nach der einzigen Handschrift in Oxford (Cat. Neubauer No. 890) zum ersten Male herausgegeben und erläutert*. Berlin: Itzkowski. In Hebrew.

_____ et al., eds. 1889. *Rav Hai ben Sherira, Gaon. Sämtliche Gedichte*. Lemberg. In Hebrew.

Halevi, A. A. 1972. *The World of the Aggadah: The Aggadah in the Light of Greek Sources*. Tel Aviv. In Hebrew.

Hallo, W. W. 1981. "Introduction" to Briggs Buchanan, *Early Near Eastern Seals in the Yale Babylonian Collection*, ix–xv. New Haven: Yale University Press.

Haran, M., ed. 1960. *Yehezkel Kaufmann Jubilee Volume: Studies in Bible and Jewish Religion Dedicated to Yekezkel Kaufmann on the Occasion of his Seventieth Birthday*. Jerusalem: Magnes.

Heinemann, I. 1949/50. *The Methods of the Aggadah*. Jerusalem: Magnes. In Hebrew.

Held, Moshe. 1965. "The Action-Result (Factitive-Passive) Sequence of Identical Verbs in Biblical Hebrew and Ugaritic." *JBL* 84: 272–82.

Heschel, Abraham Joshua. 1950. *The Earth Is the Lord's*. New York: Henry Schuman.

_____. 1951. *Man Is Not Alone*. New York: Farrar Straus.

_____. 1954. *Man's Quest for God*. New York: Charles Scribner's Sons.

_____. 1955a. *God in Search of Man*. New York: Farrar Straus.

_____. 1955b. *The Prophets*. 2 vols. Philadelphia: The Jewish Publication Society of America.

_____. 1975. *The Wisdom of Heschel*, ed. Ruth Marcus Goodhill. New York: Farrar, Straus and Giroux.

Hinke, William J. 1907. *A New Boundary Stone of Nebuchadrezzar I. from Nippur*. The Babylonian Expedition of the University of Pennsylvania. Series D. Researches and Treatises 4. Philadelphia: The University of Pennsylvania.

Hoffmann, David, ed. 1908–9. *Midrasch Tannaïm zum Deuteronomium*. Berlin: Iṭzkowski. In Hebrew.

Horovitz, H. S., ed. 1917. *Siphre d'be Rab. I. Siphre ad Numeros adjecto Siphre zutta*. Corpus Tannaiticum. III. Continens Veterum Doctorum ad Pentateuchum Interpretationes Halachicas. 3. Leipzig: Fock; rpt. 1966, Jerusalem: Wahrmann.

_____ et al., eds. 1929. *Sifre Zutta*. Lodz: Masorah.

_____ and I. A. Rabin, eds. 1931. *Mechilta d'Rabbi Ismael*. Frankfurt am Main: Kauffmann; rpt. 1960, Jerusalem: Bamberger and Wahrmann.

Hunt, A. S., and C. C. Edgar. 1934. *Select Papyri with an English Translation. 2. Official Documents*. Loeb Classical Library. London: William Heineman.

Hurvitz, Avi. 1972. *The Transition Period in Biblical Hebrew*. Jerusalem: Mosad Bialik. In Hebrew.

Ibn Janaḥ. 1875. *The Book of Hebrew Roots*, ed. Adolf Neubauer. Oxford: Clarendon; rpt. 1968, Amsterdam: Philo Press.

Jacob, Benno. 1934. *Das erste Buch der Tora: Genesis*. Berlin: Schocken.

Jacobsen, Thorkild. 1970. *Toward the Image of Tammuz and Other Essays on Mesopotamian History and Culture*, ed. William L. Moran. Harvard Semitic Series 21. Cambridge: Harvard University Press.

_____. 1976. *The Treasures of Darkness: A History of Mesopotamian Religion*. New Haven: Yale University Press.

_____. 1987. *The Harps that Once . . . : Sumerian Poetry in Translation*. New Haven: Yale University Press.

Japhet, Sara. 1977. *The Ideology of the Book of Chronicles and Its Place in Biblical Thought*. Jerusalem: Mosad Bialik. In Hebrew. Translated as Japhet 1989.

_____. 1989. *The Ideology of the Book of Chronicles and Its Place in Biblical Thought*. Frankfurt: Peter Lang.

Jastrow, Marcus. 1903. *A Dictionary of the Targumim, the Talmud Babli and Yerushalmi, and the Midrashic Literature*. 2 vols. New York: Putnam Judaica Press; rpt. 1975, New York: Judaica Press.

Jean, Charles-F. 1941. *Archives royales de Mari II*. Textes cunéiformes du Louvre 23. Paris: Imprimerie Nationale.

Jellinek, Adolph, ed. 1853. *Midrash Eleh ezkerah*. Leipzig: Colditz.

Jeremias, Alfred. 1917. "Die sogenannten Kedorlaomer-Texte." In *Orientalistische Studien Fritz Hommel . . . beigetragen I*, 69–97. Mitteilungen der Vorderasiatische Gesellschaft 21. Leipzig: Hinrichs.

Jonas, Hans. 1970. *The Gnostic Religion: The Message of the Alien God and the Beginnings of Christianity*. 3d ed. Boston: Beacon Press.

Judah Halevi. 1946. *The Book of Kuzari: An Argument for the Faith of Israel*, trans. Hartwig Hirschfeld. New York: Pardes; rpt. 1964, New York: Schocken.

Kadushin, Max. 1932. *The Theology of Seder Eliahu: A Study in Organic Thinking*. New York: Bloch.

_____. 1938. *Organic Thinking: A Study in Rabbinic Thought*. New York: The Jewish Theological Seminary of America.

_____. 1960. "Introduction to Rabbinic Ethics." In *Yehezkel Kaufmann Jubilee Volume: Studies in Bible and Jewish Religion Dedicated to Yehezkel Kaufmann on the Occasion of his Seventieth Birthday*, ed. M. Haran, 88–114. Jerusalem: Magnes.

_____. 1965. *The Rabbinic Mind*. New York: Blaisdell.

Kappaḥ, Yosef, ed. 1962/63. *Perushei rabbenu Saʿadya Gaʾon ʿal ha-Torah*. Jerusalem: Mosad ha-Rav Kook. In Hebrew.

Kasher, Menahem Mendel. 1949. *Torah shelemah ve-huʾ ha-Torah shebikhtav ʿim beʾur Torah shebaʿal peh*. New York: American Biblical Encyclopedia Society. In Hebrew.

Kasowski, Chaim Josua. 1959–80. *Concordance of the Language of the Talmud*. 41 vols. Jerusalem: Ministry of Education and Culture and the Jewish Theological Seminary of America.

Kaufman, Stephen A. 1971. "Akkadian and Babylonian Aramaic: New Examples of Mutual Elucidation." *Leshonenu* 36: 28–33. In Hebrew.

_____. 1974. *The Akkadian Influences on Aramaic*. Assyriological Studies 19. Chicago: The Oriental Institute.

Kaufmann, Yehezkel. 1937–1956. *Toledot ha-ʾEmunah ha-Yisraelit: Mimei Qedem ʿad-Sof Bayit Sheni*. 8 vols. Tel Aviv: Mosad Bialik (Dvir).

_____. 1955. *Joshua*. Jerusalem: Mosad Bialik. In Hebrew.

_____. 1960. *The Religion of Israel: From Its Beginnings to the Babylonian Exile*, trans. and abridged by Moshe Greenberg. Chicago: University of Chicago Press.

_____. 1962. *Judges*. Jerusalem: Kiryat Sefer. In Hebrew.

_____. 1970. *The Babylonian Captivity and Deutero-Isaiah* (*History of the Religion of Israel. Volume IV. Chapters 1, 2*), trans. C. W. Efroymson. New York: Union of American Hebrew Congregations.

Kempinski, Aharon, and Silvin Košak. 1969–70. "Der Išmeriga-Vertrag." *Welt des Orient* 5: 191–217.

Kierkegaard, Søren. 1941. *Concluding Unscientific Postscript*, trans. David F. Swenson with Walter Lowrie. Princeton: Princeton University Press.

King, Leonard William. 1912. *Babylonian Boundary-Stones and Memorial-Tablets in the British Museum.* London: British Museum.

Koehler, Ludwig, and Walter Baumgartner. 1958. *Lexicon in veteris testamenti libros.* Leiden: Brill.

Kopf, Lothar. 1958–59. "Arabische Etymologien und Parallelen zum Bibelwörterbuch." *Vetus Testamentum* 8: 161–215, 9: 247–87. Rpt. in Kopf 1976: 133–228.

_____. 1976. *Studies in Arabic and Hebrew Lexicography*, ed. M. H. Goshen-Gottstein with S. Assif. Jerusalem: Magnes.

Korošec, Victor. 1931. *Hethitische Staatsverträge.* Leipzig: Hinrichs.

Koschaker, Paul. 1928. *Neue keilschriftliche Rechturkunden aus der El-Amarna-Zeit.* Abhandlungen der Philologisch-historischen Klassen der Sächsischen Akademie der Wissenschaften 39.5. Leipzig: Hirzel.

Kraeling, Emil G. 1953. *The Brooklyn Museum Aramaic Papyri.* New Haven: Yale University Press. Abbreviated BP.

Krückmann, Oluf. 1931. *Babylonische Rechts- und Verwaltungs-Urkunden aus der Zeit Alexanders und der Diadochen.* Weimar: Hof-buchdruckerei.

Kutscher, E. Y. 1946–48. "Concerning the Terminology of Legal Documents in the Talmud and in Gaonic Literature." *Tarbiz* 16 (1946) 125–27, 19 (1947/48) 53–59, 125–18. In Hebrew. Rpt. in Kutscher 1977, Hebrew section, 416–30.

_____. 1951. "Is Biblical Aramaic Eastern or Western Aramaic?" *Leshonenu* 17: 119–22. In Hebrew.

_____. 1954. "New Aramaic Texts." *JAOS* 74: 233–48. Rpt. in Kutscher 1977: 37–52.

_____. 1957. "Review of G. R. Driver et al., *Aramaic Documents.*" *JBL* 76: 336–38.

_____. 1961. *Words and Their History.* Jerusalem: Kiryat Sefer. In Hebrew.

_____. 1964. "The Aramaic Calque in Hebrew." *Tarbiz* 33: 118–30. In Hebrew. Rpt. in Kutscher 1977, Hebrew section, 394–45.

_____. 1967. "Mittelhebräisch und Jüdisch-Aramäisch im neuen Köhler-Baumgartner." In *Hebräische Wortforschung: Festschrift zum 80. Geburtstag von Walter Baumgartner* (Supplements to Vetus Testamentum 16; Leiden: Brill, 1967), 158–75. Rpt. in Kutscher 1977: 156–73.

_____. 1968. "Marginal Notes to the Biblical Lexicon." *Leshonenu* 32: 343–46. In Hebrew. Rpt. in Kutscher 1977, Hebrew section, 342–59.

_____. 1971. "Aramaic." In *Current Trends in Linguistics. 6. Linguistics in South West Asia and North Africa*, ed. T. A. Sebeok, Charles A. Ferguson, Carlton T. Hodge, and Herbert H. Paper (The Hague: Mouton) 347–412. Rpt. in Kutscher 1977: 90–155.

_____. 1977. *Hebrew and Aramaic Studies*, ed. Zeev Ben Ḥayyim, Aharon Dotan, and Gad Sarfatti with Moshe Bar-Asher. Jerusalem: Magnes Press.

Landsberger, Benno. 1928–29. "Das gute Wort." *Mitteilungen der Altorientalischen Gesellschaft* 4: 294–321.

_____. 1939. "Die babylonischen termini für Gesetz und Recht." In *Symbolae ad iura orientis antiqui pertinentes Paulo Koschaker dedicatae*, ed. J. Friedrich et al., 219–34. Studia et documenta ad iura orientis antiqui pertinenta 2. Leiden: Brill.

Lane, Edward. 1863–93. *Arabic-English Lexicon.* 8 vols. London: Williams and Norgate.

Lauterbach, Jacob Bezalel ha-Kohen. 1933. "Midrash Va-yiseʿu or the Book of the Wars of the Children of Jacob." In *Abhandlungen zur Errinerung Hirsch Perez Chajes*, ed. V. Aptowizer and A. Z. Schwarz, Hebrew section, 205–22.

Veröffentlichungen der Alexander Kohut Memorial Foundation 7. Vienna: The Alexander Kohut Memorial Foundation.

Lautner, Julius Georg. 1939. "Rechtsverhältnisse an Grenzmauern. Studien zum Miteigentum im altbabylonischen Recht I." In *Symbolae ad iura orientis antiqui pertinentes Paulo Koschaker dedicatae.* Studia et documenta ad iura orientis antiqui pertinenta 2, ed. J. Friedrich et al., 76–95. Leiden: Brill.

Leemans, W. F. 1968. "King Hammurapi as Judge." In *Symbolae ivridicae et historicae Martino David dedicatae. 2. Iura orientis antiqui,* ed. J. A. Ankum et al., 107–29. Leiden: Brill.

Levine, Baruch A. 1968. "*Mulūgu/Melûg*: The Origins of a Talmudic Legal Institution." *JAOS* 88: 271–85.

_____. 1975. "On the Origins of the Aramaic Legal Formulary at Elephantine." In *Christianity, Judaism and Other Greco-Roman Cults. Studies for Morton Smith at Sixty. Part Three. Judaism before 70,* ed. Jacob Neusner, 37–54. Studies in Judaism in Late Antiquity 12. Leiden: Brill.

Levy, J., and H. L. Fleischer. 1876–89. *Neuhebräisches und chaldäisches Wörterbuch über die Talmudim und Midraschim.* 4 vols. Leipzig: Brockhaus.

Licht, Jacob. 1956/57. *The Sect of the Judean Desert and Its Writings.* Jerusalem: The Jewish Agency of Israel, Division of Youth Aliyah, Guidance Unit. In Hebrew.

Liddell, Henry George, and Robert Scott, rev. Henry Stuart Jones and Roderick McKenzie. 1968. *A Greek-English Lexicon.* Oxford: Clarendon.

Lieberman, Saul. 1939. "Ḥazzanut Yannai." *Sinai* 4: 221–30.

_____. 1940. *Midrash Devarim Rabbah.* Jerusalem: Wahrmann.

_____. 1942. *Greek in Jewish Palestine: Studies in the Life and Manners of Jewish Palestine in the II–IV Centuries.* New York: The Jewish Theological Seminary of America.

_____. 1944. "Roman Legal Institutions in Early Rabbinics and in the *Acta Martyrum.*" *Jewish Quarterly Review* 35: 1–57.

_____. 1950. *Hellenism in Jewish Palestine: Studies in the Literary Transmission, Beliefs and Manners of Palestine of the I Century* B.C.E.*–IV Century* C.E. New York: The Jewish Theological Seminary of America.

_____. 1963. "How Much Greek in Jewish Palestine?" In *Biblical and Other Studies,* ed. Alexander Altman, 123–41. Philip W. Lown Institute of Advanced Judaic Studies, Brandeis University, Studies and Texts 1. Cambridge: Harvard University Press.

_____. 1965. "Afterlife in Early Rabbinic Literature." In *Harry Austryn Wolfson Jubilee Volume on the Occasion of his Seventy-fifth Birthday,* ed. S. Lieberman, Vol. 2, pp. 495–532. Jerusalem: American Academy for Jewish Research.

_____. 1967. "Forgotten Teachings." *Leshonenu* 32: 89–102. In Hebrew.

_____. 1968a. *Siphre Zutta (The Midrash of Lydda).* New York: The Jewish Theological Seminary of America.

_____. 1968b. "A Rebuttal to Mishor." *Leshonenu* 33: 78. In Hebrew.

_____. 1973. *Toseftah ki-Feshutah.* New York: The Jewish Theological Seminary of America.

Liver, J. 1960. "The Half-shekel Ransom." In *Yehezekel Kaufmann Jubilee Volume: Studies in Bible and Jewish Religion Dedicated to Yehezkel Kaufmann on the Occasion of his Seventieth Birthday,* ed. M. Haran, Hebrew section, 44–57. Jerusalem: Magnes. In Hebrew.

_____. 1963. "The Half-shekel Offering in Biblical and Post-Biblical Literature." *Harvard Theological Review* 56: 173–98.

Loewenstamm, Samuel E. 1960. "What is above and what is below, what is before and what is after." In *Yehezel Kaufmann Jubilee Volume: Studies in Bible and Jewish Religion Dedicated to Yehezkel Kaufmann on the Occasion of his Seventieth Birthday*, ed. M. Haran, Hebrew section, 112–21. Jerusalem: Magnes Press. In Hebrew.

_____. 1978. "Ugarit and the Bible II [Review of Fisher 1975]." *Biblica* 59: 100–22.

_____. 1980. *Comparative Studies in Biblical and Ancient Oriental Literatures*. Alter Orient und Altes Testament 204. Kevelaer and Neukirchen-Vluyn: Verlag Butzon und Bercker and Neukirchener Verlag.

Luzzatto, Samuel David. 1874. *Il Pentateuco volgarizzato e commentato*. Padua: Sachetto; rpt., 1965, Tel Aviv: Dvir. In Italian and Hebrew.

McCarthy, Dennis J. 1963. *Treaty and Covenant*. Analecta Biblica 21. Rome: Pontifical Biblical Institute Press. Revised as Analecta Biblica 21a, 1978.

_____. 1964. "Three Covenants in Genesis." *Catholic Biblical Quarterly* 26: 179–89.

Maisels, Moshe. 1956. *Thought and Truth: A Critique of Philosophy*, trans. and condensed by Abraham Regelson. New York: Bookman Associates.

Malamat, Abraham. 1960. "The Ban in Mari and in the Bible." In *Yehezkel Kaufmann Jubilee Volume: Studies in Bible and Jewish Religion Dedicated to Yehezkel Kaufmann on the Occasion of his Seventieth Birthday*, ed. M. Haran, Hebrew section, 147–58. Jerusalem: Magnes. In Hebrew.

Mann, Jacob. 1925. "Genizah Fragments of the Palestinian Order of Service." *HUCA* 2: 269–338. Rpt. in Petuchowski 1970: 379–448.

_____. 1940. *The Bible as Read and Preached in the Old Synagogue. A Study in the Cycles of the Readings from Torah and Prophets, as well as from Psalms, and in the Structure of the Midrashic Homilies. I. The Palestinian Triennial Cycle. Genesis and Exodus.* Cincinnati: Hebrew Union College. Rpt. 1971, New York: KTAV.

_____ and Isaiah Sonne. 1966. *The Bible as Read and Preached in the Old Synagogue. A Study in the Cycles of the Readings from Torah and Prophets, as well as from Psalms, and in the Structure of the Midrashic Homilies. II. The Palestinian Triennial Cycle. Leviticus and Numbers to Seder 106.* Cincinnati: Hebrew Union College-Jewish Institute of Religion.

Marcus, Ralph, and I. J. Gelb. 1948. "A Preliminary Study of the New Phoenician Inscription from Cilicia." *Journal of Near Eastern Studies* 7: 194–98.

Margulies, Mordechai, ed. 1947. *Midrash ha-Gadol*. Jerusalem: Mosad ha-Rav Kook. In Hebrew.

Mauss, Marcel. 1954. *The Gift: Forms and Functions of Exchange in Archaic Societies*, trans. Ian Cunnison. Glencoe, Illinois: Free Press; rpt. 1967, New York: Norton.

Meek, Theophile J. 1969. "The Code of Hammurabi." In *Ancient Near Eastern Texts Relating to the Old Testament*, ed. J. B. Pritchard, 163–80. Princeton: Princeton University Press.

Melamed, E. Z. 1945. "Hendiadys (*hen dia duoin*) in the Bible." *Tarbiz* 16: 173–89. In Hebrew.

_____. 1954. "Comments on the Language of *Avot*." *Leshonenu* 20: 106–11. In Hebrew.

Mendenhall, George E. 1954a. "Ancient Oriental and Biblical Law." *Biblical Archaeologist* 17(#2): 26-46. Rpt. in Campbell and Freedman 1970: 3–24.

_____. 1954b. "Covenant Forms in Israelite Tradition." *Biblical Archaeologist* 17(#3): 50-74. Rpt. in Campbell and Freedman 1970: 25–53.

_____. 1955. *Law and Covenant in Israel and the Ancient Near East*. Pittsburgh: The Biblical Colloquium.

_____. 1962. "Covenant." In *The Interpreter's Dictionary of the Bible*, 1.714–23. Ed. G. A. Buttrick et al. Nashville: Abingdon.

Milik, Josef Tadeusz. 1954. "Un contract juif de l'an 134 après Jésus-Christ." *Revue biblique* 61: 182–91.

_____. 1957. "Deux documents inédits du désert de Juda." *Biblica* 38: 245–68.

Miller, Jr., Patrick D. 1973. *The Divine Warrior in Early Israel*. Harvard Semitic Monographs 5. Cambridge: Harvard University Press.

Mirkin, Moses Aryeh, ed. 1959. *Shemot Rabbah*. Tel Aviv: "Yavneh" Publishing House.

_____. 1962. *Bemidbar Rabbah*. Tel Aviv: "Yavneh" Publishing House.

_____. 1966. *Va-yiqra Rabbah*. Tel Aviv: "Yavneh" Publishing House.

Mishor, Mordechai. 1968. "A Note on Kutscher's Contribution on *drk*." *Leshonenu* 33: 78.

Montgomery, James A. 1951. *A Critical and Exegetical Commentary on the Books of Kings*. International Critical Commentary. Edinburgh: T. & T. Clark.

Moulton, J. H. 1908–63. *A Grammar of New Testament Greek*. Edinburgh: T. & T. Clark.

Muffs, Yochanan. 1969. *Studies in the Aramaic Legal Papyri from Elephantine*. Studia et documenta ad iura orientis antiqui pertinenta 8. Leiden: Brill; rpt. 1973, New York: KTAV.

_____. 1973. "Two Comparative Lexical Studies." *Journal of the Ancient Near Eastern Society* 5: 287–98. Rpt. in this volume.

_____. 1975. "Love and Joy as Metaphors of Willingness and Spontaneity in Cuneiform, Ancient Hebrew, and Related Literatures. Part I. Divine Investitures in the Midrash in the Light of Neo-Babylonian Royal Grants." In *Christianity, Judaism and Other Greco-Roman Cults. Studies for Morton Smith at Sixty. Part Three. Judaism before 70*, ed. Jacob Neusner, 1–36. Studies in Judaism in Late Antiquity 12. Leiden: Brill. Rpt. in this volume.

_____. 1978. "A History of Mesopotamian Religion." *Numen* 25: 80–84. Rpt. in this volume.

_____. 1979. "Love and Joy as Metaphors of Willingness and Spontaneity in Cuneiform, Ancient Hebrew, and Related Literatures. Part II. The Joy of Giving." *Journal of the Ancient Near Eastern Society* 11 (Bravmann Memorial Volume) 91–111. Rpt. in this volume.

_____. 1982. "Abraham the Noble Warrior: Patriarchal Politics and Laws of War in Ancient Israel." *Journal of Jewish Studies* 33(#1–2 = Essays in Honour of Yigael Yadin) 81–107. Rpt. in this volume.

_____. "Bein Din La-Raḥamim: Tefillatan shel Nevi'im." In *Torah Nidreshet*, ed. A. Shapira, 39–87. Tel Aviv: Am Oved.

Musil, Alois. 1928. *The Manners and Customs of the Rwala Bedouins*. American Geographical Society, Oriental Explorations and Studies 6. New York.

Neusner, Jacob. 1965–70. *A History of the Jews in Babylonia*. 5 vols. Studia Post-Biblica 9. Leiden: Brill.

Neusner, Jacob, ed. 1968. *Religions in Antiquity: Essays in Memory of Erwin Ramsdell Goodenough*. Supplements to Numen 14. Leiden: Brill.

_____. 1975. *Christianity, Judaism and Other Greco-Roman Cults: Studies for Morton Smith at Sixty*. Studies in Judaism in Late Antiquity 12. Leiden: Brill.

Noth, Martin. 1967. *The Laws in the Pentateuch and Other Studies*, trans. D. R. Ap-Thomas. Philadelphia: Fortress.

Nougayrol, Jean. 1955. *Le Palais royal d'Ugarit III*. Mission de Ras Shamra 6. Paris: Imprimerie Nationale.

_____. 1956. *Le Palais royal d'Ugarit IV*. Mission de Ras Shamra 9. Paris: Imprimerie Nationale.

Oppenheim, A. Leo. 1935. "Ein Beitrag zum Kassitenproblem." *Analecta Orientalia* 12: 266–74.

_____. 1955. "A Note on *Ṣôn Barzel*." *Israel Exploration Journal* 5: 89–92.

_____. 1969. "Babylonian and Assyrian Historical Texts." In *Ancient Near Eastern Texts Relating to the Old Testament*, ed. J. B. Pritchard, 265–317, 556–67. Princeton: Princeton University Press.

Orr, William F., and James Arthur Walther. 1976. *I Corinthians*. Anchor Bible 32. Garden City, New York: Doubleday.

Otto, Walter F. 1979. *The Homeric Gods: The Spiritual Significance of Greek Religion*, trans. Moses Hadas. New York: Thames and Hudson.

Paul, Shalom. 1978. "Adoption Formulae: A Study of Cuneiform and Biblical Legal Clauses." *Eretz Israel* 14 (H. L. Ginsberg Volume) 31–36. In Hebrew.

_____. 1979–80. "Adoption Formulae: A Study of Cuneiform and Biblical Legal Clauses." *Maarav* 2: 173–85.

Payne Smith, R., et al., eds. 1879–1901. *Thesaurus syriacus*. 2 vols. Oxford: Clarendon.

Pedersen, Johannes. 1914. *Der Eid bei den alten Semiten in seinem Verhältnis zu verwandten Erscheinungen sowie die Stellung des Eides im Islam*. Strassburg: K. J. Trübner.

_____. 1926. *Israel: Its Life and Culture, I–II*. London: Oxford University Press.

_____. 1940. *Israel: Its Life and Culture, III–IV*. London: Oxford University Press.

Petuchowski, Jakob J., ed. 1970. *Contributions to the Scientific Study of the Jewish Liturgy*. New York: KTAV.

Philo Judaeus. 1928–1962. *Works*, trans. F. H. Colson and G. H. Whittaker. Loeb Classical Library. London: William Heinemann.

Pick, H. 1908. "Drei neue Veröffentlichungen zu den Privaturkunden aus der Hammurabi-Zeit." *Orientalistische Literaturzeitung* 11: 315–18.

_____. 1903. *Assyrisches und Talmudisches: Kulturgeschichtliche und lexikalische Notizen*. Berlin: Calvary.

Pineles, Hirsch Mendel. 1861. *Sefer Darkah shel Torah*. Vienna: F. Förster. In Hebrew.

Poebel, Arno. 1932. *Das appositionell bestimmte Pronomen der 1. Pers. Sing. in den westsemitischen Inschriften und im Alten Testament*. Assyriological Studies 3. Chicago: University of Chicago Press.

Polotsky, H. J. 1962. "The Greek Documents from the 'Cave of the Letters.'" *Yediʿot beḥaqirat Eretz Israel ve-ʿatiqoteha* 26: 237–41. In Hebrew.

_____. 1967. "Three Greek Documents from the Family Archive of Babtha." *Eretz Israel* 8 (E. L. Sukenik Volume) 46–51.

Porten, Bezalel. 1968. *Archives from Elephantine: The Life of a Jewish Military Colony*. Berkeley: University of California Press.

Pritchard, James B., ed. 1969. *Ancient Near Eastern Texts Relating to the Old Testament*. 3d ed. Princeton: Princeton University Press. Abbreviated ANET.

Rabinowitz, J. J. 1952/53. "Jewish Elements in Babylonian Formulae of the Persian Period." In *Sefer ʾAssaf*, ed. U. Cassuto et al., 433–43. Jerusalem: Mosad ha-Rav Kook. In Hebrew.

_____. 1956. *Jewish Law: Its Influence on the Development of Legal Institutions*. New York: Bloch.

_____. 1958. *Studies in Legal History*. Jerusalem: R. H. Cohen.

von Rad, Gerhard. 1958. *Der heilige Krieg im alten Israel*. 3d ed. Göttingen: Vandenhoeck und Ruprecht. Translated as von Rad 1991.

_____. 1972. *Genesis*, trans. John H. Marks. 2d ed. Old Testament Library. Philadelphia: Westminster.

_____. 1991. *Holy War in Ancient Israel*. Grand Rapids, Michigan: Eerdmans. Translation of von Rad 1958.

Roberts, J. J. M. 1975. "Divine Freedom and Cultic Manipulation in Israel and Mesopotamia." In *Unity and Diversity: Essays in the History, Literature, and Religion of the Ancient Near East*, ed. H. Goedicke and J. J. M. Roberts, 181–90. Baltimore: Johns Hopkins University Press.

Rosenthal, Franz. 1969. "Canaanite and Aramaic Inscriptions." In *Ancient Near Eastern Texts Relating to the Old Testament*, ed. J. B. Pritchard, 653–62. Princeton: Princeton University Press.

Rowton, Michael B. 1965. "The Topological Factor in the Habiru Problem." In *Studies in Honor of Benno Landsberger on His Seventy-fifth Birthday*, ed. H. G. Güterbock and Th. Jacobsen, 375–87. Assyriological Studies 16. Chicago: The Oriental Institute of the University of Chicago.

San Nicolò, Marian. 1931. *Beiträge zur Rechtsgeschichte im Bereiche der keilschriftlichen Rechtsquellen*. Oslo: H. Aschehong.

Sanders, James A. 1965. *The Psalms Scroll of Qumrân Cave 11 (11QPs[a])*. Discoveries in the Judaean Desert 4. Oxford: Clarendon.

Schacht, Joseph. 1927. "Vom babylonischen zum islamischen Recht." *Orientalistische Literaturzeitung* 30: 664–69.

Schechter, Solomon, ed. 1887. *Avot de-Rabbi Nathan*. Vienna; rpt. 1945, New York: Feldheim.

Scheil, Vincent. 1930–33. *Actes juridiques susiens*. Memoires de la Délégation en Perse 22–24. Paris: Leroux.

Scherman, Nosson. 1988. *Artscroll Weekday Siddur*. Brooklyn: Mesorah.

Scholem, Gershom. 1965. *Jewish Gnosticism, Merkabah Mysticism and Talmudic Tradition*. 2d ed. New York: The Jewish Theological Seminary of America.

Schorr, Moses. 1913. *Urkunden des altbabylonischen Zivil- und Prozessrechts*. Vorderasiatische Bibliothek 5. Leipzig: Hinrichs.

_____. 1914. "Review of J. Kohler and A. Ungnad, *Assyrische Rechtsurkunden im Umschrift und Übersetzung*." *Zeitschrift der Deutschen Morgenländischen Gesellschaft* 68: 625–35.

Seeligmann, I. L. 1954. "On the History and Nature of Prophecy in Israel." *Eretz Israel* 3 (M. D. U. Cassuto Volume) 125–32. In Hebrew.

_____. 1963. "Menschliches Heldentum und göttliche Hilfe." *Theologische Zeitschrift* 19: 385–411.

Segal, M. Z. 1958. *The Complete Book of Ben Sirah*. 2d ed. Jerusalem: Mosad Bialik.

Seidl, U. 1968. *Die babylonischen Kudurru Reliefs*. Baghdader Mitteilungen 4. Berlin: Deutsches Archäologische Institut, Abteilung Baghdad.

Skehan, Patrick W., and Alexander A. Di Lella, o. f. m. 1987. *The Wisdom of Ben Sira*. Anchor Bible 39. New York: Doubleday.

Skinner, John. 1910. *A Critical and Exegetical Commentary on the Book of Genesis*. International Critical Commentary. Edinburgh: T. & T. Clark.

Slingerland, H. Dixon. 1977. *The Testaments of the Twelve Patriarchs*. Society of Biblical Literature Dissertation Series 21. Chico: Scholars Press.

von Soden, Wolfram. 1959. "Review of *Archives royales de Mari* VI, XV, and VIII." *Orientalia* 28: 314–17.

_____. 1965–81. *Akkadisches Handwörterbuch*. Wiesbaden: Harrassowitz. Abbreviated *AHw*.

_____. 1969. *Grundriss der akkadischen Grammatik*. Analecta Orientalia 33/47. Rome: Pontifical Biblical Institute.

_____. 1970. "*Mirjām*–Maria '(Gottes)geschenk'." *Ugarit-Forschungen* 2: 269–72.

Speiser, E. A. 1934. "A Figurative Equivalent for Totality in Akkadian and West-Semitic." *JAOS* 54: 200–3.

_____. 1953. "Cultural Factors in Social Dynamics in the Near East." *Middle East Journal* 7: 133–52.

_____. 1955. "Ancient Mesopotamia." In *The Idea of History in the Ancient Near East*, ed. Robert C. Dentan, 35–76. New Haven: Yale University Press.

_____. 1960. "Leviticus and the Critics." In *Yehezkel Kaufmann Jubilee Volume: Studies in Bible and Jewish Religion Dedicated to Yehezkel Kaufmann on the Occasion of his Seventieth Birthday*, ed. M. Haran, 29–45. Jerusalem: Magnes.

_____. 1964. *Genesis*. Anchor Bible 1. Garden City, New York: Doubleday.

Sperling, S. David. 1968. "The Akkadian Legal Term *dīnu u dabābu*." *Journal of the Ancient Near Eastern Society* 1(#1): 35–40.

_____. 1989. "Biblical *rḥm* I [to be compassionate] and *rḥm* II [to love]." *Journal of the Ancient Near Eastern Society* 19 (Semitic Studies in Memory of Moshe Held) 149–59.

Spiegel, Shalom. 1945. "Noah, Danel and Job: Touching on Canaanite Relics in the Legends of the Jews." In *Louis Ginzberg Jubilee Volume*, ed. S. Lieberman, 305–55. New York: The American Academy for Jewish Research.

Stein, Edmund. 1931. *Philo und des Midrasch. Philos Schilderung des Gestalten des Pentateuch verglichen mit der das Midrasch*. Beihefte zur Zeitschrift für die Alttestamentliche Wissenschaft 57. Giessen: Töpelmann.

Steinmetzer, Franz Xaver. 1912. "Eine Schenkungsurkunde des Königs Melišichu." *Beiträge zur Assyriologie und semitischen Sprachwissenschaft* 8(#2): 1–38.

_____. 1922. *Die babylonischen Kudurru (Grenzsteine) als Urkundenform untersucht*. Studien zur Geschichte und Kultur des Altertums II.4–5. Paderborn: F. Schöningh.

Stern, David. 1985. "The Function of the Parable in Rabbinic Literature." *Jerusalem Studies in Hebrew Literature* 7: 90–102. In Hebrew.

Stern, David, trans. 1990. "Midrash Eleh ezkerah." In *Rabbinic fantasies* [see following entry] 143–65.

Stern, David, and Mark Jay Mirsky, eds. 1990. *Rabbinic Fantasies: Imaginative Narratives from Classical Hebrew Literature*. Philadelphia: The Jewish Publication Society of America.

Strack, H. L., and P. Billerbeck. 1922–56. *Kommentar zum Neuen Testament aus Talmud und Midrasch*. 5 vols. Munich: Beck.

Tadmor, Hayim. 1958. "The Campaigns of Sargon II of Assur: A Chronological-Historical Study." *Journal of Cuneiform Studies* 12: 22–40, 77–100.

Tal, Abraham. 1981. *The Samaritan Targum*. Tel Aviv: Tel Aviv University Press.

Talmon, Shemaryahu. 1961. "Synonymous Readings in the Textual Traditions of the Old Testament." In *Studies in the Bible*, ed. Ch. Rabin, 335–83. Scripta Hierosolymitana 8. Jerusalem: Magnes.

Taubenschlag, R. 1953/54. "Das babylonische Recht in den griechischen Papyri." *Journal of Juristic Papyrology* 7/8: 169–85.

Theodor, Julius, and Albeck, Chanoch. 1903–29. *Midrasch Bereschit Rabba mit kritischem Apparat und Kommentar*. 3 vols. Berlin: Itzkowski; rpt., 1965, Jerusalem: Wahrmann.

Thompson, Thomas L. 1974. *The Historicity of the Patriarchal Narratives: The Quest for the Historical Abraham*. Beihefte zur Zeitschrift für die Alttestamentliche Wissenschaft 133. Berlin: de Gruyter.

Thureau-Dangin, François. 1919. "Une acte de donation de Marduk-zâkir-šumi."*Revue d'Assyriologie* 16: 117–56.

_____. 1937. "Trois contrats de Ras-Shamra." *Syria* 18: 245–55.

Townsend, John T. 1976. "Minor Midrashim." In *Bibliographical Essays in Medieval Jewish Studies 2*, ed. Yosef Hayim Yerushalmi, 333–92. New York: Anti-Defamation League of B'nai Brith/KTAV.

Tur-Sinai, Naphthali H. 1967. *Peshuto shel Miqra*. Jerusalem: Kiryat Sefer. In Hebrew.

Unger, Eckard. 1975. "Diadem und Krone." In *Reallexikon der Assyriologie und vorderasiastischen Archäologie*, 2.201–11. Ed. E. Ebeling et al. Berlin: de Gruyter.

Van Seters, John. 1975. *Abraham in History and Tradition*. New Haven: Yale University.

Wakin, Jeanette A. 1972. *The Function of Documents in Islamic Law: The Chapters on Sales from Ṭahāwi's Kitāb al-Shurūṭ al-Kabīr*. Albany: State University of New York Press.

Wehr, Hans. 1958. *Arabisches Handwörterbuch für die Schriftsprache der Gegenwart*. 3d ed. Leipzig: Harrassowitz. Translated as Wehr 1971.

_____. 1971. *A Dictionary of Modern Written Arabic*, trans. J Milton Cowan. 3d ed. Ithaca, New York: Spoken Languages Services.

Weidner, Ernst F. 1923. *Politische Dokumente aus Kleinasien. Die Staatsverträge in akkadischer Sprache aus dem Archiv von Boghazköi*. Boghazköi Studien 8–9. Leipzig: Hinrichs.

Weinfeld, Moshe. 1970. "The Covenant of Grant in the Old Testament and the Ancient Near East." *JAOS* 90: 184–203.

_____. 1971/72. "'Bond and Grace'—Covenantal Expressions in the Bible and the Ancient World—A Common Heritage." *Leshonenu* 36: 85–105. In Hebrew.

_____. 1971. "Pentateuch." *Encyclopaedia Judaica* 13.231–64.

_____. 1972. *Deuteronomy and the Deuteronomic School*. Oxford: Clarendon; rpt. 1991, Winona Lake, Indiana: Eisenbrauns.

_____. 1975. *Genesis*. Tel Aviv: S. L. Gordon. In Hebrew.

Weisberg, David. 1968. "Some Observations on Late Babylonian Texts and Rabbinic Literature." *HUCA* 39: 71–80.

Wernberg-Møller, P. 1957. *The Manual of Discipline*. Studies on the Texts of the Desert of Judah 1. Leiden: Brill.

Widengren, Geo. 1961. *Mani und der Manichäismus*. Stuttgart: W. Kohlhammer.

_____. 1965. *Mani and Manichaeism*. London: Weidenfeld and Nicholson.

Wiseman, Donald J. 1953. *The Alalakh Tablets*. Occasional Publications of the British Institute of Archaeology at Ankara 2. London: British Institute of Archaeology at Ankara. Abbreviated AT.

Wolfson, Harry Austryn. 1947. *Philo: Foundations of Religious Philosophy in Judaism, Christianity, and Islam.* Cambridge: Harvard University Press.

_____. 1970. *The Philosophy of the Church Fathers.* 3d ed. Cambridge: Harvard University Press.

Wright, G. Ernest. 1952. *God Who Acts: Biblical Theology as Recital.* Studies in Biblical Theology 8. London: SCM Press.

_____. 1969. *The Old Testament and Theology.* New York: Harper and Row.

Wright, William, with W. Robertson Smith and M. J. de Goeje. 1896-98. *A Grammar of the Arabic Language.* Cambridge: Cambridge University Press.

Yadin, Yigael. 1961. "Expedition D." *Yediʿot he-Ḥevra ha-ʿIvrit le-Ḥaqirat Eretz Israel* 25: 49–64. In Hebrew.

_____. 1962. "Expedition D—Cave of the Letters." *Yediʿot be-Ḥaqirat Eretz Israel ve-ʿatiqoteha* 26: 204–36. In Hebrew.

_____. 1965. *The Ben Sira Scroll from Masada.* Jerusalem: Israel Exploration Society.

Yalon, H. 1971. *Pirqe Lashon.* Jerusalem: Mosad Bialik. In Hebrew.

Yaron, Reuven. 1957a. "On Divorce in Old Testament Times." *Revue internationale des droits de l'antiquité* 3e série, 4: 117–28.

_____. 1957b. "The Schema of the Aramaic Legal Documents." *Journal of Semitic Studies* 2: 33–61.

_____. 1958. "Aramaic Marriage Contracts from Elephantine." *Journal of Semitic Studies* 3: 1–39.

_____. 1958a. "Notes on Aramaic Papyri." *Revue internationale des droits de l'antiquité* 3e série, 5: 299–310.

_____. 1958b. "On Defension Clauses of Some Oriental Deeds of Sale and Lease, from Mesopotamia." *Bibliotheca Orientalis* 15: 15–22.

_____. 1959. "Jewish Law and Other Legal Systems of Antiquity." *Journal of Semitic Studies* 4: 308–31.

_____. 1960a. "Aramaic Deeds of Conveyance." *Biblica* 41: 248–74, 379–94.

_____. 1960b. "Aramaic Marriage Contracts: Corrigenda and Addenda." *Journal of Semitic Studies* 5: 66–70.

_____. 1960c. *Gifts in Contemplation of Death in Jewish and Roman Law.* Oxford: Clarendon.

_____. 1960d. "Review of Benoît et al. 1961." *Journal of Jewish Studies* 11: 157–71.

_____. 1961. *The Law of the Aramaic Papyri.* Oxford: Clarendon.

_____. 1961. "Notes on Aramaic Papyri II." *Journal of Near Eastern Studies* 20: 127–30.

_____. 1963. "A Royal Divorce at Ugarit." *Orientalia* 32: 21–31.

_____. 1970. "Review of Muffs 1969." *Revue biblique* 77: 415–17.

Ziegler, Ignaz. 1903. *Die Königsgleichnisse des Midrasch, beleuchtet durch die römische Kaiserzeit.* Breslau: S. Schottlaender.

Zimmerman, Frank. 1958. *The Book of Tobit.* New York: Harper.

Zuckermandel, M. S., ed. 1937. *Toseftah,* with a supplement by Saul Lieberman. Jerusalem: Wahrmann.

Zulay, Menahem, ed. 1938. *Piyyuṭe Yannai. Liturgical Poems of Yannai Collected from Geniza-Manuscripts and Other Sources.* Berlin: Schocken/ Jewish Publishing Company.

INDEX OF SUBJECTS

INDEX OF AUTHORITIES

INDEX OF WORDS

Greek

apantē toward, 158
apekhō to receive in full, 100, 108n23, 108n29
bia strength, 188n3
doron gift, 189n8
dotēs giver, 182
epitropos guardian, 113–14
eudokimeō to be genuine, 107n15
eulogia willing gift, 182
ekhō to have, receive, 108n23
hilaros cheerful, 182
katadikē fine, sentence, 189n9
kurios guardian, 113–14
pleoneksia exaction, 182
khairō to rejoice, 136n33
kharizomai to give, 188n3
kharis joy, gift, 163

Latin

familia family, 52
probatus tested, 107n15

Ugaritic

drk to exercise authority, 117
drkt power, 113
mlk kingship, 113
spr deed, 91n38

Arabic

baraka blessing, endowment, 92n46, 188n1
djinn demon, 11
ḫišer divided, sorted out, 91n39
dhimma protection, 183
zakāt alms tax, 183
ṣadaqa voluntary alms, 183
ṣāra to become; *ṣāra ilā PN*, *ṣara fī yadi PN* (the money/property) came to PN, 107n22
ṭāba to be good, happy; do willingly, 137n36, 148; *ṭība* goodness, free will, 148
ṭāqa ability, power, 183
ʿafw superfluity, 183
ghaṣaba to constrain, 137n36
ghaḍiba to be vexed, 137n36; *ghaḍab* anger, 137n36, 148
faḍl surplus, 183
qabaḍa to receive (property), 108n28
qad hereby, 107n22
kariha to feel disgust, 124, 150; *karh*, *kurh* disgust, 150; *karāha* disgust, 137n36, 148, 150; *karāhiya* discomfort, 124
kahin priest, 11, 38–39, 47n19

Akkadian

abbūtu fatherhood, 38
aḫāzu to take, 38, 47n16
akalu food; *akal ḫarrānišunu* their rations for a military campaign, 73
alāku to go; (with another verb, an inceptive marker; a Canaanism in a text from Ras Shamra, cf. Hebrew *hlk*), 89n12
anāḫu I, to be exhausted, 75
anāḫu II, to perform feudal service, 75, 91n38
apālu to pay; *apil* (the owner) is paid, 3, 98

Aramaic

Hebrew

אבות fatherhood; אחזי אבות intercessors, 38

אביר mighty; אביר יעקב Powerful One of Jacob, 83

אדון master, owner (Ben Sirah), 113

אדרכתה a deed (שטר) of empowerment (?) or delegating (?), 114, 118n11; **see further** דרך III

אהבה love, 188n6; volition, 163, 180, 186–87; gift, 168, 186–87, 189n8; באהבה willingly, 123, 180, 187

אהה aha!, oh no!, 28–29, 32

אוי oy!, woe!, 29

אור **hifil** to cause to shine; **see** פנים

אזור loincloth, 51

אחד one; **see** לב

אחז to seize; **see** אבות

אין there is not; Y אלא X אין, X is nothing other than Y (with paraphrase), 137n38, 156–57, 189n10

אלה / אלון oak, 86

אלמחה compulsion, 189n9

אמה cubit, 147

אמץ **piel** to harden (of לבב), 181

אנגריא duress, 155

אנח to groan, 75; אנח groaning, 174

אני I (with *va-*, *hinne*, and suffixing form, 'I hereby &c.'), 127–28, 135n33, 155–61; **see also** הנה

אנן to mourn; אונן bereaved, 174; אנינה mourning, 174

אנס to compel; אונס coercion, 169, 172–74, 189n9; אנוס forced, 177

אנפטי welcoming, 158–59

אסון compulsion (?), 173

אסמכתה exegetical support, 155–61

אף **conjunction**; **see** הנה

אפר ashes, 52

אצבע finger, 147

אצטלא garment, 59n24

אשל tamarisk, 86

בגד to betray, 94n55

בוא to come, enter; PN בא אל (the money) came to PN, viz., PN received (it), 97–103; ביאה intercourse, 120n21

בן son; בן בית steward, 135n29

בעל lord; בעלי ברית allies, 71

ברזל iron; **see** צאן ברזל

ברית alliance, 71; covenant of grant, 134n28

ברך to bestow, 178; ברכה endowment, 92n46; gift, 188n1

גדל to grow rich, 79

גזרה decision; גזרה שוה inference from analogy, 106n5

גל heap, 80

דבק to cleave, cling, 51

דבר word; **see** דין

דון (uncertain; Gen 6:3), 160

דופי deception, 173

דיבה lawsuit, 174

דין judgment, lawsuit; דין ודברים litigation, 174

דרך I **verb** to tread

דרך II **noun** (*derekh*) road; military campaign, 73; custom, manner, 114–16, 120n19, 118n11. Is *drk* II from *drk* I or is it the source of *drk* I?

דרך III **verb** to have or delegate or exercise power, 113–20. Or is *drk* III to be glossed as 'to send, delegate' and so perhaps taken to be related to *drk* I/II, 114? Or is *drk* III a metaphorization of *drk* II (whence *drk* I?), 118n11? And are *drk* III and derivatives found in the Bible, 113–14? **See also** אדרכתה **and** נדרך.

דרך IV **noun** (*dorekh*??) master, guardian (Ben Sirah), 113–14

דרך V **noun** (*derekh*?) power, prerogative (in Midrash), 114–16, 119n13, 120n21; (in Bible??), 118n11; אין דרכן, they have no right, 115

דרש interpretation, 135n32, 157

הוי hoy!, pay attention!, 29

השג reach; **see** נשג

הון sufficiency, wealth, 180

הלך to walk; (inceptive marker), 89n12; הלכה precept, 106n5, 140

הנה behold; הנה . . . אף כי (biblical marker of inference *a fortiori*), 106n5; הנה

נשא to carry, 21–23, 41; נושא עון he bears sin, 21, 23, 41; נשא פנים **see** פנים
נשג **hifil** to suffice, reach, 178–79; השגת יד reach of the hand (Ben Sirah), 178–79; השג יד ditto (Mishnah), 178
נתן to give; **see** מתנה **and** מחת **and** קנה **and** שמחה
סבר **hifil** to brighten; **see** פנים
עבד servant, agent, 10
עבר **hifil** to transfer, 42
עברי Hebrew, 86
עגם to be sad, grieved, 177; עגם נפש doleful of spirit, 137n36
עון sin, 21, 28; **see also** נשא
עז anger (Qoheleth, Ezra), 103–5
עזז to be strong, angry; **see** פנים
עין eye; **see** טוב
על with, against, 170; **see also** נפל **and** שמח
עלילה deed, action, 22–23
עצב I to grieve, **qal**, 137n36, **hitpael**, 160–61; עצב frowning, niggardly, 146–47; עצבות grief, 130
עצב II to constrain (dubious), 137n36
עצל **hitpael, nitpael** to delay, 167, 192n58
עצם to be numerous, 79
עצר to restrain, 137n36
עשק to extort; עושק extortion, 173
עשות coercion, 173
פאר turban, 52–54
פה mouth, 36
פחד to fear; פחד יצחק He Who Inspires Fear in the Heart of Isaac's Enemies, 83
פנים face, mood, 146–47; האיר פנים to illumine the face, make happy (Qoheleth, Ben Sirah), 104, 124, 178; זעף פנים niggardly, 190n28; worried, 133n17; נשא פנים to exhibit partiality (Ben Sirah), 113; סבר פנים cheerful face, 146; מסבר פנים to look on favorably, 105; מעז פנים to be insolent toward, (perhaps rarely) to look on angrily, 105; הרע פנים to make the face sad, 124, 133n17; שנה פנים **(piel/pual)** to make the face sad, dark, 104; **see also** נפל
פשט interpretation, 135n32, 137n38, 156, 159, 189n10
צאן flock; צאן ברזל property held under certain conditions, 139
צביון volition, 176
צידה provisions; צידה לדרך rations for a campaign, 73
צעק to cry out, 11, 25–26; צעקה cry, 11
צפה to keep watch, 80
קוץ to dread, 83
קל light; קל וחמר inference *a fortiori*, 106n5
קלון disgrace, 160
קנא to be zealous, 41
קנה to acquire; קנה ונתן to give as final property, 129, 138n40, 155
קרא to call, pray, 27
ראה = רוה to be sated (Qoheleth), 133n15
רכוש property, goods, 74
רע friend, adviser, 92n43; **see** מרע
רעע to be bad, sad; הרע לב to be sad or rude in doing something, 133n17, 179–80, 185–86—**see also** פנים; רע bad, sad; רע לב(ב) sorrowful(ness), 123–24, 133n17; לב רע sad disposition, 133n17; רעה sorrow, 123
רצון (free) will, volition, acceptance, 136n33, 145, 180, 182; ברצונו in his willingness, willingly, 3, 124, 127, 136n30, 156, 172, 176, 179, 186–87, 189n13; כרצונו according to his will, 177; לרצונו on his behalf, according to his will, 145, 177; תם לרצונו perfect with/in his volition, 176; מרצונו of his own free will, 128
רצפה coal, 36
רצץ to crush, break, 36
רשה: רשאי permitted, 116; רשות permission, 115
שוה: בשווי quickly, 172; שווי in haste, quickly, 190n21
שבע to be sated, 180; שבע satiety, 180
שוב to repent, 30
שחק smiling, generous, 146–47
שטר deed; **see** הרשאה, אדרכתה
שלם: שלום I peace, 90n20; שלום II ally, 89n13; שלם unharmed, 81; perfect (in intent), appropriate, 176, 179,

INDEX OF CITATIONS

Inscriptions and Papyri

Aramaic

Phoenician

Bible

Genesis

Midrashic Sources *continued*